THE RACE

TIM ZIMMERMANN

THE RACE

THE FIRST NONSTOP,

ROUND-THE-WORLD,

NO-HOLDS-BARRED

SAILING COMPETITION

ORION

Copyright © 2002 Tim Zimmermann

All rights reserved

The right of Tim Zimmermann to be identified as the author
of this work has been asserted by him in accordance with
the Copyright, Designs and Patents Act 1988.

First published in United States of America 2002
by Houghton Mifflin Company

First published in Great Britain in 2002 by Orion Books,
an imprint of the Orion Publishing Group Ltd
Orion House, 5 Upper St Martin's Lane, London WC2H 9EA

This book is an independent account; it is not authorized
or sponsored in any way by Bruno Peyron or The Race
Event, SARL. Bruno Peyron is the owner of the trademarks
THE RACE and THE RACE logo. Any licensing inquiries
should be directed to The Race Event, SARL, Paris, France.

A CIP catalogue record for this book is available
from the British Library

ISBN 0 75284 165 3

Printed in Great Britain by
Butler & Tanner Ltd, Frome and London

For my grandfather,
    who taught me the joys of sailing
And for Ilana,
    who shares in the joys of life

No game was ever yet worth a rap
For a rational man to play
Into which no accident, no mishap,
Could possibly find its way.

— Adam Lindsay Gordon

ACKNOWLEDGMENTS

This book represents the work of many people. First and foremost, I owe thanks to the skippers who took part in The Race. Grant Dalton, Steve Fossett, Loïck Peyron, Cam Lewis, and especially Skip Novak spent many hours patiently answering questions and recounting their experiences. Fossett and Dalton (along with his coskipper, Franck Proffit) helped me get a feel for the power and speed of their maxi-catamarans by welcoming me aboard for several outings. The *PlayStation* crew — including Ben Wright, Brian Thompson, Stan Honey, Peter Hogg, Nick Moloney, Damian Foxall, Mark Callaghan, David Scully, and Tom Weaver — were gracious, humorous, and informative. Stuart Radnofsky was always willing to help arrange rides on the boat and track down far-flung sailors. The *Club Med* crew — including Neal McDonald, Ed Danby, Mike Quilter, Steffano Rizzi, and Jan Dekker — were equally accommodating when it came to educating a multihull neophyte. The cast of *Team Philips* — Pete Goss, Mark Orr, Alex Bennett, Andy Hindley, Gary Venning, Vicky Bartholomew, and Patricia Juarez — demystified their fascinating Race design for me. Randy Smyth of *Team Adventure* explained the intricacies of driving a large catamaran in the Southern Ocean. With good humor and an eye for detail Rick Deppe, also of *Team Adventure,* answered endless questions — some obscure, some mundane, almost all random — on life at sea aboard a racing boat. The crew of *Innovation Explorer* — Roger Nilson, Elena Caputo-Novak, Yves Loday,

Julien Cressant, and others — also provided essential information, in some cases tactfully overcoming my abysmal French, the international language of multihull racing.

Special thanks are also due to *PlayStation*'s designers, Gino Morrelli and Pete Melvin. Pete spent considerable time walking me through the design of a maxi-catamaran from start to finish (and even offered to show me how to surf), and Gino filled in the gaps whenever I caught up with him in port or on the phone. Franck Martin of Multiplast also spent many hours explaining the development of the Ollier catamarans, and the yard's David Palmer proved an invaluable and knowledgeable bridge to the French sailing world. Nigel Irens, one of the busiest multihull designers, added a crucial outsider's perspective from the pleasant vantage of a café in Vannes.

Keeping up with the moving parts of The Race — getting in and out at the start in Barcelona and the finish in Marseilles with a wealth of information and details, a minimum of confusion, and plenty of good fun — was the miraculous accomplishment of The Race's press staff, headed by the tireless Mireille Vatine, assisted on the front lines by the inimitable Isabel Genis and the unflappable Bénédicte Etienne. David Adams, a Race director, also gave me a better understanding of the operation and management of a worldwide competition.

You can't understand sailing without understanding, or at least trying to understand, the weather. Whatever insight I gained into that somewhat unknowable phenomenon I owe to Lee Bruce, who showed me how a person with a roomful of computers in Wolfeboro, New Hampshire, can peek at the weather thousands of miles away and accurately route a sailboat through and around storms and calms. Lee also contributed greatly — and generously — to my depiction of *Team Philips* and her battle with the North Atlantic. On the other side of the globe, first from Sydney, Australia, then from Auckland, New Zealand, Roger "Clouds" Badham took time from his numerous forecasting commitments to guide me on *Club Med*'s 27,000-mile voyage through the world's major weather zones. Gilles

Chiorri, of France's Météo Consult, also gave me his highly informed bird's-eye view of the tactical war on the water, gleaned from his perch as weather consultant to The Race.

My thanks also to the hospitable staffs of *Sailing World* in Newport, Rhode Island, and *Yachting World* in London for letting me rummage through their magazine archives, which contained the colorfully told stories of many races long past. Trixie Wadson was a godsend when it came to tracking down photographs.

Most of all, this book could never have been started or finished without the enormously patient guidance and wise counsel of Bonnie Nadell at the Frederick Hill / Bonnie Nadell Literary Agency and of Eamon Dolan at Houghton Mifflin, so ably assisted by Emily Little. Larry Cooper, senior manuscript editor at Houghton, was a consummate pro and seemingly unfazed by any change or addition, no matter how small or how late. Whitney Peeling, senior publicist, was creative and impressively resourceful. Finally, nothing would have been possible without the generous and loving understanding of my wife, Ilana, who calmly negotiated all manifestations of stress, unburdened me of any chore she could take on, and provided a steady and soothing stream of encouragement when it was needed most — and even when it wasn't, which was nice too.

CONTENTS

THE RACE

INTRODUCTION

I tell you naught for your comfort,
Yea, naught for your desire,
Save that the sky grows darker yet
And the sea rises higher.

— G. K. Chesterton

AT FIRST it looked like a cloud, stretched low and benign along the horizon. From the helm of *Team Adventure,* a twin-hulled sailing catamaran hissing across the Southern Ocean, skipper Cam Lewis peered forward and muttered, "What the hell is that?" He took a distracted swipe at his goggles to clear the salt spray that 35-knot winds had speckled across the lens. He was rewarded with a glint of blue. Suddenly it wasn't a cloud at all. It was an iceberg, directly ahead. *Team Adventure* was closing at 30 knots, just minutes from a collision with the frozen mass.*

Ice is one of the Southern Ocean's most lethal and unpredictable dangers. Calving off the Antarctic ice pack, icebergs

---

*A nautical mile, which corresponds to a minute of latitude, is slightly longer (6,080 feet) than a statute mile (5,280). Boat speeds and wind speeds at sea are measured in knots. A knot, which is the speed it takes to travel one nautical mile in an hour, is equal to 1.15 miles per hour. The term "knot" does not come from "nautical mile." It derives from the practice, first used in the fifteenth century, of measuring a ship's speed with a "chip log." A chip log consisted of a length of line on a reel with knots tied every 47 feet 3 inches. To measure a ship's speed, the line, usually weighted with a chip of wood at the end, would be thrown overboard. The number of knots that ran out in a 28-second period (measured with a sandglass) would indicate the ship's speed in "knots." Throughout the text, knots will be used for wind and boat speeds. Any reference to miles indicates nautical miles.

larger than Rhode Island sometimes wander hundreds of miles
north into the shipping lanes around the bottom of the world,
carried by fingers of current from the frozen Weddell and Ross
Seas. The berg in *Team Adventure*'s way was a baby compared
to some of the monsters recorded over the years, but massive
nevertheless, perhaps four hundred feet long and one hundred
feet high. Running into it would be like driving a bus into the
side of an apartment building. That was not the only concern.
Big icebergs often leave a trail of crumbling smaller chunks bobbing at the surface like floating mines. These "growlers," some
the size and weight of a minivan, are virtually invisible to radar
and all but the sharpest lookout. At the speed *Team Adventure*
was sailing, even a fifty-pound chunk of ice could shatter her
brittle carbon-fiber skin or tear away a rudder. Anything bigger
could rip her hulls right open, crippling her and stranding the
fourteen-man crew halfway between Africa and South America,
almost fifteen hundred miles from assistance.

Barely twenty-four hours earlier, *Team Adventure* crossed latitude 40° south, the line that serves in sailors' minds as the informal gateway to the Southern Ocean, the uninterrupted belt of
stormy water encircling Antarctica. Finding a large iceberg at
45° south, in water that measured 12°C, well above freezing,
was an unwelcome danger. "They are just as hard whether they
are melting or not," observed conavigator Larry Rosenfeld.

The last thing Lewis and his crew wanted was to be dodging
ice. They were racing nonstop around the world in a high-tech
catamaran that they had sailed for the first time just two months
earlier. Surviving ten thousand miles of windy, frigid Southern
Ocean intact and alive to Cape Horn was going to be difficult
enough without ice appearing where no ice was expected. Lewis,
at forty-three one of America's top multihull sailors, had in fact
hoped that *Team Adventure* might get all the way through the
Southern Ocean's austral summer — it was January 2001 —
without ever seeing the telltale flash of sun on frozen water. But
it would be hard to make a living predicting the anomalies of
one of the globe's least understood bodies of water. Ice, like any

other danger in the Southern Ocean, simply had to be accepted and endured. In "the South," as sailors liked to call it, stoicism was a necessary virtue.

The crew, almost exclusively professionals who sailed for a living, knew enough to respect the Southern Ocean. They were also out to conquer it. *Team Adventure* was one of three identical sister ships that had been designed to sail around the world faster than any boat in history. At 110 feet in length, she was one of the largest catamarans ever built. Her mast soared almost 150 feet above the water, tall as a fourteen-story building, and her rig could carry enough sail to blanket three tennis courts. The result was a theoretical top speed greater than 40 knots, faster than all but the swiftest passenger liners. That sort of power was hard on the crew. The mainsail alone weighed around a thousand pounds. In heavy winds it put a fifteen-ton load on the lines that controlled it, a load that could crush body parts and rip skin off hands if it was not handled carefully. Routine procedures — changing the headsails up front, reducing or increasing the size of the mainsail by lowering or raising it, adjusting the sails to come to a new course — required brute muscle power and the mechanical advantage of multiple giant winches.

The crew was divided into watches, with each sailor spending four hours on then four hours off. In theory, that meant twelve hours a day on deck and up to twelve hours resting. But weather and the big catamaran had little respect for neat schedules. Sail handling was so labor intensive that sleeping crew were frequently roused from their bunks to help out on deck. Cooking, cleaning, and routine maintenance also ate into spare hours. Meals were something of a chore too, a bland parade of freeze-dried entrées, scooped out of bowls and formulated to deliver maximum nutrition for minimum stored weight. Even so, it was hard to choke down enough to replace the constant calorie burn of racing the big boat. When the chance for sleep did arrive, the tired sailors wedged themselves into bunks stacked closely together in tiers of three. Everyone slept with his feet forward to protect against the danger of a broken neck if the boat slammed into anything at high speed. Just outside, the ocean rushed by with a dull roar that earplugs — not usually standard sailing gear — could only muffle. In rough seas the boat launched off waves and crashed back into the water with a violence that bounced bodies around in the bunks like popcorn. For some, silence was even worse. It meant that the hull you were trying to sleep in had lifted clear of the water. If it kept going, the boat would flip over. Time slowed until it came back down. If you were in the hull and a sudden gust or freak wave capsized the boat, you faced a potential death sentence. On deck, where you could see what was happening, the cat seemed more stable and secure. Down below, in the tomblike confines of the living spaces, it was sometimes harder to convince yourself.

If *Team Adventure* was grueling and at times unnerving to sail, she was also exhilarating. The twin hulls accelerated with the quick surge of a high-performance car. In the right conditions, sailing seven hundred miles in one day was not impossible, and average speeds of 20 knots or more were routine. For the first time in sailing history, a boat could play the weather systems sweeping across the oceans, running from dangerous storms and seas or sprinting into the path of favorable winds. Once hooked into a weather system, the catamaran had the raw speed to "surf" it for days. The only hard question was whether *Team Adventure,* a prototype design, could survive the constant abuse of sailing at high velocity over twenty-eight thousand miles of open ocean. Cam Lewis and the crew had been learning more every day about *Team Adventure*'s handling and performance, but it takes months, even years, to truly know a boat's nuances and limits. With just a few weeks of experience behind them, the crew was now facing the wind, waves, and ice of the globe's most unforgiving test tank.

The transition to the Southern Ocean had been abrupt. Just two days earlier, the crew had been bouncing across the enormous trampoline nets stretched between the catamaran's hulls in shorts and T-shirts, doing laundry and drying clothes in the warm, almost windless torpor of a high-pressure bubble planted off the South American coast. Jacques Vincent, a thirty-eight-year-old veteran ocean racer from France who had sailed the Southern Ocean with Lewis once before, stripped down on the starboard hull to take what might be his last full-body scrub for a month. The light weather was also a final opportunity to ready the boat for the ten-thousand-mile sleigh ride that lay ahead. The mainsail was dropped so that the worn strop that locked it in place at the top of the mast could be replaced. It took seventeen minutes and all fourteen crew taking turns at the winch handles to get the huge sail back up, and that was a boat record. Steering systems were double-checked. Rob Myles, a thirty-three-year-old rigger from Newport, Rhode Island, worked into the night by the light of a headlamp to fashion spare halyards and lines. Smaller storm sails were brought out on deck for the first time, ready for use.

From a racing perspective, though, the calm winds had been slow torture. Rolling swells from weather systems long gone or far away slopped the giant boat around with such force that sail battens broke, and the crew sometimes had to crawl on hands and knees to get around safely. Speeds dropped into the single digits. *Team Adventure* had arrived in this weather divot after seventeen days of flat-out dueling with *Club Med,* one of her sister ships. Since the New Year's Eve start in Barcelona, the two boats had dogged each other the length of the Atlantic, trading the lead back and forth over thousands of miles, rarely finding themselves more than a few hours' sailing time apart. Winning the headlong sprint to the South's powerful west winds was perhaps the single most important strategic goal in the race. Those winds would slingshot the boats eastward around Antarctica toward Cape Horn. The first boat that caught them would likely be the first to escape the Southern Ocean. Any lead after Cape Horn meant a big tactical advantage during the stretch run up the Atlantic toward the Mediterranean finish in Marseilles.

Entering the Southern Ocean had been a blessed relief, like crossing into another ocean world. The Global Positioning System steadily ticked off the minutes of latitude toward 40° south.

As if on cue, albatrosses appeared overhead, soaring on nearly motionless wings in the rapidly accelerating winds. Air temperatures started to drop toward freezing, beading areas of *Team Adventure*'s minimalist interior with cold condensation. On deck, the chill wind and stinging spray required a complete change of uniform. A layer of fleece replaced thin summer clothing. Waterproof ocean suits were piled on top to keep the frigid water from sneaking close to the skin. A wild assortment of headgear — a garish lime-green neoprene hood, a sensible balaclava, a favorite baseball cap — was enlisted in a never-ending battle to stay warm and dry.

The real battle had just started, though. *Club Med*'s highly experienced crew had somehow managed to sniff out a faster route into the South. For twelve hours, while *Team Adventure* continued to wallow in light winds, *Club Med* sailed into a corridor of solid breezes that quickly rose to 35 knots and rocketed her away to a lead approaching two hundred miles. Cam Lewis was a world-champion small-boat sailor four times over, known for his love of speed, his competitive fire, and an instinctive skill for making boats sail really fast. *Club Med*'s coup was galling. Over the length of the Atlantic, *Team Adventure* had shown flashes of a slight but critical speed edge. Now *Club Med* had sneaked — or lucked — into a commanding lead and was threatening to break a tight race wide open. Lewis was used to boats chasing *him,* not the other way around. When *Team Adventure* finally felt the 25-knot punch from the westerly winds that had carried *Club Med* away, he set off in hot pursuit. A lot of the sailors on board had spent most of their careers on slower, more stable, monohull boats. The sensation of sailing at 25 to 35 knots in Southern Ocean conditions was unsettling, even shocking, and took some getting used to. When the call came to reduce sail after a night of hurtling over the dark seas, there were more than a few private sighs of relief.

Still, hour after hour Lewis and the crew pressed for as much pace as they dared, driving, tweaking the trim of the enormous sails, sleeping only sporadically. With every gust of wind the liquid-crystal digits of the speed readout cycled rapidly toward 40 knots. The twin bows sliced the tops off waves, flinging sheets of salt spray back to the cockpits, stinging bare skin and testing the waterproof seals of the crew's dry suits. To protect their eyes, some drivers wore ski goggles. Crossing almost sixty feet of trampoline from one hull to the other became a game of both skill and chance. Waves shot up through the netting with enough force to knock a crewman down or even wash him over the stern. You had to tether your harness to the safety line, pick your moment, and sprint. Sometimes you made it safely. Sometimes you were dumped by a wave. And sometimes you called for a "taxi," signaling the driver at the helm to slow the boat for a few brief seconds to make it all easier.

Every four hours new position reports arrived via satellite. Almost every update had *Team Adventure* averaging a knot or two faster than *Club Med*. The effort and concentration were paying off. *Team Adventure* had sailed almost 615 miles in twenty-four hours, the best run of the race so far and just 10 miles shy of the world record, set by *Club Med* during training seven months earlier.

But now there was ice, and ice warranted caution. Lewis, for the first time in a long sailing career, was responsible for thirteen other lives. A bad decision or bad luck could put those lives in jeopardy. He ordered the headsail dropped to the deck. *Team Adventure* immediately slowed, and Lewis maneuvered to pass upwind of the floating mountain. It meant a detour, but the easier downwind side was growler territory. Rosenfeld dutifully contacted race headquarters in France with an ice warning for the area. Soon *Team Adventure* came upon a second iceberg and then a third. One was enormous, perhaps a mile long. To get to the windward side meant an even longer detour. The crew pressed their luck and passed to leeward. It was a mistake. Growlers slid past the hulls.

The unsettling run through the ice was a perfect example of the relentless dilemma the Southern Ocean throws at racing sailors: how to balance speed against safety. The sailing condi-

tions — large waves to surf on and strong following winds —
are an almost irresistible invitation to push boats to the limit.
That's why sailors love to go there. But high speed means esca-
lating loads on masts, rigging, and mechanical hardware and the
risk of breakage. It means less time to see and avoid ice, debris,
even whales, and more damage if there is a collision. And, particularly on a catamaran that might be surfing down a wave face
at almost 40 knots, it means the possibility that the boat will
bury its bows in the wave just ahead. Southern Ocean sailors la-
conically call this "going down the mine," which doesn't quite
do justice to the violence of the event. As the bows submarine,
the boat sharply slows and the sterns start to lift from the water.
The sudden deceleration sends an enormous shock through the
rig as the mast tries to whip forward. Sometimes it is enough to
snap the mast in two. Any sailors not well braced or safely in
their bunks are sent tumbling. The boat might even have enough
momentum or enough assistance from the wave behind to som-
ersault over its own bows, coming to a stop upside down. This
is known as pitchpoling, and for any multihull it is the end of the
game. With mast, sails, and rigging hanging into the depths like
a sea anchor, the boat is more stable upside down than right side
up. A flipped catamaran tends to stay that way.

Team Adventure had been designed for speed above all else,
and it was hard to resist that pedigree. Lewis had matched well-
designed sails, made out of a superlight, superstrong material
called Cuben Fiber, with skilled drivers. One of them, a forty-
six-year-old American named Randy Smyth, a.k.a. "Dr. Speed,"
was a two-time Olympic silver medalist and one of the best multihull sailors in the world. No one on board doubted Team Adventure could run Club Med down. But Lewis initially sounded
a cautious note. "Where can we expect to compress on them?
Where is a passing lane?" he mused in an e-mail as he sat in one
of the custom-built racecar seats installed in Team Adventure's
navigation station. "You have to finish to win. We must use
good seamanship and enjoy good luck."

As Lewis saw it, he had two choices. Team Adventure could

play it safe and try to nibble away at *Club Med*'s lead — after all, ten thousand miles of Southern Ocean sailing lay ahead. Or he could press *Club Med* hard, perhaps forcing her to throttle back or risk breakdown. The two boats were locked in a game of high-seas chicken, and Lewis got to choose the pace. Mostly he just wanted to stay in the same weather system to prevent a decisive breakaway. But he also knew the Southern Ocean was a drag race. And in any drag race Lewis was determined to be as fast or faster than the competition. Nibbling wasn't his style. Soon after *Team Adventure* cleared the third iceberg she was back up to top speed, carving through the waves at 25 to 30 knots, all her lines stretched rigid, the hulls creaking and groaning.

And here the boat offered a warning. For the first time since arriving in the South, she buried the bows. Everyone held his breath as the catamaran slowed sharply and then relaxed as she took off again, the buoyancy of the bows bringing them back to the surface. Rick Deppe, a Southern Ocean veteran and full-time racing sailor who was shooting film and photos for the voyage, was safely in his bunk at the time. But he was starting to worry that the catamaran was being pushed past sensible limits. Deppe had no illusions about the dangers of the Southern Ocean. He knew that any sailor who agreed to race here was putting his or her life on the line. Still, the sudden encounter with ice had crystallized a nagging sense that the big catamaran had not yet found the right balance between speed and prudence.

Icebergs are unpredictable, and sailors have to nurture a certain degree of fatalism: if you hit one, you hit one. But good sailors will also do whatever they can to minimize the risks. The first line of defense, especially at night, is radar, which can be set to sound an alarm if it detects an obstacle at predetermined ranges. When the first iceberg appeared directly in *Team Adventure*'s path, Deppe ran below to the wall of instruments in the nav station to see whether the iceberg was visible on the screen. He was shocked to discover that the radar wasn't even turned on.

Deppe once told a reporter that his credo was "Scare yourself at least once a day." He could live with the risk of ice, but he had a harder time dealing with his concern that *Team Adventure* seemed unprepared for it. The chances of hitting ice at high speed so early in the Southern Ocean were small, but the consequences would have been catastrophic. The dormant radar symbolized to Deppe a lack of discipline regarding the dangers *Team Adventure* faced. "I was flabbergasted, horrified. Words can't explain what I was thinking. If it had been at night we would have hit it, we would have sailed straight smack down into it," he recalled. "That really had a big effect on me." Deppe was thirty-six, with a wife and two young children. He was looking to get out of professional sailboat racing and begin a more stable career in video and film. He had done a lot of dangerous sailing in his life, yet he had always promised his family that he would not be reckless.

Racing a brand-new maxi-catamaran design to the edge of its potential in the Southern Ocean was beginning to scare him more than once a day. He was having trouble sleeping during his off watch, sometimes imagining the dark, the panic, the icy water down below if the boat flipped over. He developed a gnawing premonition that signing on with *Team Adventure* had been a fateful, spur-of-the-moment mistake. Just before the start in Barcelona, Deppe had landed awkwardly on the deck, severely injuring his right ankle (he later discovered it was broken). Even after he went to the hospital, he resisted the inner voice urging him to pull out. Now, careening around the bottom of the world, he regretted his stubbornness and joked morbidly to himself that the leering gargoyles he had seen in the old quarter of Barcelona had been trying to warn him.

With each watch, the wind kept building and *Team Adventure*'s average speeds kept increasing. When Deppe next came on deck, Randy Smyth was at the helm doing what he did best — pushing a multihull at maximum speed, in this case 30 knots and more. Deppe sat in the cockpit worrying that the boat was being pressed too hard for the conditions and was in danger of wiping out. "Jackie," he called out over the roar of the wind to Jacques

Vincent, the watch leader on deck. "What about reducing some sail to slow down a bit or finding a different angle through the waves?"

Vincent was one of the most experienced ocean racers in the world, with four circumnavigations to his credit and a swashbuckling style that reflected his pure love of sailing. He considered the wind and the boat's violent passage through the roaring seas. "Yeah, yeah, you are probably right." He paused, then added, "Maybe we will wait a little while." And finally came "It's okay. I think it is okay."

Deppe couldn't contain his nervous energy. "Whatever," he muttered under his breath. He left the cockpit to help shift some sails on the trampoline.

Down below, Cam Lewis was lying awake in his bunk, listening to the loud thrum of water racing past the hull. It was a sound that meant the catamaran was devouring the miles. The boat was going really fast, maybe too fast. There is a fine line between racing hard and racing recklessly. Lewis wasn't on deck, but he was in charge. And he too was starting to wonder whether *Team Adventure* was speeding into danger.

Meanwhile, thousands of miles away, in Paris, a man named Bruno Peyron was closely monitoring the high-speed duel under way between *Team Adventure* and *Club Med* in the South. Peyron, a record-setting multihull sailor himself, could almost feel the stress and doubt that Lewis and his crew were experiencing as they juggled speed, safety, racing tactics, and the unpredictable waters. As a survivor of Southern Ocean sailing, Peyron empathized. As an observer, he was thrilled. This was exactly the sort of drama — the test of sailor versus sailor, of technology versus the elements, the demonstration of pure speed — he had in mind years earlier when he first envisioned this round-the-world sprint, which had come to be known simply as The Race.

1

CLIPPERS, TOFFS, AND AN AMERICAN ORIGINAL

Where lies the land to which the ship would go?
Far, far ahead, is all her seamen know.
And where the land she travels from? Away,
Far, far behind, is all that they can say.

— Arthur Hugh Clough

THE INSPIRATION for what would become The Race can be traced to the cramped navigation station of a boat heaving itself through the same waters *Team Adventure* and *Club Med* now faced. It was an environment unlikely to evoke casual inspiration, but Bruno Peyron was not the sort of man, or sailor, to let his thinking be restricted by noise and discomfort. In 1993 he was skipper of *Commodore Explorer,* an eighty-six-foot catamaran chasing after a literary ghost named Phileas Fogg. Fogg, in Jules Verne's popular nineteenth-century novel *Around the World in Eighty Days,* used trains, ships, a balloon, and an elephant to circle the globe. Peyron was out to match or exceed Fogg's feat using only a state-of-the-art racing catamaran, launched in 1987.

Circumnavigating by sailboat in eighty days, even with the technology available in 1993, was an ambitious goal. Advances in sail design and materials technology had by the 1980s produced light, powerful racing multihulls that could easily exceed the estimated average of 14 knots or so that the record-setting trip would require. But as with Fogg's proposition, it was widely considered to be a fool's errand.

Sailing a catamaran at blistering speeds for a few days, or even across the Atlantic, was one thing; racing it nonstop around the world through storms and calms for eighty days was quite another. Engineers design gear to withstand predicted loads, but predicting the stress and wear inflicted on a delicate racing machine by every extreme of weather over the course of a circumnavigation is a black art. If a fast-moving multihull sailed through an average of just fifteen waves a minute, its hulls would be twisted and its rig pumped like a wand almost two million times in a voyage around the globe. Some sea conditions would of course be much worse than others. But every passing swell would exert some part of its considerable power on the complex, highly integrated structure of the boat, inexorably prodding and probing every connection and bond for weaknesses to exploit. These dynamic loads are extremely difficult to model accurately and therefore difficult to predict.

Before 1993 at least four sailors had attempted to sail multihulls around the world nonstop. All failed. The extant record for a nonstop circumnavigation, set in 1990 by a monohull, stood at 109 days and 8 hours. If Bruno Peyron could whip *Commodore Explorer* around the globe in eighty days while keeping the boat in one piece, he would not only become the first multihull sailor ever to complete a nonstop circumnavigation (a major sailing milestone in itself), he would also improve the existing circumnavigation record by a nearly unbelievable 27 percent.

It would be an extreme test of speed sailing skills and seamanship, which meant knowing when to throttle back at times. If anyone could pull it off, however, Bruno Peyron was a reasonable gamble. He was the son of a tanker captain, and grew up on the west coast of France, near the border between the Brittany and Loire regions, a breeding ground for many of France's greatest offshore sailors. Peyron became one of them. Thirty-seven years old in 1993, he had sailed across the Atlantic almost thirty times — more than ten times solo — and in both 1987 and

1990 he claimed the single-handed west-to-east transatlantic record, completing the 1990 voyage in just under ten days.

To chase after Phileas Fogg, Peyron scraped together enough money to buy a seventy-five-foot transatlantic record-setting catamaran named *Jet Services V* (which he intended to lengthen by about eleven feet) and recruited a small crew of four crack sailors. One of the four was Jacques Vincent. Another was Cam Lewis. That Peyron chose an American was a reflection of his belief in sailing as a sport that breaks down national barriers. Lewis was also one of the fastest multihull drivers anywhere, and well known in France. In 1986 he had hooked up with Randy Smyth to win the Formula 40 championship, the top French multihull racing circuit. This stunned fiercely partisan French enthusiasts, but they could recognize talent when it went sailing by. Peyron and Lewis became friends and started doing some racing together.

When Peyron bought *Jet Services* — which he renamed *Commodore Explorer,* for her new sponsor — to chase after Phileas Fogg, his friend Cam seemed a natural choice to help him. But Peyron hesitated at first. Building good crew chemistry is a critical and somewhat mystical art. On a long, stressful voyage there is plenty of time for minor personality differences to erupt into confrontations that can undermine morale and the efficiency of crew work. Lewis had a high-energy style that Peyron thought might be painfully amplified in the catamaran's narrow hulls. Still, there weren't many sailors who could drive the boat as fast, and speed was what the voyage was all about, so Lewis was invited to join the five-man crew. To keep him humble, he was also put in charge of cooking, a decision that his French crewmates sometimes regretted.

On January 31, 1993, *Commodore Explorer* crossed an imaginary line that runs north across the English Channel from Île d'Ouessant, at France's northwest corner, to the Lizard, Great Britain's southernmost point. Fewer than nine days later, she had sailed from the channel to the equator, faster than any boat in history (a good passage to the equator for the clipper ships of the nineteenth century was twenty-one days). Thirty days later, she was deep in the Southern Ocean, running hard between Africa and Australia and on course to break the eighty-day target. The miles had not been easy for either the boat or the crew. In the South Atlantic the cat was almost pitchpoled. In the South Indian Ocean two rogue waves cracked the starboard hull. Peyron was spending a lot of time in what Lewis called the office, in the starboard hull, chasing after more sponsorship dollars over the telex and worrying that any more damage to the boat — like a toppled mast — would leave him destitute, a near pioneer with a large and debilitating debt. To take his mind off his woes, Peyron would drift off into a fantasy he had nurtured for years: building a futuristic maxi-catamaran that was more than a hundred feet long and could sail faster than anyone believed possible. In 1985 he had asked *Commodore*'s designer, Gilles Ollier, to draw up the lines for such a multihull, but the project had never been completed. Now, holed up in *Commodore Explorer*'s cramped instrument space, suffering constant back and neck pain from the punishing motion of the boat as the Southern Ocean roared by the hulls, he doodled sketches of fantastic craft worthy of Jules Verne.

The best thing to do with spectacular boats is set them against one another in a test. And Peyron also started to imagine a race around the world over this same route, a race between giant multihulls created by the world's best designers and sailed by the world's top sailors. There would be no design restrictions, no speed limits, and no stopping. The Race, as Peyron began to think of it, would be unprecedented: the first organized nonstop, fully crewed sailing sprint around the world. If he could pull it off, The Race would be an exciting test of how far technology and skill could push the art of sailing. It would launch the sport into a new millennium, but it would also pay tribute to what had come before. The crews, despite sophisticated navigational software and weather forecasting technology, would follow routes first sailed 150 years earlier by another generation of tough, adventurous seafarers, the clipper men. They would be engaged in

a form of competition — racing nonstop — that had been pioneered decades earlier by single-handers, the eccentrics of the
sport. And they would race in a design class — multihulls —
that had been elevated to premier ocean-racing status, despite
concerns about safety, thanks to a persistent clique of sailors
dedicated above all else to the pursuit of speed across the oceans.

THE CLIPPER WAY

By the mid-nineteenth century, trade with three disparate parts
of the world demanded, as never before, fast sailing ships. In Europe and the United States, the growing thirst for China tea
placed an enormous premium on the first and freshest cargoes of
the year to reach London and New York. The discovery of gold
in California and Australia and the ensuing explosion of immigration and economic growth had shipping companies scrambling to build vessels that could shorten the long voyages from
Europe and the eastern United States. The result, first from the
drawing boards and yards of the American shipping industry
and then from Europe as well, was a spectacular refinement in
nautical design: the clipper ship.

The clippers — so called, it is believed, for their ability to
move at such a rapid clip — were sharp-bowed, narrow in the
hull, and carried an enormous press of sail, usually on three
masts. They were an elegant fusion of form and function, rang-
ing in size from 120 feet overall to around 300 feet. The *Sea
Witch,* launched in New York City in 1846 for the China run
and considered by many historians to be the first true American
clipper, was almost 200 feet overall and capable of sailing 16
knots or more. Over a good ten days' run she might average
more than 12 knots, faster than most sailing ships of the previous decade could manage even in a brief burst.

The speed and beauty of the clippers caught the public imagination and inspired a frenzy of wagering and record-keeping

that remains the basis for many sailing-record routes today. In March 1849 *Sea Witch* sailed home to New York with a cargo of tea from Hong Kong after a voyage of seventy-four days and fourteen hours. An older packet ship might take four or five months to complete the 15,500-mile voyage. At first the semaphore operator at Navesink Highlands, off the entrance to New York Harbor, refused to believe the ship was a tea clipper. It seemed impossible for any ship to be in so soon with China's January crop. "Never in the United States has the brain of man conceived or the hand of man fashioned so perfect a thing as the clipper ship," the noted historian Samuel Eliot Morison observed.

The discovery of gold in California in 1848, and in Australia in 1851, only intensified the boom in clipper ship building and design. From April 1847 to April 1848, a total of 2 ships and 9 whalers from the eastern seaboard put in to San Francisco Harbor. In 1849, after President James Polk's December 1848 announcement that gold had been found in California, 775 ships sailed out of Atlantic ports bound for San Francisco, carrying more than 91,000 immigrants. By 1852 the number was 220,000. Shipping companies and builders rushed to meet the insatiable demand for both cargo capacity and speed. New York shipbuilders turned out 13 clippers in 1850 and 54 in 1851.

The stormy fifteen-thousand-mile route around Cape Horn, which before the clippers often took 150 days or more, became a celebrated passage. Clipper ship captains who made the run in record time became public figures and were encouraged by shipowners and their own egos to drive their ships harder than any that had ever been sailed. Passage logs for the voyage around Cape Horn are replete with accounts of falling masts, shredded sails, and drowned crew. Captain Robert Waterman, well known as the skipper of the *Sea Witch,* was said to padlock the sheets and halyards that controlled the sails, to prevent nervous crew from reducing sail before he gave the order. The clippers and their fantastic voyages came to symbolize America's rising maritime achievement. When in 1851 the *Flying Cloud* sailed from New York to San Francisco in a record eighty-nine days, it was front-page news.

In Australia it was much the same. Before 1851, immigration to the Australian colonies averaged about 100,000 people a year. Between 1851 and 1854, the number jumped to almost 350,000 a year. With the population boom came a boom in shipping, and the profits associated with fast passages once again rewarded clippers and the companies that built them. British ships had been making the passage to Australia and New Zealand for years, carrying emigrants and finished goods on the way out and wool and other raw materials on the way back. The most direct route out and back, recommended by the British Admiralty, took these ships close to the Cape of Good Hope, at Africa's southern tip, where they could put in to Cape Town for additional cargo or repairs, if necessary. Just as the clipper ships were starting to make the Australia run in the 1850s, though, the preferred route was undergoing a dramatic revision, thanks to an obscure U.S. Navy lieutenant named Matthew Maury. Without skippering a single clipper, Maury, from the musty archives of the Depot of Charts and Instruments in Washington, D.C., revolutionized the routes on which first merchant ships and eventually racing sailors attacked the world's oceans.

In the middle of the nineteenth century, deep-ocean sailors were familiar with some of the earth's more obvious weather patterns and currents, such as the trade winds, the Pacific monsoon, and the Gulf Stream. But navigators knew less when it came to the nuances of myriad local currents and wind patterns that might affect a ship's passage time. Much of what passed for conventional wisdom about routes was a mix of lore and gut instinct, with only a smattering of real science and direct observation. But in 1839 a stagecoach crash started a chain of events that would change all that.

In the accident, Matthew Maury broke his leg, putting an end to his seagoing career in the navy. Maury, then thirty-three, was a dedicated student of navigation who already had some impor-

tant treatises on the subject to his name. He passed his conva-
lescence writing a series of pseudonymous articles, published in
the *Southern Literary Messenger*, which took the navy to task
over such things as graft and the need for a naval academy anal-
ogous to the army's West Point. Not surprisingly, the articles
irritated the navy leadership, and when Maury's true identity
was eventually revealed he had good reason to fear that even his
shorebound naval career would end.

Instead, the navy decided in 1842 to appoint the fractious
Maury to its Depot of Charts and Instruments. Whether this
represented mercy on the part of the navy brass or a desire to
punish Maury by exiling him to the dungeons of the navy's vast
bureaucracy, it was a fortuitous decision. The depot's main purpose was to provide accurate time for the navy's shipboard chro-
nometers, which were used to find longitude at sea. It was also
a haphazard repository for navigational instruments and old
logs collected from warships. The logs contained daily, even
hourly, reports of the ships' tracks and locations, along with observations about winds, currents, and any other notable oceano-
graphic characteristics.

No one in the navy had much use for the growing shelves of
logs; a previous depot administrator had in fact contemplated
selling them as scrap paper. But Maury, with his long interest in
navigation and sailing routes, quickly grasped the hidden value
of the information he now had under his supervision. He and his
staff began collating the logs by area and converting the data in
them into pictorial representations of the currents, average wind
speeds, and wind directions experienced by U.S. Navy ships over
all the routes they had sailed since the service's inception. Maury
assembled these pictorial representations into easily readable
charts, using arrows of various sizes to depict average wind
speeds, strengths, and directions for specific locations during different seasons of the year. Maury's first Wind and Current Charts
were produced in 1847. They were accompanied by an explanation and analysis that came to be called *Sailing Directions*.

At first Maury offered his charts and directions only to U.S.

Navy ships. A few commercial skippers heard talk about them and, always on the lookout for any advantage, asked for copies. One, Captain Jackson of the bark *W.H.D.C. Wright,* used them during an 1848 voyage from Baltimore to Rio de Janeiro. They helped him decide where best to cross the Doldrums, the windless belt that lies across the equator, and encouraged him to hug the Brazilian coast while rounding Cape São Roque (virtually every captain and navigator of the time would do the opposite, sailing across the South Atlantic toward Africa, then doubling back, fearful of being trapped against the cape). Jackson tucked in along the coast, dramatically shortening his route, and, contrary to received wisdom, found favorable wind and current. The *W.H.D.C. Wright* made it to Rio in just thirty-eight days, a voyage that usually took Jackson about fifty-five days. His return trip took just thirty-seven.

When Jackson arrived home in Baltimore more than a month ahead of schedule, the news quickly spread. Commercial skippers up and down the Atlantic coast, including the highly competitive clipper captains, fast became Maury converts and requested copies of his charts and *Sailing Directions.* Maury distributed about five thousand copies of the first edition of his work. In return, he shrewdly asked skippers using his charts to fill out an abstract log he had designed so he could compile even more information about wind and current patterns. He used the results to update subsequent editions of his charts and *Sailing Directions* and expand their coverage beyond the Atlantic and Pacific Oceans. By 1851, he was receiving abstract logs from about one thousand American ships. By 1856, captains and officers from thousands of ships in navies and merchant marines in Europe were also participating in Maury's project, and the picture of the world's oceans, currents, and winds steadily grew more detailed (today's popular Pilot Charts are direct descendants of Maury's original work).

Estimates of how much Maury's Wind and Current Charts shaved passage times are somewhat subjective. Some historians claim that his charts helped reduce the tricky passage from northern ports to the equator by about ten days. In 1859 shipping reports from San Francisco indicated that in that year 124 ships sailed direct to San Francisco from the U.S. Atlantic coast via Cape Horn. Of those ships, 70 were known to have carried the Wind and Current Charts. Their average passage was 135 days, 11 days faster than ships arriving without the charts. One business magazine in 1854 argued that as a result of faster passages, Maury's *Sailing Directions* was saving American ships $2.5 million a year, and the global fleets perhaps more than $10 million a year.

It was on voyages to Australia that Maury's advice proved particularly valuable. Instead of the usual route past the Cape of Good Hope, Maury directed captains and navigators to head well to the south in the Atlantic, all the way to latitude 48°, before turning east. That kept ships clear of the capricious winds in the middle of the South Atlantic and on a direct route to the booming westerlies of the Southern Ocean. With the wind favorably behind them, the ships could "run their easting down" over the thousands of miles to Melbourne and Sydney. Instead of reversing course for the passage home, Maury suggested it would be faster just to keep going east, to ride the great westerly winds all the way to Cape Horn and then turn north.

Sailing out to Australia and back via the Cape of Good Hope could take 120 days or more each way, a sometimes tortuous passage in crowded ships with poor food and water. Maury's directions and charts, in the hands of the clipper sailors, markedly reduced the total sailing time. The first British clipper built specifically for the Australia run was the *Marco Polo*, launched in 1851 at 185 feet long. She sailed from Liverpool for Melbourne in July and arrived there in just 68 days, making a best day's run of 364 miles. Her return journey, via Cape Horn, was made in 74 days. Not only did her fast passages net higher freight rates, a ship like the *Marco Polo* could now make the Australia run twice in one year. That ships on the Australia run

ended up sailing around the world was a coincidence; captains and shipping companies cared only about getting their cargoes home faster. But year after year the clipper ships defined and refined the fastest sailing route around the world, work that did not pass unnoticed by sailboat racers more than a century later.

Maury's Australia route also introduced sailing ships and their crews to the harsh realm of the Southern Ocean. American clippers rounding Cape Horn on the passage to California and back battled the frigid, stormy climes, sometimes for weeks, during the middle third of their voyage. A clipper on the Australia run endured Southern Ocean conditions for months. The ships were massively built and brutal to work. The 244-foot-long *Lightning,* which once sailed a record 436 miles in twenty-four hours, had a mainmast that was 3½ feet in diameter and towered 164 feet above the deck. Her lower stays, which held up the mast, were made of hemp rope 11½ inches in diameter. She could spread more than an acre of sail before the wind. Almost every square foot of it had to be set and taken in by her crew, high above the deck, as they clung precariously to footropes suspended below the massive horizontal yards to which the sails were attached.

Much of the work was done in freezing temperatures, and skippers on the Australia run — obsessed only with making a fast passage — would steer their ships deep to the south in order to sail the shortest route possible. Wool clothing and stiff oilskins were all the sailors had to protect themselves from rain, snow, sleet, and winds that sometimes reached hurricane force. Richard Henry Dana, in *Two Years Before the Mast,* described how, even in freezing weather, the sailors had to work aloft with bare hands because they couldn't grasp the frozen ropes with mittens. Volleys of heavy hail frequently rained down, cutting open their hands and the exposed skin of their faces. In the high Southern Ocean latitudes, the noise of the wind through the rigging was oppressive and unrelenting. Sailors started referring to the "Roaring Forties," "Furious Fifties," and "Screaming Sixties." Clipper captains flew as much sail as the ships could stand, calling for sail changes to match every variation in wind strength. The constant slog stole sleep from the off watches and exhausted the crews to the point of collapse.

Full of cargo, the clippers sailed very low to the water. Large waves frequently swept the decks, threatening to wash over the side any sailor too slow to leap for the rigging. Seas in the Southern Ocean, with no land masses to stop them and plenty of wind to fuel them, are higher on average than anywhere in the world. Thirty-footers are not uncommon, and freak waves of one hundred feet or more have been reported. "It is strange but true: in the high southern latitudes, where the seas can be 50 feet high and 2000 feet long, they roll forward in endless procession, with occasionally one sea of abnormal size towering above the others," reported Captain W.H.S. Jones in *The Cape Horn Breed*. Sometimes the mountains of water rushing up from behind were so intimidating that captains ordered their helmsmen not to look back. The deeper south the ships went, the more dangerous the sailing became, as they encountered ice fields and fog. Sometimes ships simply disappeared.

These conditions demanded the toughest of men. One of them, Captain Alan Villiers, described what it was like to try to survive aloft while handling sails in a Southern Ocean storm: "We dug our fingers — or tried to dig our fingers — into that canvas until it was wet with our blood in parts, as well as with the sprays and the rain; and always we had to try again . . . Perhaps it took a little courage to carry on up there, with a suspicion of ice about the rigging, and hands that were blue with cold and wet with blood. We had not time to think of courage then; we had only time to fight on." Villiers recounted one incident in which a whipping steel cable knocked one of the crew senseless, leaving him unconscious across the yard high above the deck. His mates only had time to lash him to the yard before returning to their struggles. When they thought to glance at him a short while later, they found that he had come to and was working away again. "Game? I don't know," Villiers wrote. "It was no use any being in the ship-of-sails who was not like that."

With passage after clipper passage, the myth and lore of the Southern Ocean grew. "Below 40 degrees south there is no law; below 50 degrees south there is no God," the clipper sailors liked to say. Veterans of Cape Horn proudly took to piercing their left ear with an earring, the ear closest to the cape when rounding west to east, to signify their accomplishment. Tales of Southern Ocean sailing, many no doubt apocryphal, circulated in ports around the world. When in 1854 the *Lightning* made a torrid record run from Melbourne to Cape Horn in just over nineteen days, passengers disembarking in Liverpool claimed that her captain, "Bully" Forbes, had stationed himself on deck with a pistol in each hand to keep his petrified crew from shortening sail. Yet for all the dangers, for all the hardships, injuries, and deaths, there was also the clear sense that Southern Ocean sailing was the most exhilarating sailing on the planet. "How the wind roars through the sailing ship's rigging! How magnificent is its sound!" Villiers wrote. "Though it brings us only work — hard, dangerous, tremendous, Herculean work of a kind people ashore can never know — we yet can feel the glory of the roar of the wind."

Offshore yacht racing, in its infancy during the clipper era, was cause for excitement in the yachting world. Yet Captain Arthur Clark, a clipper veteran and historian of the era, could not bring himself to concede more than a token acknowledgment of the growing sport: "It must be frankly admitted that yacht racing, even across the Atlantic, in comparison with the old clipper ship racing, resembles snipe shooting as compared with big game in the wilds of Africa, while the gold and silver yacht cups appear as mere baubles beside the momentous stake of commercial supremacy for which the clippers stretched their wings." Clark would no doubt be more respectful of the ocean racers who eventually set out across the clipper tracks in the

Southern Ocean. But that sort of racing would not begin for almost a century after the clippers first dramatized the thrills and risks of Southern Ocean sailing.

THE YACHTING WAY

Clark's dismissal of yacht racing was biased but not entirely gratuitous. At the time, sailboat racing in Europe and the United States was mostly a coastal affair, dominated by industrialists who raced mainly to build extravagantly gilded sailing yachts and hired professional crew to run them. The American hub for most of this racing — as well as the prodigious betting that went along with it — was the New York Yacht Club. It was formed in 1844 on the initiative of John Cox Stevens, a wealthy businessman, patron of the arts, and avid sportsman, with the collaboration of eight of his wealthy, boat-owning friends. The club organized races on the Hudson River, with bets from enthusiastic punters running as high as $5,000.

Stevens's love of racing led to the formation, in 1850, of a NYYC syndicate to build the schooner *America,* to be sailed across the Atlantic in 1851 to race against England's fastest yachts. Her builder, George Steers, was so confident of *America's* speed that he proposed the NYYC pay him $30,000 if she beat every boat her size, but agreed to take her back free of charge if she lost just once. In a race around the Isle of Wight, with Queen Victoria and Prince Albert among the spectators, the *America* crushed the gathered fleet of fourteen English yachts, winning a silver ewer known as the Hundred Guinea Cup.

Stevens perhaps overstayed his welcome, hanging around in England for weeks and offering to take on any comers at wagers up to $50,000. Eventually, he was forced to offer one-to-five odds to tempt potential challengers (he got only one taker and happily pocketed £200). On the strength of her reputation, *America* was then sold to an English lord for $25,000. Stevens returned to New York with his silver cup, which was renamed America's Cup and offered as a prize for any yacht that could best the NYYC in a match race.

The America's Cup competition, staged every few years, quickly became a focal point of top-level American yacht racing. But the dearth of true ocean racing was not lost on New York newspapers, ever in search of more exciting spectacles to cover. In 1866 they started to complain that racing giant schooners across New York Harbor was a tad ludicrous. Two NYYC members, George Osgood (married to a Vanderbilt) and tobacco magnate Pierre Lorillard, Jr., agreed. In October of that year, over bowls of turtle soup at the Union Club, Osgood and Lorillard got into a debate over whose sailboat was faster. The argument grew heated, and possibly well lubricated with drink. The only way to resolve it, they decided, was to wager $30,000 each (the equivalent of more than $300,000 today) on a transatlantic race that would pit their two great schooners, *Fleetwing* and *Vesta,* both well over one hundred feet long, against each other. The course would run from Sandy Hook, New Jersey (just outside New York Harbor), to the Needles, a rock formation off the Isle of Wight. The two sportsmen blithely decided that the race would start on December 11, subjecting the boats and their crews to the North Atlantic's fierce winter weather. It was a decision made somewhat easier by the fact that neither owner actually planned to be aboard for the race. They were seeking prestige, not personal adventure.

Their proposal for the first transatlantic race — and the obscene amount of money at stake — had dramatic appeal. As soon as he got wind of it, James Gordon Bennett, Jr., the twenty-five-year-old son of the owner of the *New York Herald,* added $30,000 to the pot so he could race his yacht, *Henrietta.* Bennett Sr., the man who would send Stanley to the wilds of Africa to find Livingstone, assigned one of his star reporters, Stephen Fisk, to be aboard with the following terse instructions: "This race. Yachts. One of 'em me son's. Cover it. No fooling about. Fall in the sea for all I care but get the news. Properly. Understood?"

A $90,000 stake for a yacht race across the Atlantic sent the public into a betting frenzy that added an estimated half million dollars to the wagering. Fisk's friends were convinced that the reporter would be killed at sea and tried to get him subpoenaed as a witness in a court trial that was in progress. Fisk, however, was more afraid of his boss than the North Atlantic in winter and managed to steal onto the *Henrietta* with a succession of bribes and disguises concocted to evade court officers.

More than two hundred steamers with spectators aboard were at Sandy Hook for the start. *Henrietta,* under the command of another Bully, retired merchant skipper "Bully" Samuels, arrived in Cowes, on the Isle of Wight, just under fourteen days later, beating *Fleetwing* and *Vesta* to the finish by about eight hours. Fisk and the *New York Herald* managed to get 500,000 words out of the event, which was as harrowing as expected. The schooners were repeatedly bludgeoned by gale winds and high seas during the crossing. One storm sent a sluice of solid water careening along *Fleetwing*'s decks, sweeping eight men overboard. Only six were recovered. In 1870 Bennett, now owner of the 117-foot *Dauntless,* raced the British America's Cup challenger *Cambria* across the Atlantic east to west, finishing at New York's Ambrose Lightship two hours behind *Cambria.* During the rough crossing two sailors were plucked from *Dauntless*'s bowsprit, adding to transatlantic racing's death toll.

Despite the loss of life, or perhaps because of it, the thrill of transatlantic racing proved hard to resist, and sporting yachtsmen began keeping careful records of times and distances. In March 1887 *Dauntless,* now owned by the firearms heir Caldwell H. Colt, raced the 123-foot *Coronet* from New York to Ireland. *Dauntless* lost but managed to post the best twenty-four-hour run yet recorded by a yacht, 328 miles, a record that would last almost twenty years. Rich men and rough racing produced some odd moments. About halfway across the Atlantic, *Dauntless* lost most of her fresh water thanks to a leaky tank, forcing the thirsty sailors to tap into Colt's abundant champagne reserves for the remainder of the voyage.

Additional transatlantic races followed. The most famous was a 1905 race from Sandy Hook to the Lizard, off Britain's southwest coast. The race was organized by Wilhelm II of Germany, a yachting enthusiast. He offered as a prize a gold cup, so the race became known as the Kaiser's Cup. It received tremendous publicity in both Europe and the United States. Eleven yachts, the largest transatlantic race fleet to date, showed up at the starting line, including a 185-foot, three-masted schooner called *Atlantic,* owned by Wilson Marshall of New York. Marshall hired as captain a forty-one-year-old Scottish immigrant, Charlie Barr, a three-time defender of the America's Cup who was considered the world's top racing skipper. Marshall and six of his friends went along for the ride, but left the work to a professional crew of fifty.

The start off Sandy Hook on May 17 found the glamorous yachts gliding along in very light winds. Shortly after the race began, strong winds filled in, sending *Atlantic* and her rivals charging across the North Atlantic at a record clip. Barr was notorious for his fiercely competitive nature and ability to drive a boat hard. *Atlantic* could carry a staggering 18,500 square feet of sail, and despite the howling winds he was determined to make use of every scrap he could. On the seventh day, *Atlantic* posted a run of 341 nautical miles, breaking *Dauntless*'s 1887 record at an average speed of more than 14 knots. By the eighth day, the North Atlantic was serving up a full gale as *Atlantic* thundered east through huge seas and ice, her leeward rail constantly underwater. Two men were lashed to the wheel to try to keep her under control. At this point Marshall ventured out on deck to advise Barr that perhaps it would be wise to shorten sail. According to legend, Barr answered, "You hired me, sir, to win this race, and by God that is what I am going to do," and ordered the owner back below. And win the race Barr did, whipping *Atlantic* to the finish in the astonishing time of twelve days and four hours. It would take seventy-five years and a new generation of professional sailors, racing with the latest in sailboat design and technology, to eclipse that record.*

Transatlantic racing possessed many of the elements that would eventually lure adventurous sailors to around-the-world racing: fast sailboats, driven crews, a preoccupation with records, and an incessant battle between man and the seas. It was just that no one at the time, particularly the rich men who preferred the comforts ashore of Newport and Cowes to the hard life aboard a racing yacht at sea, thought to race much beyond the Atlantic. Instead, it would take a charismatic old sea captain named Joshua Slocum to open the sailing world's imagination to distant horizons and the concept of sailing for adventure itself.

THE REAL SALT

Slocum was born on a farm in Nova Scotia in 1844 but always had an eye for the sea. At the age of twelve he was beaten for whittling a ship model instead of sorting potatoes. Before long he turned his back on the farm he considered an "anchor" and shipped out in the local fishing fleet as a cook. By the age of thirty-five he was master of the bark *Washington,* a salmon-fishing vessel out of Alaska. Slocum's seafaring career then progressed in the usual pattern of wide-ranging voyages, the occasional stranding and shipwreck, and a succession of wives. By the 1880s he was part owner of one of America's greatest clipper ships, *Northern Light,* which was followed by full ownership of a fast bark named *Aquidneck.* In 1887 Slocum wrecked the *Aquidneck* on a sandbar in Brazil. He and his family survived and made their way back to the United States in a thirty-five-foot sailing canoe, dubbed *Liberdade,* that Slocum had built

---

*Twelve years after the Kaiser's Cup race, at the height of World War I, Marshall raised money for the war effort by smashing the gold cup in front of President Woodrow Wilson and a paying audience at New York's Metropolitan Opera House. The sledgehammer revealed that the trophy was in fact made of pewter, covered by thin gold plate and worth about $35. "I wish it had been made of lead, and then we could have melted it down and fired it back at the faker," Marshall said.

from the wreckage. That experience was more than enough for
the current Mrs. Slocum. Back in New England she announced
that she had had enough of the life afloat.

In 1894, at the age of fifty, Captain Slocum thus found himself faced with a shipping recession, the steady replacement of
the commercial sailing fleet by unromantic steam-powered ships,
and a profound lack of direction in life. Herman Melville, whom
Slocum much admired, wrote at the beginning of *Moby-Dick:*
"Whenever I find myself growing grim about the mouth; whenever it is a damp, drizzly November in my soul . . . then, I account it high time to get to sea as soon as I can." When a friend,
a whaling captain, came across the brooding Slocum in Boston
and offered him a ship if Slocum would repair it — it had been
left to rot in the port of Fairhaven, Massachusetts — he did not
hesitate. Thirteen months of sweat (and $553.62 in cash for ma-
terials) later, the thirty-seven-foot *Spray,* a trim little sloop, was
ready to sail again.

Slocum at first tried to fish for a living with his new command. After discovering he had "not the cunning to properly
bait a hook," he resolved instead to set out around the world.
Slocum never explained how he hit upon this unique plan. Perhaps it seemed logical to a man used to seeking out foreign
ports, a man who was supremely confident in his own seamanship and in need of some excitement. On April 24, 1895, Slocum
and the *Spray* set out from Boston, with his friends and fellow
sailors questioning his sanity. The resolute old captain paid them
no mind. "I felt that there could be no turning back, and that I
was engaging in an adventure the meaning of which I thoroughly understood. I had taken little advice from any one, for I
had a right to my own opinions in matters pertaining to the
sea," he later wrote.

More than three years later Slocum returned to the United
States, having completed a westabout circumnavigation that
wandered over some 46,000 nautical miles, more than twice the
earth's circumference, which is 21,600 miles. He made harbor
in Newport, Rhode Island, one pound heavier and by his own

reckoning "at least ten years younger than the day I felled the first tree for the construction of the *Spray*." Along the way, Slocum sailed with aplomb in gales and calms, passed twice through the tricky Strait of Magellan at the southern tip of South America (after being forced back into the strait by hurricane-force winds in the Pacific), and escaped from pirates and Fuegian marauders (he scattered tacks on the deck as a primitive but effective alarm system). He stopped everywhere, from the island of Juan Fernández in the South Pacific (also known as Robinson Crusoe's island) to Cape Town in South Africa, where President Kruger insisted Slocum's voyage was impossible, since the earth was flat. Slocum gave lectures to raise money, made dozens of friends, and was generally accorded the astonishment his voyage warranted. The *Sydney Morning Herald* compared him to the polar explorers and interpreted his wide popularity as a statement on human nature: "This could hardly be the case if the ideal were not still at the long last and in the deep inner heart of humanity a more powerful motive than the real — if adventure and danger, now as formerly were not regarded as finer qualities than comfort and ease."

Slocum's wry and self-effacing account of his adventure made no effort to bludgeon the reader with melodrama and philosophizing. "The worst pirate I met on the whole voyage," he insisted, was a goat (put aboard *Spray* on the island of St. Helena), "which threatened to devour everything from flying-jib to stern davits." The goat's feast included Slocum's West Indies chart and straw hat, forcing him to make a sunburned landfall in the coral-strewn Antilles from memory. Yet despite his Yankee humility, his circumnavigation ranks as one of the greatest voyages ever completed. Before his 1895 voyage, any number of explorers and commercial captains had sailed ships around the globe, but Slocum was the first sailor ever to circumnavigate alone, the first to do it in such a small boat, and the first to do it for his own pleasure. Today's sailing technology — black boxes spitting out pinpoint positions from satellite navigation systems at the push of a button (or the click of a mouse); electric winches that take most of the sweat out of handling a boat; space-age materials that make sailboats and their sails strong and light; Gore-Tex fabric, microwave ovens, and all the other comforts that help keep sailors warm and dry — makes it easy to underestimate Slocum's feat.

In his day, and up until the 1980s, finding a ship's position in the middle of an ocean involved an elaborate procedure using a sextant to calculate the altitude of the sun and other celestial bodies above the horizon. A lot of trigonometry followed, made somewhat easier for Slocum and his generation by precalculated tables that eliminated the need to solve equations in longhand. Although the science and mathematics behind this sort of navigation was sound, a certain margin of error was inevitable because of the difficulty of taking precise sextant readings at sea. A "sight" required the sailor to hold the sextant steady enough to bring the target (whether sun, moon, or stars) into focus and then manipulate the sextant so that the target appears to brush the surface of the sea. That was easy enough on a sunny day in a flat calm. But what about when the sun or stars appeared fleetingly in an overcast sky or simply disappeared for days? What if the ship was tossing about in a heavy sea? Or both? In these sorts of conditions a skilled navigator was lucky if his fix of the ship's position was only a few miles off. Even that margin of error could make the difference between survival and shipwreck when approaching a coast or an island.

Slocum, of course, had a lifetime of sextant navigation behind him when he set out, but his ability to make a safe landfall time after time along coastlines and amid islands bespoke a mastery of his craft. He had such confidence in his skills that he left his trusty chronometer behind when he discovered it would cost $15 to service it so it would run accurately. Instead, he sailed with a tin clock that he bought for a dollar in Nova Scotia. It had a smashed face, and he had to dip it in boiling oil while crossing the Indian Ocean to get it running. Such an unruly timepiece would have been the death of many a sailor. Slocum resorted to calculating his longitude using the lunar distance method, an extremely complicated procedure that had largely been abandoned over the previous century as accurate seagoing chronometers, which allowed for a simpler alternative, became widely available. Slocum succeeded splendidly with the lunar method, nailing a landfall at the small Pacific island of Nukahiva in the Marquesas and in the process even identifying some errors in his lunar tables. Typically, the further Slocum wandered from conventional practice, the happier he became: "I was *en rapport* with my surroundings, and was carried on a vast stream where I felt the buoyancy of His hand who made all the worlds . . . The work of the lunarian, though seldom practiced in these days of chronometers, is beautifully edifying, and there is nothing in the realm of navigation that lifts one's heart up more in adoration."

Although Slocum struggled on occasion, with only himself for company, sailing solo had its benefits. "I found no fault with the cook, and it was the rule of the voyage that the cook found no fault with me. There was never a ship's crew so well agreed," he reported. But with passages of up to seventy-two days (crossing the Pacific), it was inevitable that loneliness would creep aboard. To ward it off and keep his spirits above the waterline, Slocum read, sang, talked to the man in the moon, and traded confidences with a ghostly alter ego, the pilot of Columbus's ship *Pinta,* whom he first conjured while ill in a gale. His solitude sometimes got the better of him, however. Approaching the Keeling Islands in the Indian Ocean after a twenty-three-day passage, Slocum found himself overwhelmed with emotion and sat crying on the deck. "To folks in a parlor on shore this may seem weak indeed, but I am telling the story of a voyage alone," he explained.

Loneliness, while sometimes profound, was not the least of the challenges. Books provided diversion, but they could not help Slocum sail the *Spray.* Seamanship is sometimes a vague concept, but at its core it means taking good care of the ship. Even today, many sailors consider sailing across oceans with a crew of one inherently unseamanlike. Too much is required — sail handling, maintenance, navigation, steering, keeping a good lookout, cooking — for one person to handle easily. Slocum somehow juggled all these responsibilities with calm efficiency.

Steering was perhaps the most obvious obstacle to sailing solo, and he knew that no vessel had ever steered itself around the globe. But a well-designed sailboat can be made to steer a straight course with no hand on the helm if the sails are carefully trimmed so that the rudder can be tied off in one position. Still, striking this delicate balance over thousands of miles of open ocean seemed impossible. Slocum and the *Spray*, to their credit, proved it was not. He never had significant steering difficulties, sometimes sleeping soundly as the *Spray* carved a steady course through narrow passages (though he did run aground once, on the coast of Uruguay, and almost drowned). Man and boat became so comfortable with each other that Slocum claimed the 2,700-mile, twenty-three-day crossing of the Indian Ocean required no more than an hour of his time at the helm. "A delightful midsummer sail," he called it.

Slocum made it all sound pretty easy. But he encountered skeptic after skeptic who refused to believe he was sailing alone. Three friendly Samoans concluded that he had eaten the other members of his crew, and port officials around the world scrutinized his ship's papers for evidence of additional human cargo. Slocum eventually settled on a somewhat offbeat solution to prove once and for all that he sailed alone. While stopped at Ascension Island in the South Atlantic, he invited a lieutenant from the local Royal Navy base to fumigate the *Spray* so thoroughly that any crew hiding below would be flushed out or asphyxiated. When none emerged, Slocum had a certificate issued to that effect, and went on his way.

Like most adventurers, Slocum was less than articulate when explaining his original motivations or ambitions in striking out to do something so out of the ordinary. But after the hardships and triumphs of the experience itself, he made it clear that his journey bestowed a sort of enlightenment on an aging sailor. At sea he frequently felt renewed, immortal. As he navigated by the sun, moon, and stars, he learned to view the physical world with wonder. And most important, he learned patience: "As for patience, the greatest of all the virtues, even while sailing through the reaches of the Strait of Magellan . . . where through intricate sailing I was obliged to steer, I learned to sit by the wheel, content to make ten miles a day beating against the tide, and when a month at that was all lost, I could find some old tune to hum while I worked the route all over again, beating as before . . . The days passed happily for me wherever my ship sailed."

Slocum achieved something that probably no sailor had ever attempted, thanks to his inventiveness, determination, and joyful spirit. And it was natural that his voyage would speak to any sailor since who suffered from wanderlust, wished to try something new, or simply had an itch to confound conventional wisdom. "To young men contemplating a voyage I would say go," he wrote. "The tales of rough usage are for the most part exaggerations, as also are the stories of sea danger . . . To face the elements is, to be sure, no light matter when the sea is in its grandest mood. You must then know the sea, and know that you know it, and not forget that it was made to be sailed over."

Slocum spent many a subsequent year happily following his own advice. Eventually, however, his unique lifestyle collided with one of the sea's grand moods. In 1909 he set out to sail the aging, rundown *Spray* through winter gales from Martha's Vineyard to the Bahamas and on to South America. He was headed for the Orinoco River, where he intended to work his way to the headwaters of the Amazon. Perhaps Slocum contemplated the possibility that he was leaving for the last time. Aboard *Spray* he carried a phonograph; he said if the Indians he met mistook him for a god he would stay and set up in business. Whatever his intentions, he never reached the Amazon. Slocum and *Spray* disappeared without a trace.

Joshua Slocum set a compelling example of how amateur sailors could make sailing an adventure that spanned all the world's oceans. His voyage was also a parable on the rewards of bucking convention, believing in one's own abilities, and pursuing a goal with unswerving determination. He set a new standard that expanded the horizon for any sailor dissatisfied with ordinary life or ordinary sport. At the same time, his circumnavigation was such an incomparable feat of seamanship that it was not a journey that many ordinary sailors could duplicate or even contemplate.

Slocum was a professional seaman turned amateur by circumstance. Yachting for decades remained a sport mostly for the wealthy, a sport preoccupied with near-shore cruising and racing. After two world wars and a global depression, though, amateur sailing and racing spread to the middle class. And it was this generation, the generation of postwar amateurs, that turned to Slocum's example for inspiration. He had single-handedly created the sport of extreme sailing. Now the new generation, looking for an antidote to the banality of postwar life, was ready to expand the genre. Slocum had voyaged alone. These sailors wanted to race alone.

2

COCKLESHELL HEROES

> He had bought a large map representing the sea,
> Without the least vestige of land:
> And the crew were much pleased when they found it to be
> A map they could all understand.
>
> — Lewis Carroll

JOSHUA SLOCUM was motivated to go to sea by a disaffection with his life ashore. In the 1960s, boredom with everyday life sent two more single-handers to the oceans for adventure, H. G. "Blondie" Hasler and Francis Chichester. If Slocum pioneered the sport of single-handed sailing, Hasler pioneered the sport of single-handed racing. In sailing, single-handers have always been happy to test conventions of seamanship and boat design. Hasler, with Chichester's help, launched the next great revolution in extreme sailing. They started by racing across the Atlantic, and Chichester ended up conquering the globe. Together they inaugurated the era of round-the-world racing, which led directly to The Race.

Blondie Hasler was an archetypal English hero: brave, adventurous, and clever. During World War II he became a national icon by leading a squad of twelve Royal Marines on a raid into Nazi-occupied France. The team was brought by submarine to the mouth of the Gironde River, in the Bay of Biscay. From there, using two-man kayaks Hasler helped design, they paddled fifty miles up the Gironde to Bordeaux Harbor and sank or severely damaged six German ships. Only Hasler and his kayak mate survived the mission. It's unclear how much impact the raid had on the Nazis' war-fighting capability, but the exploits of the "cockleshell heroes" provided an enormous boost to British morale, and Hasler was awarded the Distinguished Service Order.

In 1947 Hasler retired from the Royal Marines, convinced that the tedium of peacetime service would drive him insane. Like Slocum, Hasler soon found himself without much direction and casting about for anything that would interest him. He had no definite idea of a profession, listing, in one stock-taking exercise, "Writing, Drawing, Painting, Play and script writing, Consultant, Inventor, Lecturer" as possible sources of income. He did have a hobby, though. When he wasn't busy making lists of women he might or might not marry, he devoted his considerable energy to the innovation and design of sailboats, which he raced in the waters around England. Never satisfied with the status quo, he was always looking for something new. And in 1956, as the glory of cockleshell heroism faded, Hasler reached deep into his creative imagination and plucked forth a compelling and novel proposition: a single-handed race, sailed east to west across the Atlantic.

A single-handed race across the Atlantic was not unheard of. In 1891, before Slocum's voyage, two unbridled optimists named William Andrews and Josiah Lawlor set out to race from Boston to Europe, with the prevailing winds, aboard fifteen-foot sailboats. Lawlor arrived in England after forty-five days, and Andrews was rescued after sixty-one by a passing steamer six hundred miles from the finish. Nor was sailing single-handed east to west, against prevailing winds, a completely fresh idea: Hasler knew of at least two separate crossings going the hard way. But no one had ever staged an east-to-west transatlantic single-handed race, and even the notion of offshore solo racing remained anathema in traditional yachting circles.

The shortest route for boats sailing from the English Channel to New York followed a daunting three-thousand-mile track subject to storms, persistent headwinds, currents, fog, and ice. Hasler — compact, balding, and with an engaging smile — was determined to pull off the stunt, motivated chiefly by a desire to inspire innovations, such as self-steering and short-handed sail control systems, which would make single-handed sailing, and sailing in general, easier and more efficient. To achieve that, he could think of no better format than a race, shrewdly calculating that there is nothing like a little competition to spur creativity. He understood that lives might be lost, but told potential sponsors that the risks, in his estimation, were no greater than those of the Grand National, a particularly chaotic English steeplechase.

Hasler posted his proposal for the race on the bulletin board of the Royal Ocean Racing Club. It was soon marked up with scrawled comments, most of them skeptical. Finding sponsors for the race was also an exercise in frustration. Hasler hoped that the *Observer* newspaper, for which he wrote sailing stories, would sponsor the competition. But the *Observer*'s management politely declined, afraid of bad publicity should racers start disappearing in the middle of the Atlantic. His search for an organizing yacht club was also greeted with timidity, and he was forced to turn to the one organization bound to be sympathetic to his plans.

The Slocum Society, in the United States, which had been established in 1953 to promote single-handed and small-boat passage-making, was enthusiastic in principle. But negotiations quickly bogged down over details such as when the race would start and whether there should be a stopover in the Azores (since Slocum had stopped there). Hasler thought he had a simple, exciting idea and couldn't understand why the sailing world was making it so complicated. After undergoing one round of proposed changes, he could no longer maintain a polite English air, writing to the society that he had the "persistent impression that . . . fainthearted amendments originate from members who do not wish race to be held at all and will not enter if it is. Kindly have them assassinated and send bill to me."

Ultimately, all Hasler really needed was someone to race against, and in sailing there are always a few eccentrics ready to attempt just about anything. The first to make a commitment, in September 1959, was a doctor named David Lewis, who had recently sailed his twenty-five-foot *Cardinal Vertue* from England to Norway and back as a warm-up. "One man using his wits to get across all that water is what appeals to me," he told an interviewer. Lewis was followed by Val Howells, whom Hasler recruited after reading an account of Howells's single-handed voyage from Cork, Ireland, to La Coruña, Spain, in a twenty-five-foot Scandinavian "folkboat" — which happened to be a virtual sister of *Jester*, the boat Hasler was then sailing as a test bed for his innovations.

Hasler also heard from Francis Chichester, then in his fifty-ninth year. Chichester was an inveterate adventurer. At the age of eighteen he had journeyed from England to New Zealand, where he wandered the outdoors as a lumberjack, livestock herder, and gold prospector. While there, he got hooked on airplanes and took to the skies, pioneering flying routes and air navigation techniques. He was the first pilot to fly solo from New Zealand to Australia, and in 1931 he made the first solo flight from New Zealand to Japan. After World War II, Chichester bought a twenty-four-foot sailboat and found a new mode of transport in which to indulge his passion for navigation and exploration. He raced extensively, but in 1957 was diagnosed with a form of lung cancer. He was on his way to the hospital when he noticed Hasler's race proposal at the Royal Ocean Racing Club. It took him two years to beat back his disease, and now, with a fringe of gray hair, steel-framed eyeglasses, and a determined posture, he was ready for yet another new adventure. For Chichester, sailing had become a liberation from illness. "I sail because it intensifies life," he later explained.

Along with Hasler, Lewis, Howells, and Chichester made up the four entrants for a planned June 1960 start (a fifth, French-

man Jean Lacombe, would also eventually join the race). The
Slocum Society, although long past the possibility of overall
sponsorship, agreed to organize the finish, set for New York
Harbor. The *Observer,* at the urging of a new sports editor,
first offered to contribute a trophy and then acquiesced to general sponsorship if Hasler could find a reputable yacht club to
run the race. With Chichester's help, he continued making the
rounds and continued to encounter clubs reluctant to be, as
Chichester put it, "accused of sending the gallant sons of Old
England to their watery deaths."

Frustrated, Hasler and the three other competitors announced
that if they couldn't find a sponsoring club they would stage the
race themselves, for a half-crown. (This led to the informal es-
tablishment of the Half-Crown Club, into which all successful
transatlantic single-handers are automatically inducted.) In the
end, the Royal Western Yacht Club in Plymouth succumbed to
their lobbying and agreed to take on the race. The first Observer
Single-handed Transatlantic Race (known as the OSTAR) com-
menced on June 19, 1960. Like The Race, there were no limits
on boat size or design, and the sailing instructions were refresh-
ingly simple: "Leave the Melampus buoy [off Plymouth] to starboard and thence by any route to the Ambrose light vessel, New
York."

The OSTAR was a curious affair by modern racing standards.
The tenor was decidedly Corinthian, which is to say amateur. All
the boats had been principally designed for relaxed cruising in
European waters and had to be modified for racing. Chichester
tested his self-steering gear, which he dubbed Miranda, not at
sea but on a model he sailed on the Round Pond in London's
Kensington Gardens. All the boats measured under twenty-six
feet in length save for Chichester's *Gipsy Moth III,* which was
almost forty feet overall and considered a questionable size for
one man to handle.

Most of the entrants stocked provisions for up to eighty days
at sea and did not stint when it came to amenities such as
whiskey and beer. Chichester in particular was determined to

lead a civilized life on the water. He was happy to discover that a "survival kit" donated by the makers of Plymouth Gin contained a reserve bottle, but was chagrined to find that the velvet smoking jacket he took along became covered in mold. Hasler, who was almost overcome by tears as the boats finally set out from the start, had *Jester* floating below her designed waterline with a load of supplies that included fresh eggs, strawberries, and a ukulele.

That the five quixotic competitors (Jean Lacombe had by now joined them) had their light moments could not detract from the extraordinary seamanship they exhibited in soloing across the North Atlantic. Worst off was Chichester. With *Gipsy Moth*'s larger sails and heavier gear, sail changes took up to three hours of exhausting work, and during the voyage more than 120 were required. He endured gales, a three-day storm (with winds that at one point exceeded one hundred miles per hour), and fog over almost half the course. Still, he completed the passage in just over forty days. Communications were so rudimentary he didn't know his finishing position until he was told "You are first" as he approached Ambrose Light. To get there, Chichester had averaged just over 3 knots in conditions so relentlessly wet his only hope of drying his clothes was to sleep in them, a technique countless global racers have adopted since. Despite the hardships, solo sailing, as it had with Slocum, seemed a magical and rejuvenating experience to him. "If anyone lacks interest, exercise or excitement or suffers in any way from boredom this is the answer," Chichester noted in his log.

Hasler, whose notion of single-handing — in contrast to Chichester's more stoic approach — included experimenting with as many labor-saving devices as was practicable, had a somewhat less harrowing passage. He sailed an extreme northerly route on the theory that he might find more favorable easterly winds. His sail handling was a snap compared to Chichester's. *Jester*'s Chinese junk–style rig allowed him to raise or drop his sail like a venetian blind, and lines were rigged so he could do almost everything from the comfort of the cockpit. The cockpit itself was outfitted with a Perspex dome, which protected Hasler from the elements while he was keeping a lookout or handling sails.

He also perfected the single-hander's art of catnapping, snoozing for brief snatches when conditions allowed and waking himself up at regular intervals with an egg timer. He found that up to thirty minutes of sleep while offshore and clear of shipping lanes worked well, but that he could do with as little as two minutes at a time if necessary (he even claimed to have cultivated the "five-second catnap"). The problem of laundry was given a typically unorthodox Hasler solution. As he approached the American coast, and could no longer stand the smell, he simply started throwing his dirty clothing overboard.

Hasler came close to running *Jester* onto the rocks off Ireland, but he survived to glide into New York after forty-eight and a half days at sea. He was second to Chichester, but considered the voyage a great success. He was especially happy with the self-steering gear he had designed, which could be set to steer the boat at a specific angle to the wind.* When he arrived in New York he proudly announced he had spent only an hour of the transatlantic passage steering himself.

David Lewis sailed *Cardinal Vertue* to the finish after a tough fifty-six days, to take third. He lost his mast shortly after the start, and returned to Plymouth for repairs before setting out again. Fifty miles south of Cape Breton, Nova Scotia, a Canadian frigate brushed against him and damaged his rig. Lewis sailed on in thick fog and, like Hasler, almost ran on the rocks, tacking away at the last moment when he saw breaking waves. He later ran aground near Cape Cod and fractured his skull when the boom hit him in the head (a common problem among single-handers, even today). Val Howells turned up after sixty-three days, after stopping in Bermuda to make repairs, and Jean Lacombe appeared after seventy-four. The grueling race took its toll on all the contestants. Chichester and Hasler arrived in New

---

*The gear became the basis for many modern self-steering designs, but Hasler threw away a potential fortune because he never bothered to patent it. Asked why, he would invariably reply, "Because I didn't want to spend my life in law courts."

York ten pounds lighter. Lewis and Howells dropped almost twenty pounds each.

The OSTAR was a milestone in offshore racing, the first in a series of races and courses that would push sailors and boats far beyond the normal demands of sailing. It was an extreme challenge that tested the character and heart of the sailors, who willingly put their lives at risk, as much as it tested the design of the boats. As Hasler had hoped, over time the race became an important proving ground for new gear and sailing techniques, which trickled down to the rest of the sailing world in the form of improved self-steering systems and roller-furling sails that could be struck or reduced in size in a matter of minutes.

So offbeat was the OSTAR experience that one of the first officials to greet Chichester in New York was a U.S. Air Force captain conducting research for the space program. He wanted to know whether Chichester had exhibited any unusual behavior during his forty days of solitude. Chichester didn't have any particular insights to offer American astronauts contemplating long space flights, but his victory in the OSTAR made him a national hero in England. The *Observer*, initially so reluctant to sponsor the race, quickly announced a 1964 competition to prevent rival publications from poaching the sponsorship. That race was won by Eric Tabarly, a thirty-two-year-old French naval officer sailing a custom-built forty-four-foot boat, in just over twenty-seven days (Chichester finished second). Tabarly's victory in a "British" race earned him the Legion of Honor and ignited a passion among the French for single-handed offshore racing that led to a mastery of the sport.

Following the 1964 race the OSTAR became a major commercial event, with generous sponsorships and a slew of competitors. By 1976 there were 125 boats on the starting line, including some monstrous vessels, such as French sailor Alain Colas's four-masted, 235-foot *Club Med*. Tabarly was back, in a 73-foot boat that normally raced with a crew of fifteen. The chaos of the start, and the sight of Colas single-handing his enormous ship among the small fry, inevitably led to fresh accu-

sations that the OSTAR was inherently foolhardy and unseamanlike. Bernard Heyman, editor of Britain's *Yachting World* magazine, screeched, "Gentlemen, this time you have gone too far."
Tabarly managed a second win with a superhuman effort in
which he spent most of the race at the helm after his self-steering packed up four days into the race. Colas somehow sailed the
unwieldy *Club Med* to third place, silencing his detractors. Nevertheless, critics (whom Hasler enjoyed referring to as "the nan-
nies") were given plenty of ammunition when two competitors
drowned — the first deaths in OSTAR history — and forty-eight
starters failed to finish.

In the 1980 OSTAR, organizers answered the sniping with a
size limit of fifty-six feet and the use of tracking transmitters on
the boats. The OSTAR is still a premier transatlantic race — the
2000 edition had seventy-one competitors — but with the addition of numerous regulations and classes its fundamental nature
has been much altered from Hasler's original no-rules, no-limits
concept. Although sympathetic to some modifications such as a
size limit, Hasler refused to surrender to the "nanny" assault on
the legitimacy of single-handed racing. When it was argued that
single-handers selfishly put the lives of rescue personnel at risk,
Hasler coolly responded that sailors who participated in extreme
races should simply "die like gentlemen" if they got into trouble
and couldn't save themselves. Moreover, Hasler said, racers
shouldn't even carry radios. That way, they wouldn't be tempted
to issue a mayday call.

These sorts of arguments about risk and responsibility have
become a consistent theme in extreme ocean racing. Hasler was
adamant that society and its armchair experts should not be allowed to restrict the creativity and ambitions of sportsmen, no
matter how dangerous a game they chose to play. In return, however, he insisted that the risk takers had to accept full responsibility for the choices they made. Hasler wasn't trying to make
any grand point about extreme sport and its effect on human
values; he just wanted sailors to be free to challenge themselves
in ways that would push sailing to new experiences and better

equipment. Still, his iconoclasm and firm belief in self-reliance were the very ideals that drew many sailors to the style of sailing he was promoting. Stuart Woods, an American who raced in the ill-fated 1976 OSTAR, expressed the broader philosophy at work in a rebuttal to the barrage of criticism over the two dead sailors: "Both, in a sense, died defending the right of men to die in adventurous living. No one has proposed, with any effect, that motor racing be prohibited or that men stop trying to climb Everest. It is simply accepted that those who participate in these enterprises do so at their own risk, and good luck to them. Those of us who race single-handed ask no more than that. Leave us alone; ignore us if you like, but let us get on with it."

The OSTAR, with its humble beginnings among five like-minded adventurers, opened the oceans to anyone with a bold racing idea. Such people had to have something else as well. Hasler only succeeded in launching the sport of single-handed racing because he was a creative thinker and a charming, tireless salesman. He had a passion for the sport that infected those around him and eventually won over reluctant sponsors and a growing cadre of sailors. No sport breaks new ground without overcoming skepticism and opposition. Hasler proved that if a concept is compelling enough, it has a chance no matter how absurd it may at first seem.

The aging, angular Chichester — who looked more like a schoolmaster than an ocean racer — showed the sailing world what it took to win at this new sort of racing. He wasn't happy just trying something different; he was happy succeeding. He was a fanatic about details and planning, but out on the seas his most important quality was a fierce, unyielding determination, a refusal to surrender to adverse weather, self-pity, or pain.

These were qualities not traditionally associated with the more cerebral, tactical nature of inshore racing. And Chichester was about to demonstrate that sheer bloody-minded will was as crucial as traditional sailing skills in conquering the world's oceans. After finishing the 1964 OSTAR, he was so comfortable with single-handing a sailboat that the Atlantic Ocean no longer appeared to be the great obstacle it had been in 1960. Now a far grander idea took root in his ambitious mind. If he could solo across the Atlantic, perhaps he could also solo around the world, a distance of twenty-eight thousand miles or more, making just one stop.

CHICHESTER CIRCLES THE GLOBE

Chichester first started toying with the idea of circumnavigating alone in 1963. By that time, numerous yachtsmen had sailed around the world, some of them, following Slocum's example, single-handed. However, most of these voyages took years to complete, with many stops along the way, and most had stuck to the relatively benign latitudes of the trade winds bracketing the equator, using the Suez and Panama Canals to avoid the more dangerous passages to the south, around Africa and South America. Chichester dramatically reinvented the challenge of circumnavigating alone by modeling his intended voyage on the great clipper ship route, setting out from England with a single stop in Australia and a return passage via Cape Horn. No one had ever attempted the feat, least of all a sixty-four-year-old, but it seemed logical enough. Crossing one ocean single-handed was becoming routine, so why not cross a few oceans at a time?

Even better from his point of view, a circumnavigation by yacht would redeem an earlier personal failure. In 1929 Chichester had flown a Gipsy Moth biplane from London to Sydney, stopping only for fuel. In Sydney, he converted the Gipsy Moth to a seaplane and learned how to take off and land with floats instead of wheels. He set out again, intending to continue all the way around the world, but never made it. In 1931, as he circled the Japanese town of Katsuura, he flew into a half-mile span of telephone lines. The horrific crash almost killed him and put an abrupt end to his circumnavigation by air.

Chichester quickly moved from pondering a circumnavigation by sea to planning it. Long fascinated with the romance of the clipper trade, he dove headlong into the project with his characteristic attention to detail, submerging himself in clipper ship accounts of the route and conditions and compiling so much material he decided to produce a book (*Along the Clipper Way*, published in 1966). During this time — he could never pinpoint exactly when — Chichester decided he would "race" against the clippers' passage times from England to Sydney (a distance he estimated at fourteen thousand miles) and back via Cape Horn (another fifteen thousand miles).

Chichester knew that in sailing alone in a small boat he couldn't possibly match the best times of the swiftest clippers and their hard-driving, full crews. But he hoped he might match the times of some of the slower clippers and declared he was shooting for 100 days, a nice round number. That target would require daily averages on the order of 140 miles, which was asking a lot of both boat and crew but was not beyond the realm of possibility. And chasing after target averages, even if they turned out to be overly optimistic, would help him maintain his focus at sea.

There were also single-handed sailing records to break. Aside from attempting the fastest small-boat passage around the world, Chichester would aim for the longest nonstop single-handed passage, a record he attributed to an Argentinean named Vito Dumas. In 1943 Dumas had sailed solo from Cape Town, South Africa, to Wellington, New Zealand, a passage of 7,400 miles. Dumas had also posted the fastest overall circumnavigation time that Chichester could identify, 375 days, although Chichester observed that the route had been a short one, only 20,000 miles or so, because it had been sailed entirely in the Southern Hemisphere at high latitudes (longitude lines get closer together as they approach the poles). He also noted what he believed to be the fastest lengthy single-handed passage, which he credited to Bill Nance, an Australian sailor who in 1964 sailed 6,500 miles from Auckland, New Zealand, to Buenos Aires, Argentina, at an average of 122 miles per day. Finally, Chichester targeted a six-day run of 925 miles posted by Nance — which itself had eclipsed a seventy-year-old record of 900 miles, set by Joshua Slocum himself.

Looming above it all was the supreme challenge of Cape Horn, for seamen the grandest, most notorious, most intimidating cape in the world. "For years [the Horn] had been in the back of my mind. It not only scared me, frightened me, but I think it would be fair to say that it terrified me," Chichester later wrote. Here his research was sobering. He could find only eight small yachts that had circumnavigated via Cape Horn. That there were so few was not surprising: conventional wisdom decreed the cape's treacherous winds and waters too dangerous for any small vessel. And the conventional wisdom had some merit. Of the eight yachts he could identify, six had rolled over or somersaulted before, during, or after the attempt to round Cape Horn (two were lost entirely, along with their crews). Chichester comforted himself with the observation that most of the boats had been designed for waters much milder than the Horn. He hoped that *Gipsy Moth IV,* the custom-designed craft he was building with John Illingworth, one of England's top naval architects, would greatly increase his chances.

In this he proved to be slightly overconfident. *Gipsy Moth IV* was launched in March 1966, and from the start she was an ill-mannered, cantankerous vessel. On the day of her launching, the champagne bottle, dropped by Chichester's wife, Sheila, swung down onto her bow with a solid thunk — and did not break. Chichester considered this the worst possible omen, and his feelings of foreboding only deepened when *Gipsy Moth* stuck in the greased ways and refused to take to the water. The equally stubborn Chichester hopped down and threw his shoulder against the launching cradle, forcing the boat to wet her bottom at last. When a passing ferry sent a few wavelets rippling her way, she pitched up and down in a startling manner. "My God," Chichester and his wife exclaimed to each other, "she's a rocker."

Every new boat has teething problems, but *Gipsy Moth* seemed more blighted than most. On her first sailing trials, a moderate puff of wind laid her on her side in the flat waters of the Solent, the channel between the Isle of Wight and the English mainland. Chichester cringed at the thought of sailing such a "tender" boat through the Roaring Forties. Modifications were hurriedly made to try to stiffen her up so she could better withstand a press of wind. But *Gipsy Moth* remained an exceptionally difficult boat to settle into a stable, straight run. Ordinary, even languorous, waves set her pitching violently and slowed her down. Chichester spent endless hours fiddling with the set of the sails and the steering gear in an effort to get her to move in a straight line without ceaseless intervention. By the time he was approaching Australia during his voyage, with thousands of miles under the keel, *Gipsy Moth*'s cranky ways finally drove him to log a harsh conclusion: "I fear *Gipsy Moth* is about as unbalanced or unstable a boat as there could be."

Chichester himself was notoriously cranky, so not everyone took his sometimes impassioned abuse of *Gipsy Moth* seriously. Even so, there was no doubt that the boat's gut-wrenching movement through the seas and insatiable demand for fine tuning would have sorely taxed any solo sailor. By the time he set off on his ambitious voyage in August 1966, Chichester was just a month shy of his sixty-fifth birthday. A lifetime of adventure and physical exertion had kept him muscular and fit, but sailing a fifty-four-foot sloop over fourteen thousand miles of ocean to Australia was enough work to keep even a full crew busy. Worse, before he set out he slipped on one of *Gipsy Moth*'s spray-slicked deck skylights, badly bruising his leg. Within days he had lost feeling and coordination, but he refused to see a doctor, for fear he would be declared unfit for his arduous trip. Although he attempted homegrown physical therapy, the leg never healed properly, nagging Chichester throughout the voyage with painful cramps that frequently prevented him from sound sleep.

Despite the poor odds, flaws in the boat's design, and the handicaps of physical age, the stubborn Chichester managed to pull off an astounding voyage. On the first leg, from Plymouth to Sydney, *Gipsy Moth* lurched her way over the seas, resisting most of his efforts to settle her into a steady course. He sweated and cussed through the heat, calms, and squalls of the Atlantic until, just over seven weeks into the trip, he hit the magic line of 40° south. *Gipsy Moth* had made it to the Southern Ocean, and Chichester could finally "turn left" to run before the westerly winds for seven thousand wavy, windy miles before reaching Australia.

Unfortunately, in the Southern Ocean *Gipsy Moth*'s behavior only got worse. Chichester discovered that in a gale she refused to run downwind under bare poles, leaving him the unenviable choice of flying a small storm jib, which would send him surfing along at dangerous speeds, or simply letting *Gipsy Moth* "lie ahull" with no sails up, bobbing along at the mercy of the storm. The ocean's big rollers also had their fun with the primitive self-steering gear, effortlessly sluing *Gipsy Moth* through an arc of 60° as they swept underneath. In one storm, a massive breaking wave whipped her sideways and carried her along, with her masts nearly in the water, for a 30-knot thrill ride. Chichester could only stand on the side of his bunk — which was now his floor — helpless and wondering whether his boat was about to be driven right under. He found the sailing loud, lonely, and frightening, unlike any he had ever experienced. "I had been used to the North Atlantic," he later wrote. "Fierce and sometimes awesome, yes, but the North Atlantic seemed to have a spiritual atmosphere as if teeming with the spirits of the men who sailed and died there. Down here in the Southern Ocean it was a great void. I seemed planetary distances away from the rest of mankind."

Around three thousand miles from Sydney, *Gipsy Moth*'s balky self-steering gear finally quit, battered beyond repair by storms and waves. Tired, wet, and drained by the stress of the South, Chichester reluctantly decided to give up on Sydney. He turned his bow northeast for Fremantle, on Australia's western coast, trying to steer *Gipsy Moth* using the set of the sails alone, as Slocum had guided the *Spray*.

Yet Chichester did not accept failure for long. As his skill at keeping the boat on course by tweaking the sails increased, his innate stubbornness kicked in. He had always dreaded losing his self-steering because he assumed *Gipsy Moth* would be ungovernable without it. Now that he had lost it and discovered that he didn't really need it, he suddenly declared himself happier than at any point in the voyage. He gently guided *Gipsy Moth* back onto a course for Sydney. "That I had been able to rig up gear to make her sail herself was deeply satisfying. I hate turning back; I hate giving up; and I hate being diverted from my course; it was a seaman's job to get over the difficulties," he wrote. The failed steering gear ruined his hope of arriving in Sydney in 100 days, but neither he nor his growing horde of followers quibbled. He was doing something no sailor had ever done; how fast he did it was interesting but relatively unimportant. After almost 107 days at sea, *Gipsy Moth* arrived in Sydney Harbor. Francis Chichester had sailed nonstop for 14,100 miles, alone and at an average of almost 132 nautical miles a day.

Chichester's arrival in Australia was triumphant. Within minutes of stepping ashore, he was confronted by a horde of newspaper, radio, and television reporters. His quixotic voyage had touched the public imagination, transforming a solitary adventure into a global event. After spending so much time alone, he stumbled in answering the barrage of questions, particularly those of a metaphysical nature. He did manage one steely quip, though. Asked when his spirits were at their lowest point, he replied, "When the gin gave out."

Chichester had proved the feasibility of sailing halfway around the world alone in a small yacht. But the second half of his intended voyage featured Cape Horn, and now he was besieged by a new wave of skeptics trying to talk him out of continuing. The most serious warnings were issued by Captain Alan Villiers, the aforementioned writer and authority on Cape Horn. "I beg Chichester not to attempt it. The outward trip he has made is simple compared to this one," he told an interviewer. The Horn, he predicted in the *Guardian*, would be too much for one tired man to handle: "Sailors learned long ago that the price of survival there is constant vigilance and expert helmsmanship, with equally constant attention to the set of the sails." Another retired sea captain called Chichester a "glorious bloody fool" and rated his chances of survival at only fifty-fifty.

The fool in question appreciated all the attention and concern but never wavered. *Gipsy Moth* was overhauled and modified for her coming trial. Almost two months after he arrived, Chichester set out again, bound for Plymouth via the Horn, carrying three miniature bales of wool in honor of the clippers. Stubborn to the end, he ignored warnings about a tropical storm northeast of Sydney.

His return leg was an ode to seamanship and determination. The skeptics had been right, at least about the abuse he was in for. A day out of Sydney Heads, *Gipsy Moth* ran into the outer winds and seas of tropical cyclone Diana and was rolled by a large breaker. Chichester was below at the time and could only manage a cool "Over she goes" as the boat capsized. She immediately rolled back upright, with the usual pandemonium of flying stores and sloshing bilges, leaving him shaken but uninjured. Both Chichester and *Gipsy Moth* recovered, but endured a week of storms farther down the track to Cape Horn and at one point sailed through 66-knot hurricane-force winds. Slowly *Gipsy Moth* clawed her way south and east, drawing a snaky line across the chart toward the nether tip of South America at 56° south.

Fifty days after leaving Sydney, Chichester made his approach to Cape Horn in bucking seas and a wind that steadily kicked up above 40 knots. HMS *Protector,* a Royal Navy ship, monitored the passage, as did a light airplane chartered by reporters from the BBC and the London *Sunday Times.* They flew off with images of *Gipsy Moth* bravely forging through the rough waters under storm jib alone. ("*Muy hombre,*" the pilot was reported to have commented as the tiny figure waved from the deck.) Chichester in fact was feeling tired and seasick. "The odd thing was that I had not only no feeling of achievement whatever at having passed the Horn, but I had no more feeling about it than if I had been passing landmarks all the way from Australia," he wrote.

Perhaps the Horn took umbrage at such complacency. Six hours after passing by, Chichester was under assault by a true Southern Ocean blast. Winds gusted up to 85 knots (almost 100 miles per hour), and a huge, angry sea creamed down on *Gipsy Moth* from behind. All he could do was run before the storm and hope that a change in wind direction would not push him toward the brutal, rocky coast to the north. *Gipsy Moth* cleared this dangerous zone when an exhausted Chichester guided her past Staten Island, east of Cape Horn, and turned northeast toward the Falkland Islands.

He was finally headed for home. He would endure one more major storm and bone chips in his elbow as he plowed steadily onward, back across his outbound track, back across the equator, and back into the familiar waters of the English Channel. *Gipsy Moth* approached Plymouth in late May 1967, 119 days out from Sydney, and Chichester got a preview of the thunderous greeting he was about to receive. Aircraft buzzed by overhead, and an escort of thirteen ships, five of them Royal Navy warships, took up positions around him. Just before 9 P.M. he sailed past the Plymouth breakwater to a finishing gun. On this leg he had covered 15,517 miles at an average of 131 miles a day.

Chichester and *Gipsy Moth* had completed a solo circumnavigation of 29,630 miles, spending 226 days at sea with just one stop. No small boat, crewed or otherwise, had ever circled the world so fast or sailed so far without stopping. The feat touched a nation, and sailors everywhere. Two hundred and fifty thousand people lined the streets and harbor of Plymouth, and millions more sat by their television sets to watch the sailor set foot again on British soil. From Plymouth, Chichester and *Gipsy Moth* sailed on to London, where he was knighted at Greenwich with the sword Queen Elizabeth I had given Sir Francis Drake four centuries earlier in honor of his circumnavigation.

Chichester had invented a new type of hero: the indomitable racing sailor, denizen of the Southern Ocean and conqueror of

Cape Horn. The limits of the possible had once again been pushed outward, and the next step was obvious. Not long after Chichester returned from the sea in 1967, rumors about sailors planning to sail the world nonstop began to circulate on docks and in waterfront bars. By the following year these ambitions materialized as the Golden Globe, the first nonstop race around the world ever staged. Hasler and Chichester, pioneers of single-handed racing and heirs of Joshua Slocum, could be proud of their sailing achievements. Ocean racing now covered all the world's oceans, and a new generation of adventurers was about to launch an era of competition that would confirm the Southern Ocean and Cape Horn as the ultimate measure of any offshore racer.

Hasler and Chichester would not be part of the coming action, however. Blondie Hasler stayed involved in the organization of single-handed sailing but drifted off into other, more whimsical pursuits, including the search for the Loch Ness monster. Francis Chichester could not put his passion for sailing solo aside for retirement ashore and kept sailing the Atlantic, always trying to improve a previous time or set some new record. In 1972, at the age of seventy, he was diagnosed with a cancerous tumor on his spine. Stubborn to the last and against his doctor's advice, he set off for another OSTAR. As he sailed into the Atlantic he was weakening fast. After a week of missed scheduled radio contacts, a rescue operation was mounted to find him. His son and three Royal Navy seamen were put aboard his latest *Gipsy Moth* to help him return to Plymouth.

Chichester never sailed again, and died later that year. In recognition of his sailing achievements his name was inscribed on the Navigators' Memorial in Westminster Abbey. It was an honor that would have deeply touched the cranky old pioneer. Also on the stone were the names of Sir Francis Drake and Captain James Cook.

3

THE GOLDEN GLOBE

> O Lord God, When thy givest to thy servants to endeavor
> any great matter, grant us also to know that it is not
> the beginning, but the continuing of the same until it be
> thoroughly finished, which yieldeth the true glory.
> — Sir Francis Drake

SIR FRANCIS CHICHESTER had proved that a tenacious senior citizen and consummate seaman could sail alone around the world with a single stop. Going nonstop was the obvious next step, but it was an enormous one. *Gipsy Moth* had been battered mercilessly on the leg to Sydney. Only a full refit and weeks of rest allowed Chichester to complete the trip home. Making a circumnavigation nonstop was literally doubling the challenge, the days at sea, and the distance sailed. A boat would have to survive twice as much abuse and carry all the additional spare parts necessary to keep systems running over a longer period. It meant perhaps ten continuous months at sea. No one knew for sure whether it was possible for a small yacht and crew to survive a nonstop ordeal, and plenty of sailors and pundits doubted it was. But of course that was the lure — the chance to be first, the chance to do the seemingly impossible. Within six months of Chichester's return, at least four sailors were actively planning a nonstop assault on the world's oceans.

First was Bill King, a retired British submarine commander, who swung into action immediately. His forty-two-foot custom design, *Galway Blazer II,* was under construction by the end of 1967. Also in the hunt was a twenty-eight-year-old British merchant seaman named Robin Knox-Johnston, who was determined that if anyone was going to be first to sail around the world nonstop, it should be an Englishman — or, more to the point, not a Frenchman. Knox-Johnston had been contemplating the voyage since arriving home to England on leave in March 1967, two months before Chichester landed in Plymouth, and immediately set about trying to raise money to build a boat for the adventure. Not having much luck, he resolved to make the trip in his own boat, a thirty-two-foot ketch called *Suhaili,* the Arabic name for the southeast wind. *Suhaili* was small but seaworthy. She had been built in India from heavy mahogany, and Knox-Johnston knew all her little habits intimately, having sailed her fifteen thousand miles from India to London.

Knox-Johnston had feared that Eric Tabarly, the hero of the 1964 OSTAR, would be the Frenchman out to steal seafaring glory from Britain, but Tabarly was more interested in transatlantic racing. Instead, Knox-Johnston got perhaps a more formidable French rival, Bernard Moitessier. Moitessier was a writer and seafaring romantic, not a racer. He was, however, an accomplished seaman and master of a boat well suited to the challenge: the red, steel-hulled *Joshua* (named after Slocum). Moitessier had never circumnavigated, although he and *Joshua* had already made one remarkable passage together in 1966, a fourteen-thousand-mile nonstop voyage from Tahiti to Spain, sailed with his wife via Cape Horn. It wasn't until Chichester voyaged from Sydney to Plymouth just months later that anyone sailed a small boat farther. Finally there was John Ridgway, a British paratrooper who bravely — or foolishly — resolved to undertake the circumnavigation in a thirty-foot boat called *English Rose IV.* He had almost no sailing experience, but he was undeniably tough. In 1966 he had become a national celebrity by rowing a boat across the Atlantic with an army sergeant named Chay Blyth.

In early 1968, with all the chatter of multiple campaigns under way in the race to be first around the world nonstop, the *Sunday Times* started sniffing around for a way to take advantage of this next leap forward in offshore racing. The *Times* had sponsored Chichester's voyage and noted all the publicity its rival the *Observer* was milking from the single-handed transatlantic races. Knox-Johnston approached the paper in search of sponsorship, but it had doubts about his chances for success. (The *Times* was enamored of the prospects of a sailor known as "Tahiti" Bill Howells, who in the end did not even start.) In any case, while British newspaper readers had lapped up the Chichester saga, simple sponsorship seemed too much like covering the same territory.

Instead, the *Sunday Times* decided to invent a contest. It wouldn't be a formal race, with a fixed starting line and time, because the editors weren't sure everyone intending to sail around the world, all preparing on different schedules, would join. Instead, the *Times* would offer two prizes: the "Golden Globe," given to the first sailor who managed to circumnavigate solo and nonstop without assistance, and £5,000 to the nonstop circumnavigator with the shortest elapsed time. There were few restrictions. Participants had to start sometime between June 1 and October 31, 1968, to maximize the chances that they would sail through the Southern Ocean during the austral summer. For the £5,000 prize, the start had to be from an English port; for the Golden Globe, it just had to be a port north of 40° north (the newspaper agreed to this wrinkle in case Moitessier insisted on starting from France).

The Golden Globe was formally announced in March 1968 and immediately ignited heated commentary in the yachting press, much of it warning of disasters ahead in the Southern Ocean. "Many people will think the *Sunday Times* offer undesirable, encouraging people to drown themselves," wrote one British sailing journalist. "After all, this feat is so difficult that nobody in all the world and in all of recorded history has ever achieved it." That was only an inducement to some. Nine sailors eventually set out, over the course of the summer and fall of

1968, to sail around the world alone and without assistance. Only one, Robin Knox-Johnston, made it home successfully.

THE VOYAGE OF SUHAILI

Knox-Johnston and *Suhaili* sailed off into the unknown from Falmouth, England, on June 14, thirteen days after John Ridgway and six days after Chay Blyth (Ridgway's transatlantic rowing partner, who also jumped into the round-the-world free-for-all without any sailing experience). Knox-Johnston was a well-trained seaman and *Suhaili* a rugged vessel, but his preparations were rushed by the fact that he had to get to sea early, to compensate for the slow average speeds he expected from his small boat. He didn't have time to test his ad hoc self-steering gear or plan his route until he was under way. It took him two weeks, as he headed south past the Strait of Gibraltar, to coax more than a hundred miles from *Suhaili* over the course of a twenty-four-hour period. He was obviously in for a long voyage, and his chances of winning depended entirely on whether he could keep *Suhaili* plodding forward while other, faster competitors fell by the wayside.

Though decades had passed, life on a small sailboat at sea had not changed much since Slocum's time. To sail over the horizon was to sail into the wilderness. Navigation was still accomplished by sextant, with the weather and the navigator's skill dictating accuracy. Pilot charts, although more reliable, were still based on the original work of Matthew Maury, and the clipper route remained the favored path. Sails and ropes were perhaps more durable than those of Slocum's day, but made mostly from natural fiber and subject to chafing and wear. Hasler's steering gear and its spinoffs, if working properly, could make handling a boat easier. But as both Slocum and Chichester had proved, simply trying to balance the boat with the rudder and sails was sometimes less frustrating.

The one big change was in communications. The *Sunday*

Times encouraged each competitor to take a single-sideband, or long-range, radio so the racers could make reports and stay in touch with their backers and sponsors. (Radios also allowed the sailors to check their clocks against a time signal, which helped make navigation more accurate.) Successful radio contact depended on a host of factors, however, including a good battery charge and favorable atmospheric conditions. Knox-Johnston and the other competitors (except Moitessier, who refused to take a radio, claiming it would be an annoyance) did manage sporadic communication over the course of their voyages. News of other competitors and world events trickled in over the months, but communications technology at sea was still fairly hit or miss. The Golden Globe's contestants were largely cloaked in solitude, with very little regular information about the ongoing competition. Frequently they were unable to transmit their own positions and had to signal passing ships with the code flags MIK, the universal signal for "Please report me by radio to Lloyds, London."

For most of the racers over most of the race, the battle was with the elements, the boat, and the psyche. Many of the sailors were left wondering about the safety and welfare of the other racers. The Golden Globe was a competition, but it was also a dangerous shared adventure, and Robin Knox-Johnston, despite getting home first, had his fair share of adversity.

Just weeks into *Suhaili*'s voyage, water started filling the bilges. Most wooden boats allow a certain amount of seepage through the hull. Now Knox-Johnston, after diving over the side in a calm, discovered that two eight-foot seams had opened up on either side of the keel. He managed to stanch the flow by tacking strips of canvas and cotton coated with tar along the outside of the two leaky seams. He reinforced the repair by nailing on a strip of copper inadvertently left behind by the technicians who had installed his radio. This was no straightforward patching job. Before going back into the water to finish the work, he had to shoot a curious shark that was lurking alongside the hull.

Other problems followed throughout the voyage. The gooseneck connection between the mainmast and boom repeatedly failed, forcing Knox-Johnston to improvise repairs. His drinking water turned putrid, leaving him to catch rainwater. *Suhaili*'s self-steering broke down (like Chichester, Knox-Johnston got the boat to balance with sails and tiller alone, and ended up happier for it). And persistent troubles with his transmitter made time checks for navigation difficult to come by, and eventually rendered him incommunicado for months.

Knox-Johnston sometimes found the mental and emotional stresses of the voyage as draining as the mechanical and physical challenges. Just a month into his journey he felt listless, a symptom of boredom and loneliness. Books, such as Tolstoy's *War and Peace,* helped to occupy his mind. But it was not until *Suhaili* had been at sea for almost four months that he was able to come to terms with the daunting fact that he might spend almost a year sailing alone. He invented mental exercises such as writing and memorizing poetry or setting down a detailed description of his self-steering gear. He even tape recorded his voice so he could play it back and listen for any signs of mental deterioration in his speech. His patriotism, fueled by stirring Gilbert and Sullivan operettas, helped keep him motivated during difficult moments. "After all, in my circumstances would a Drake, Frobisher, Grenville, Anson, Nelson, Scott or Vian (note — all seamen!) have thought of giving up?" he asked himself in his log.

Off New Zealand he received word that Moitessier was steadily gaining on him, threatening a close finish. This news spurred him to greater effort. Struggling north through the Atlantic after Cape Horn, Knox-Johnston even managed to turn a BBC radio report of an arcane diplomatic dispute over the European Common Market into a trumped-up excuse for more heated sailing. "General De Gaulle's insult to our Ambassador cost my French competitors 5 miles today," he wrote with satisfaction in his log.

Of course, Knox-Johnston and *Suhaili* were subjected to the usual painful and dispiriting rigors of the Southern Ocean, arriving in the Roaring Forties on September 3 after a two-and-a-half-month trip down the Atlantic. Before reaching the South, *Suhaili* had weathered but one gale. Over the next ten days she was battered by five and suffered a knockdown that left cracks running around the edge of the deckhouse. Subsequent storms convinced Knox-Johnston that *Suhaili* would end up in pieces, and he went so far as to calculate where his life raft would drift if he had to abandon ship. After passing New Zealand astern, he even had to endure a three-week stretch of demoralizing and adverse east winds that offered only one day of favorable westerlies. "If the Frogs are meant to win — O.K.," he wrote with exasperation in his log. "But there is no need to torture me as well as allow me to lose."

Cape Horn surrendered without a fight, however, and after 218 days at sea, *Suhaili* was heading home. A long, slow trip up the Atlantic returned Knox-Johnston to Falmouth after thirty thousand miles and 313 days, delivering another heroic sailor — the first to solo nonstop around the world — home to a cheering British public. *Suhaili* was escorted into port by a Royal Navy minesweeper, and officers from Her Majesty's Customs Office in Falmouth were first on board. They playfully asked the exuberant Knox-Johnston the time-honored question: "Where from?"

"Falmouth," he answered proudly.

Suhaili had completed the longest nonstop voyage in history. The feat was so physically demanding that Knox-Johnston added seven pounds of muscle to his frame and two inches around his chest and upper arms. He and *Suhaili* hadn't broken any speed records, averaging just under four nautical miles per hour over the course of the voyage (Chichester averaged almost five and a half on his two-part circumnavigation). But as the first home, Knox-Johnston had won the Golden Globe. The fate of the £5,000 and the circumnavigation record depended a lot on how the competition, almost all sailing in faster boats, handled the challenge.

Luckily for Knox-Johnston, hardly any were up to the strain. By September, when *Suhaili* was plugging her way through the

Southern Ocean south of the Cape of Good Hope, both Ridgway and Blyth had been forced to withdraw because of structural damage and gear failure. By November, as *Suhaili* bobbed past New Zealand, the attrition list had grown. Bill King had been towed into Cape Town after a South Atlantic storm capsized *Galway Blazer* northeast of Gough Island, damaging both masts. Alex Carrozzo, an Italian sailor who jumped in late and retired early, had put in to Lisbon with a stomach ulcer. Loïck Fougeron, a Frenchman and another late entrant, had suffered a knockdown in the Roaring Forties and dropped out. That left the enigmatic Moitessier, who had set sail in August, and two trimaran sailors, both English, named Nigel Tetley and Donald Crowhurst. Each, in his own way, has a tale worth telling.

JOSHUA *SAILS AGAIN*

Bernard Moitessier was raised in the Far East, and the stamp of Eastern philosophy was strongly reflected in his attitude toward the sea. For him sailing was a journey into nature and the soul. He did not sail to compete; he sailed to grow, explore, and ponder the great questions regarding man and the natural world. His steel-hulled *Joshua* was a rugged passage-maker, and in 1967 he started planning for the ultimate voyage — nonstop around the world — shortly after his passage from Tahiti. His motivation, a sense that the world is more agreeable and coherent when viewed from the deck of a small boat, was similar to Slocum's. "I felt such a need to rediscover the wind of the high sea, nothing else counted at that moment, neither earth nor men. All *Joshua* and I wanted was to be left alone with ourselves," he later wrote in *The Long Way,* his account of the Golden Globe.

Predictably, Moitessier had no interest in a race. He was the only competitor who knew what to expect in the Southern Ocean and around Cape Horn, and in fact was annoyed at first that the *Sunday Times* had turned such a noble sailing challenge into a base competition. But the paper dispatched Murray Sayle, the reporter who had covered the Chichester story, to Toulon to speak with him, and somehow Moitessier was won over. Reportedly, he relented simply because he liked Sayle's face. Another British journalist suggested a more rational motive: "Having seen *Joshua* tied up in Toulon, there seems little doubt that Moitessier could find a use for the prize money. I don't think I have ever seen such a sorry, dilapidated yacht." Moitessier himself later admitted that he and Loïck Fougeron decided to sail to Plymouth and start there in hopes of carrying off the *Sunday Times*'s money prize for the best elapsed time, "the Good Lord willing, without risking our freedom, since the rules did not specify that we had to say 'Thank-you.'" Even then he resisted the notion of a competition between boats. "It will be a question of survival," he told another competitor in Plymouth. "Everyone who gets round will have won."

Moitessier was probably the most experienced seaman in the race. He set off from Plymouth on August 22, more than two months after Knox-Johnston, who was by then approaching the windy high latitudes. Moitessier's description of his voyage adopts none of the clinical, day-by-day efficiency of Chichester's and Knox-Johnston's accounts. Instead, it is a rambling, romantic story of a man slowly and happily giving himself over to his boat and the elements. It is full of emotion and poetic observation, with Moitessier unraveling a mystical journey in which he communes with *Joshua,* the ocean, and the sea life around him (he believed dolphins warned him away from shipwreck off New Zealand).

For all his musings, Moitessier was a highly proficient sailor, endlessly toying with *Joshua*'s trim and the set of the sails to wring the most speed from his beloved vessel as he relentlessly narrowed the distance to Knox-Johnston's unwinding wake. It took *Suhaili* 218 days to get from England to Cape Horn, a nonstop run that *Joshua,* bigger and faster at forty-six and a half feet, polished off in just 167 days. Moitessier rounded the sentinel of the Horn on February 5, 1969, just three weeks after Knox-Johnston, who was only fifteen hundred miles ahead.

Given the relative performances of the boats to that point, Moitessier and *Joshua* were poised to return to the English Channel, as predicted, in a tight race with Knox-Johnston. The chance to upend the British sailing world by slipping away with both the Golden Globe and the £5,000 beckoned. It took Knox-Johnston and *Suhaili* another seventy-five slow, tortuous days to sail the remaining six thousand miles or so through the equatorial belt's calms and contrary winds to the finish. If Moitessier and *Joshua* could continue to average just twenty miles a day more than *Suhaili*—less than one knot per hour more—he would be in line, à la Tabarly, for his own Legion of Honor.

Yet prizes and awards were the last things on Moitessier's sea-soaked mind as he rounded Cape Horn. For months he had been retreating from the rest of humanity, traveling toward an infinite horizon in his floating cocoon. Week by week he cast aside the trappings of the quotidian world, evolving into a kind of sea creature himself. He allowed his hair and beard to grow so long that he had to trim around his lips now and then so he could eat porridge without smearing it all over himself. From the equatorial Doldrums on, he shunned soap in the belief that bathing sapped virility. He began practicing yoga naked in his cockpit, soothing an ulcer and achieving a state of well-being he had never experienced before. He occasionally wet himself while lost in reverie, only to express gratitude for the sudden warmth and for the fact that he had not been distracted from a potentially important insight by the need to fumble with his fly. He had entered the Golden Globe on a whim, eager for any excuse to return to the sea. He had no settled goals other than a nonstop circumnavigation. Halfway to Cape Horn, in the Pacific portion of the Southern Ocean, an epiphany announced itself. "I found something more. A kind of undefinable state of grace," he wrote in *The Long Way*. "I know, I have known since the Indian Ocean, that I no longer want to go back."

The Horn itself seemed to confirm Moitessier's extraordinary decision to drop out of the Golden Globe — and the human race — and simply keep sailing. "I no longer quite know how far I have got, except that we long ago left the borders of too much behind," he logged on the final approach to the Horn. "But never have I felt my boat like that; never has she given me so much." And with the Horn behind him he could only note, "Plymouth so close, barely 10,000 miles to the north . . . but leaving from Plymouth and returning to Plymouth seems like leaving from nowhere to go nowhere." Moitessier set *Joshua*'s bow for the Cape of Good Hope, deciding to continue his circling of the globe and Southern Ocean until he could head north in the Pacific to Tahiti. On he sailed, into a kind of euphoria, only occasionally interrupted by physical exhaustion and questions about whether the world, his wife, Françoise, and his children would understand what he had done. He paused just long enough off Cape Town, as he rounded the Cape of Good Hope for the second time, to get a message to the *Sunday Times* by way of explanation. It was terse but complete, reading only, "The Horn was rounded February 5, and today is March 18. I am continuing non-stop towards the Pacific islands because I am happy at sea, and perhaps also to save my soul."

The news befuddled the yachting world. When Knox-Johnston eventually heard it from a French ship, off the Azores and just two weeks from the finish, he had trouble believing it. At first he suspected the French crew of playing a cruel joke on an Englishman. But the report was soon confirmed by the first radio contact he had managed in five months. "So of the nine who set out, only three of us were left, all British, which I thought to be a Good Thing," he concluded.

In June 1969, after 37,455 miles of nonstop sailing and 307 days at sea, Moitessier finally dropped anchor in Tahiti. He had circled the globe one and a half times and sailed farther nonstop than any sailor in history, surpassing Knox-Johnston's 30,000-mile mark, set just two months earlier. It was a record that would stand almost twenty years. In Tahiti Moitessier sank into a kind of eco-mysticism. He would fill the last pages of *The Long Way* with colorful screeds about the blindness of the human race and its assault on the environment. He instructed his publisher that all royalties from his book be sent to the pope.

.   Yet all the sermonizing in the world could not diminish Moitessier's superb show of seamanship or the charm inherent in his decision to freely trade glory for purity of soul. Perhaps the day-to-day loneliness at sea drove him to an eccentricity not far short of insanity, or perhaps the solitude allowed him to see the world with unusual clarity (his log books were crammed with impassioned arguments defending his choice). Whatever the explanation, Moitessier's actions transformed him into a cult hero to voyaging sailors all over the world, many of whom sought him out as they passed through Tahiti.

MULTIHULL MADNESS

Although in 1968 the notion of racing a small, conventional monohull through the Southern Ocean was considered dangerous, racing a multihull through the same waters seemed downright preposterous. The reason was simple: any nonstop circumnavigator was almost certain to run into winds and seas severe enough to threaten capsize. In fact, the majority of participants in the Golden Globe suffered at least one knockdown. Moitessier recorded that *Joshua* was rolled over seven times in the course of his voyage, three times to the horizontal (with the masts parallel to or in the water) and four times well past horizontal (with the masts submerged and the keel up to 40 percent out of the water). They all survived intact enough to sail on or into port because their heavy lead keels rolled the boats back upright. Since a multihull would not come back up on its own, if one capsized, it would mean almost certain death. There was no margin for error. A solo sailor who couldn't tend to the boat at all times was particularly vulnerable to this nasty fate. Somehow that didn't stop two of the contestants, both Englishmen, from making the attempt in a trimaran: Donald Crowhurst, an electronics engineer, because he hypothesized that a multihull would be faster than a monohull; and Nigel Tetley, a naval officer, because a trimaran happened to be the boat he was living on.

Crowhurst was a manic dreamer with a failing business who saw the Golden Globe as a chance to make his mark in life. At first he tried to secure Chichester's *Gipsy Moth IV* for the voyage, but when his increasingly plaintive entreaties were rebuffed, he turned to the idea of building a Victress-class trimaran for the voyage. A well-tested and popular design, the Victress had been produced by an innovative American multihull innovator named Arthur Piver. Piver himself had recently disappeared at sea while testing one of his trimarans — a pointed reminder of the dangers of multihulls. Nevertheless, the irrepressible Crowhurst planned to engineer away the knockdown problem with a homemade, self-actuating buoyancy bag, to be attached to the top of the mast (theoretically, it would inflate if the trimaran capsized and keep it from inverting).

As with many of the grand projects and ideas he applied to the preparation of his boat, *Teignmouth Electron,* this invention came out half-baked.* The night before his scheduled departure, Crowhurst broke down in tears, admitting to his wife that he and the boat were a shambles. Only later did she realize that this was a plea for her to insist that he put an end to the voyage, since Crowhurst himself was too proud to pull the plug. But she misunderstood, and instead tried to comfort her petrified husband. Despite nagging doubts, Crowhurst managed to maintain a brave public face and put to sea in his disorganized, untested boat as the deadline for departure approached.

Tetley, in contrast, had embarked with all the aplomb to be expected of a Royal Navy officer. He had read the *Sunday Times* announcement of the Golden Globe while lolling about his trimaran *Victress* (the same Piver design Crowhurst had chosen) with his wife on a cold morning in March. Within minutes, based solely on a surge of excitement and almost no reflection,

---

*The definitive account of Crowhurst's voyage, from which this section draws, is Nicholas Tomalin and Ron Hall's closely reported *The Strange Last Voyage of Donald Crowhurst.*

he had asked for and received her permission to participate. He set out to raise sponsorship money for a larger, more suitable multihull, but when his solicitations yielded nothing he decided to beef up his *Victress* and sail her around the world instead. Up to that time, the most arduous voyage he and the boat had undertaken was a race around Britain.

Tetley, who knew the catamaran inside and out, was not overly concerned. While preparing for the voyage in Plymouth, he fell in with Moitessier and Loïck Fougeron, also readying for departure. The Frenchmen took a liking to the British naval commander but had misgivings about the wisdom of sailing a multihull across the Southern Ocean and around Cape Horn. It had never been done before, and throughout his voyage Moitessier would worry about Tetley's progress. Moitessier generously provided all the helpful hints his experience at sea could offer. He presented Tetley with a packet of his specially formulated underwater cement in case Tetley needed to plug a hole. The French sailors also tried to talk him into taking along a big saw. If he found himself irreversibly upside down or otherwise incapacitated, they suggested, he could cut off one of the trimaran's floats to make a canoe that could be paddled or sailed to safety. Tetley dismissed this idea as a joke (it wasn't), but did agree to take a second life raft and a wetsuit. He set out on September 16, three weeks after Moitessier and two weeks before Crowhurst.

After all the fretting, Tetley's voyage south through the Atlantic was relatively mundane. He had been hoping to sail about 120 miles a day, but averaged only about 100 as he settled in to life at sea alone. In November, after one uneventful radio report, his disappointed contact at the *Times* asked, "Haven't you fallen over the side or anything else exciting?"

When *Victress* worked her way into the Southern Ocean, though, the sailing did get exciting. In December, Tetley broke the two-hundred-mile barrier over the course of twenty-four hours, a run that included wild surfing at speeds of 12 knots and more. Sensitive to the delicate nature of his lightly built floating home, he tried to stay as far north as possible in an effort to avoid the dangerous winds of the Roaring Forties. Even so, he ran into numerous gales. In the Pacific, Tetley came close to capsizing in an enormous breaking wave, which rolled *Victress* to an angle of almost 50 degrees. A subsequent storm smashed his Perspex cabin windows and flooded the cabin. Still, he pressed on, growing more confident in his boat with each mile he survived.

Tetley rounded Cape Horn in mid-March and learned that Moitessier had dropped out. Knox-Johnston had not been heard from in months — his transmitter was still down — and was considered overdue. That put Tetley in a position to win both the Golden Globe and the cash prize, an extraordinary possibility given his essentially casual entry into the race. Such was his sense of camaraderie, though, that even the heady prospect of a double victory did not prevent him from feeling sincere relief when a few weeks later he heard that Knox-Johnston had been sighted off the Azores. That meant he would finish first and win the Golden Globe, but Tetley and the doughty *Victress* were still on track to post a faster elapsed time and pocket the £5,000. In fact, with everyone else out of the race, he had only one competitor who might steal the cash: Donald Crowhurst, who was reportedly going well and homing in on Cape Horn.

Tetley was a good sport who could contemplate a Crowhurst victory with equanimity. But he was loath to lose to a boat of similar design and kept pushing his weary trimaran toward the finish. As he clawed north in the Atlantic, the toll on his liveaboard cruiser started to show in the form of structural damage to the port float. He briefly contemplated heading for a port and repairs. But having almost completed the course, he decided instead to keep sailing for home, nursing *Victress* when necessary and sailing for speed to keep ahead of Crowhurst when conditions allowed.

Just off the Azores, Tetley's luck and skill ran out. Pounded by a fierce gale, *Victress*'s port bow tore away in the night, crippling the trimaran and holing the main hull. Tetley surrendered to the inevitable, put out a distress call, and jumped into his life raft. Twelve hours later he was picked up by an Italian steamer on its way to Trinidad. From his raft he sadly watched *Victress*'s lights extinguished by the rising sea. It was a tragic sight. He was just eleven hundred miles from the finish, on the verge of becoming the first sailor in history to sail a multihull nonstop around the world. Worse, he had pushed *Victress* beyond her limits for no reason. Donald Crowhurst, it transpired, was nowhere near where he said he was.

At his most optimistic, Crowhurst had calculated that he and *Teignmouth Electron* might cover 220 miles per day and complete the circumnavigation in a mere 130 days. It was a ridiculous expectation — a 70 percent improvement over Chichester's average speed — and a reflection of Tetley's wildly unrealistic approach to the race. Crowhurst scaled his expectations back to just under 150 miles per day as the start approached, but even that was vastly overoptimistic. In the first sixteen days of the voyage Crowhurst was beset by a variety of problems, including balky steering. He averaged a miserable 50 miles a day, a rude shock that intensified his self-doubt. He refused to let those doubts show in the public façade he had constructed, and continued to report steady progress even as he privately compiled arguments in favor of dropping out. Over time, his actual progress diverged more and more from the expectations he had raised. Soon he crossed over into outright deception. One and a half months into the voyage, sailing in the trade winds, Crowhurst falsely reported a solo twenty-four-hour record of 243 miles. This claim was generally accepted in England, although it did arouse the suspicions of Chichester, who called up the *Sunday Times* and warned that Crowhurst should be carefully watched.

From this initial lie, Crowhurst steadily and tragically slipped into a crazed scheme to con the world. Afraid to challenge the Southern Ocean in a suspect boat, he sailed large circles in the South Atlantic while broadcasting vague and intermittent information about his position. His cunning reports were calculated to convince the newspapers covering the Golden Globe that he was speeding around the globe.

This elaborate fraud wasn't easy to pull off, probably requiring Crowhurst to keep two logs — one with his true position, one with his false one, buttressed by made-up celestial navigation sums.* He also had to avoid being sighted by any ship that might recognize his trimaran and report his real location. All this was cloaked in long periods of radio silence (Crowhurst claimed transmitter problems) because it would be suspicious if a relay station in South America, say, picked up his broadcast when he was supposed to be off Australia. In April 1969, after more than five months at sea, he broke radio silence to transmit an ambiguous message that suggested he was on course for the island of Diego Ramírez, just southwest of Cape Horn. The critical moment had arrived. Crowhurst was planning for a "rounding" of the cape on April 18, which would put him hard on the heels of Tetley on elapsed time and allow him soon after to rejoin the race from his South Atlantic position.

Crowhurst's reemergence as a contender for the elapsed-time prize was greeted with barely a ripple of skepticism back in England. His family and friends began planning elaborate celebrations. He wasn't in the clear, though. There was no outright suspicion of his claimed location and speed, but it was unlikely that even an artfully rendered fake log would ultimately withstand the close examination of race officials and a vigilant Francis Chichester. Tomalin and Hall suspected that Crowhurst realized this and started to slow down so Tetley would win the elapsed-time prize and he himself would win admiration for his circumnavigation but prompt little scrutiny.

That plan might have worked if Tetley's *Victress* had been able to withstand the punishment she was absorbing in the duel with her phantom competition. When Crowhurst heard that Tetley had been forced to abandon, he was cruelly trapped by his own machinations. Without Tetley he was fairly assured the

*Tomalin and Hall present evidence that this log existed; however, it was never found.

elapsed-time prize unless he could somehow lose enough weeks to fall behind *Suhaili*'s snailish mark and concoct a believable explanation for his sudden slowdown. He was certain to be exposed as a fraud, suffering unbearable humiliation and crushing his wife and loyal supporters. Crowhurst was still off Brazil when this reality hit home, and the stress and guilt of his actions slowly and inevitably drove him over the edge.

During the final weeks of his race, he scribbled tens of thousands of words in his log about God, fate, and physics. In early June, after more than two hundred days alone with his troubles and demons, his radio transmitter failed, cutting him off for good from his loving wife and the rest of the world. The journals and tape recordings Crowhurst made revealed that he spent much of his time below, sitting naked at his chart table as he obsessively tried to repair his transmitter and purged his fevered mind onto paper. The cabin was a shambles, and his writings tracked a steady descent into madness and self-loathing.

No one heard from Donald Crowhurst again. On June 24 he made his last navigational log entry, on June 29 his last radio log entry. On July 1 he sat down and wrote a minute-by-minute account of his final thoughts. "I am what I am and I see the nature of my offence," he scrawled. "It is finished . . . It is finished . . . IT IS THE MERCY."

Ten days later, the Royal Mail vessel *Picardy,* on her way across the Atlantic from London to the Caribbean, spotted *Teignmouth Electron* ghosting along. She drew alongside, but no crew was visible. The captain ordered his chief officer into a small boat to make an inspection. He found a cabin in disarray — dirty dishes in the sink, radio parts lying around — but no signs of life. *Teignmouth Electron* had been abandoned. There was no sign of a storm or any other violent event that might account for the missing crew. Crowhurst had apparently stepped off the side and into oblivion.

The *Picardy* winched the mysterious trimaran aboard and continued on her way. As news of Crowhurst's disappearance spread, so did a circus of speculation over how he met his end and whether he was really dead. The BBC and the newspapers prepared to tell his heroic tale. The *Sunday Times* started an appeal fund for the Crowhurst family, and Robin Knox-Johnston donated the £5,000 he had now won. It was not until the logs were scrutinized over the following weeks that the true nature of Donald Crowhurst's voyage and its sad end were finally revealed. The story of the hoax was an international sensation, and the revelation cast a pall over the Golden Globe. In the end, though, no one lost sight of the humanity in Crowhurst's story of hubris and failure. "None of us should judge him too harshly," Knox-Johnston — one of the few people on earth who had any sense of what Crowhurst had gone through — advised.

The Golden Globe delivered drama, tragedy, danger, and excitement. Despite Crowhurst's shocking story, sailors and the general public wanted more. The modern era of round-the-world racing was launched. It was an era in which hundreds of sailors would undergo the physical ordeals of the high latitudes, an era in which amateur adventurers would be replaced by full-time professionals, sailing for syndicates and sponsors every bit as sophisticated as those of professional car racing. Robin Knox-Johnston, after briefly considering a run for Parliament, embarked on a sailing career in which he would spend at least nineteen birthdays at sea. Single-handers, the most daring and imaginative of sailors, had introduced the world to a new form of extreme sailing. It was unconventional and posed unprecedented dangers. But the Golden Globe had moved Southern Ocean racing into the mainstream. It would soon become the most vibrant, compelling competition in the sport of sailing.

4

Modern Mayhem

> No man will be a sailor who has contrivance enough to get himself into a jail. For being in a ship is being in a jail, with the chance of being drowned . . . A man in jail has more room, better food, and commonly better company.
>
> — Samuel Johnson

IN 1973, England's Whitbread Brewery and the Royal Naval Sailing Association teamed up to stage the first crewed round-the-world race. The Southern Ocean would no longer be the private domain of solo specialists. Eighteen boats and more than one hundred sailors set out from Southampton on this inaugural circumnavigation, which broke the course into four legs, with stops in Cape Town, Sydney, and Rio de Janeiro.

The Whitbread was fundamentally different from a solo race. Boats with full crews could be driven hard all the time. Where the solo sailor had to combat loneliness and fatigue, the Whitbread crews, wedged into small, often damp spaces, had to battle claustrophobia, exhaustion, and sometimes each other. Though the Whitbread eschewed the purity of nonstop racing, the Southern Ocean continued to cement its reputation as the most formidable challenge a racing sailor could face. Three sailors were killed during the 1973 race, including one who was swept from the deck of Chay Blyth's *Great Britain 2,* the first yacht to finish. "It's a risk sport," Blyth commented. "If you don't want to take it, fine."

The Whitbread was an immediate hit, and has been staged every four years since. In 1982, another solo race was established, the British Oxygen Challenge (or the BOC, later renamed the Around Alone). Like the Whitbread, the BOC was broken into legs, losing some of the intensity and extreme effort attached to a nonstop event. It wasn't until 1989 that Philippe Jeantôt, a two-time BOC winner, dared organize another nonstop race, again for single-handers, which he called the Vendée Globe. It is the world's most grueling sailing race, and, as in the Golden Globe, the attrition rate, owing to gear failure, injury, even death, is high.

Taken together, these races, despite the varied formats, set a new standard of drama and risk that made inshore races like the America's Cup look pedestrian. The New Zealand sailor Peter Blake was so appalled by his experience in the 1973 Whitbread that he quit sailing for six months. Blake returned for the 1985 race, but on the way to Auckland he hit a whale at 11 knots, destroying the boat's rudder. (He came back yet again, and finally won in 1990.) The competition in these races was so cutthroat that sailors were prepared to take almost any risk to steal an advantage. In the Southern Ocean so many dove south to dangerous latitudes, to shorten the track as the clipper captains had, race organizers started adding restrictions to the route. Design formulas were also implemented, to promote closer racing and safer boats.

Even so, nail-biting rescues and heroic seamanship became a staple of Southern Ocean racing. In the 1997–98 Vendée Globe one sailor vanished and three others had to be rescued from the depths of the South. English racer Tony Bullimore survived for five days in an overturned boat — his keel had fallen off — half full of freezing water before the Australian Navy could get to him. Another, Frenchman Raphael Dinelli, was pulled from a life raft by a British competitor, Pete Goss, after his boat disappeared beneath the waves (the grateful Dinelli climbed aboard Goss's boat clutching a bottle of champagne). During the 1998–99 Around Alone race, Isabelle Autissier of France was also saved by a competitor. Her boat capsized fifteen hundred miles from Cape Horn, and her only hope for survival was Italian racer Giovanni Soldini. "I am not letting up until I have found Isa," Soldini told race organizers. When he finally located her upturned boat, he threw a hammer against the hull to attract Autissier's attention. To keep her mind off death, she had spent the days since the capsize calmly organizing the upside-down cabin. Soldini went on to win the race, becoming the first non-Frenchman to win a solo round-the-world event since Knox-Johnston. After he rescued Autissier, he captured the spirit of camaraderie the Southern Ocean breeds by saying, "I've already won the race . . . I think a hero is somebody who risks his life to save the life of somebody else. I just passed over there and picked up my friend."

Sailors hated the privations of the Southern Ocean — the cold, the wet, the fear — but somehow always went back for more. Harry Harkimo, a three-time Whitbread veteran, confided to a video camera during the 1989–90 race that "I don't actually know what I am doing here anymore. Once should be enough. Everyone who is down here says it all the time. But the next time they come again." No other place on earth offered the same combination of wind and waves, speed and adrenaline. The Southern Ocean was also a special place that had yet to be softened and diminished by the modern world. Life there was simple, raw, and always on the edge. Cornelius Van Rietschoten, a successful businessman and two-time Whitbread winner who was known as the Flying Dutchman, could never get enough of it. "The highlight in sailing is the Southern Ocean," he stated simply. Few sailors who had been there disagreed.

The Whitbread, Around Alone, and Vendée Globe introduced hundreds of sailors to the bottom of the globe, who in turn perpetuated the mystique of the Southern Ocean. In the early years these races attracted a large number of amateur sailors. Boats sailed with tons of stores and plenty of booze, some had designated cooks and running bridge games, and one boat bunkered coal to keep a heavy stove blazing in an attempt to ward off the cold. As sponsorship and recognition grew in proportion to that mystique, the round-the-world circuit increasingly became the domain of professional sailors and well-tuned racing campaigns. Cigarette and food companies, banks, and all sorts of manufacturers put their money behind racing boats in order to associate their brands with the rugged adventure of Southern Ocean sailing. Salaries for the top professionals in the Whitbread climbed well above six figures. Competition grew so intense that by 1993 boats were stripped of all excess weight — some didn't even have toilets — and many crew were limited to just one pair of boots or shoes and were allowed no books and personal stereos. Some boats carried only one tube of communal toothpaste, and whispers about shared toothbrushes or toothbrushes with sawn-off handles padded the wild Whitbread lore.

The fanatical attention to detail, all in the pursuit of the smallest increments of additional speed, got the racers around the world at ever-increasing speeds. Even so, the best round-the-world times, whether sailed nonstop or in stages, stayed above one hundred days (the 2000 Vendée Globe finally broke the one-hundred-day mark). That's very fast, considering it took Robin Knox-Johnston 313 days to complete his voyage. But it wasn't fast enough for some. While multitudes of monohull sailors were circling the globe, chasing after Knox-Johnston, Tabarly, and Moitessier, another cult of extreme ocean racing was rapidly developing: record-setting in multihulls.

MULTIHULL MANIA

Nigel Tetley had opened the round-the-world course to multihulls. Tetley survived the Southern Ocean in his commodious trimaran Victress, built for casual cruising, and technically completed the first multihull circumnavigation when, off the coast of Brazil, his outbound and inbound tracks crossed after 179 days of sailing. But appreciation for Tetley's accomplishments seemed to sink with Victress off the Azores. He became known more for failing just short of the finish — and for being a victim of Donald Crowhurst's madness — than for the precedents he set, with quiet modesty, during his impetuous cruise.* *Victress*'s design suggested a multihull could handle a nonstop circumnavigation, an important statement. However, it did not reveal much about the potential speeds. *Victress* was a houseboat, not a racing boat. She made some good runs when the wind was behind her, but overall she was slow, and in fact was outpaced by Moitessier's well-sailed *Joshua*.

If Tetley's near success and Crowhurst's tragic example failed to establish the promise of multihulls in round-the-world racing, another multihull adventure through the Southern Ocean helped push the argument. In 1973, Alain Colas, a protégé of Eric Tabarly and winner of the 1972 transatlantic single-handed race, set out in a purpose-built aluminum ocean-racing trimaran to retrace (and improve upon) Chichester's one-stop voyage around the world. Colas and his seventy-foot *Manureva* ("Bird of Passage" in Polynesian) set out from St. Malo, France, on the Brittany coast, in September and sailed 14,640 miles to Sydney in seventy-nine days (an average of 185 miles per day, or 7.7 knots). Along the way, he sailed 326 miles in one day, a new record for a single-hander. On the return journey from Australia to Europe, Colas ran from Sydney to Cape Horn in thirty-eight days — Chichester had taken fifty — and saw the Brittany coast again after ninety days.

Colas's voyage was a revelation. He had proved that a racing multihull could successfully circumnavigate the world, albeit with a stop — a point he wished to make to the Whitbread race organizers, who had banned multihulls. And by sailing 30,067 miles in 169 days (for an average of 7.41 knots), Colas also suggested that if let loose on round-the-world races, multihulls, as they had started to do in the transatlantic races, would soon be leaving monohull boats bobbing in their speeding wakes.

---

*Tetley never truly regained his emotional balance after the stress, exhilaration, and trauma of his Golden Globe experience. Sadly, for reasons never understood, he took his own life in 1971.

Colas's 169-day circumnavigation caused monohull adherents and multihull skeptics to take notice. He had slashed Chichester's elapsed time by almost two months and put 180 miles a day below the horizon (in contrast to Chichester's 131). In his sleek trimaran, Colas had demonstrated the enormous potential speed advantages awaiting anyone who had the guts to race a multihull through the deep ocean. Of course, the speed potential of a multihull was no secret. In fact, for racers it was the main point. And it was a point that had been splashed in the face of monohull advocates as early as 1876.

That was the year that Nathaniel Herreshoff, who would become America's most renowned yacht designer, entered an open New York Yacht Club regatta with a twenty-five-foot catamaran called *Amaryllis*. Small and not very maneuverable, *Amaryllis* was slow when sailing to windward but was a screamer on a reach — when the wind came from the side instead of from ahead. Sailing off the Battery in New York, *Amaryllis* found the right wind angle and beat a fleet of some ninety conventional racing monohulls. The disconcerted race committee did what any hidebound organization does when confronted with a threatening innovation: they hid behind a rulebook. Herreshoff was strongly discouraged from any further racing on the grounds that his little catamaran did not have the required "accommodations" — that is, a toilet. Herreshoff didn't take it too hard and went on to design five winning America's Cup boats for the NYYC. From his home in Bristol, Rhode Island, he continued to dabble in catamarans, once beating Narragansett Bay's fastest passenger steamer in a match race.

It wasn't until after World War II that ocean-voyaging multihulls started to take off. In 1947 two American multihull designers in Hawaii named Woody Brown and Rudy Choy collaborated on the construction of a series of pathbreaking multihulls. Brown had spent the war in the Pacific and been fascinated by the oceangoing outrigger canoes the Polynesians had been building for centuries. His first effort with Choy was a thirty-eight-foot catamaran called *Manu Kai* ("Sea Bird"), which reached a top speed of 28 knots and was put into service off Waikiki, sailing tourists around. Eight years later, Brown and Choy built another thirty-eight-foot cat, called *Waikiki Surf,* which sailed the twenty-three hundred miles to the U.S. mainland in just fifteen days. When she showed up at the start of the Transpacific Yacht Race, *Waikiki Surf* was given the *Amaryllis* treatment and multihulls were banned from the race. She sailed unofficially, for the fun of it, and came in fifth, beating much larger monohulls. Two years later, Choy's *Aikane* beat the lead monohull by more than a day.

Elsewhere, other multihull designers and advocates were also taking to the high seas. In 1957 a twenty-three-foot catamaran was sailed across the Atlantic. In 1960 Arthur Piver, the designer of Tetley's and Crowhurst's Victress model, sailed a thirty-foot trimaran from Massachusetts to England via the Azores in hopes of competing in Hasler's OSTAR race the same year. Piver arrived too late to qualify, but in 1964 a sailor named Derek Kelsall sailed the first trimaran in the OSTAR.

After that, the gates were open and multihulls quickly proved their edge over monohulls. By 1968, designer Bruce Kirby was declaring on the pages of *One Design & Offshore Yachtsman:* "It has now been proven beyond a shadow of a doubt that for any given length a good catamaran or trimaran will beat the best monohull upwind or down." Thirteen multihulls sailed in the 1968 OSTAR, with one taking third place. The first OSTAR multihull win came in 1972, when Colas finished first in the trimaran he was about to sail around the world. Since then, a monohull has won the transatlantic race just once, in 1976, when Eric Tabarly slipped into Newport first after the fleet of 120 had been hammered by five successive gales during the crossing. By 1980, the top six finishers were multihulls, and the first monohull arrived at the finish almost two days after the winner.

Multihulls were still not allowed in the single-handed and crewed round-the-world races that followed the Golden Globe.

So in addition to the OSTAR, they also started to attack speed-sailing records. In 1980 Eric Tabarly finally broke the schooner *Atlantic*'s seemingly indestructible 1905 Kaiser's Cup Atlantic crossing record, sailing his fifty-five-foot, three-hulled *Paul Ricard* from Ambrose Light to the Lizard in just over ten days. Today, multihulls own every outright ocean speed-sailing record on the books.

If no one ever really doubted the speed of multihull sailors, more than a few questioned their sanity. Engineering the connections between two or three hulls to withstand the relentless shearing and torquing created by different wave patterns on the different hulls — all the while using the lightest gear possible in order to keep weight down — can be a guessing game. It takes just one blast of wind and an inattentive sailor to send a multihull toward what is blithely known as the "angle of vanishing stability." That is the point at which it will roll over instead of coming back down onto its hulls. There is no elegant solution to this problem of inverted stability. When Alain Colas was preparing for his 1973 voyage around the world, he ran into Golden Glober Loïck Fougeron. As he had with Tetley, Fougeron expressed concern about the safety of a multihull at sea and made a close inspection of Colas's *Manureva*. He looked slightly less grim when Colas showed him the hole in the bottom of the boat through which the paddlewheel for the speed log passed. "Ah," Fougeron said, "you'll be able to use that for fresh air, and for your antenna in case you capsize. But since you are still working on the boat, why don't you simply make a hatch in the bottom?" That struck Colas as a sound idea, and he did. Today, the multihull solution to a capsize remains the same: an escape hatch and a good emergency beacon.

Escape hatches, rescue beacons, and other safety and survival equipment can mitigate the risks to multihull sailors. But even with the best gear, multihull racing is a dangerous, sometimes deadly sport. During the 1976 OSTAR, one catamaran broke up (the skipper was rescued) and another was lost along with its skipper. In 1978 Colas himself vanished while racing *Manureva* in the inaugural 3,700-mile Route du Rhum, started as a French transatlantic answer to the OSTAR. In 1984 Chay Blyth, also one of the original Golden Globe adventurers, capsized in a trimaran west of Cape Horn while trying to break the 1851 New York–San Francisco record set by the clipper ship *Flying Cloud,* and was rescued. One year later, the eighty-five-foot French catamaran *Jet Services IV* somersaulted in an 80-knot gale off Spain while trying to set the transatlantic record, killing one crew member and seriously injuring two others. In 1987 another well-known French catamaran, *Royale,* flipped in a transatlantic race, killing her skipper. In 1990 the sixty-foot trimaran *Great American* was also rolled over near Cape Horn. The waves were so enormous that in this rare instance the trimaran was rolled back upright again, although the two-person crew needed to be rescued from their swamped boat.

The list goes on, with French sailors, who found the swashbuckling excitement involved in multihull sailing irresistible, paying the heaviest price. "We're not sailors anymore, we are pilots," Loïck Peyron, Bruno's younger brother and a multihull ace, once said. In France, where multihull racing quickly developed a rabid national following, sailing fans could tick off the names of the multihull sailors the sea had taken in the same way that motor sports fans could reel off the names of Formula 1 drivers who have been martyred on the track: Alain Colas, Loïc Caradec, Daniel Gilard, Olivier Moussy, Rob James, Jean Castenet, Paul Vatine, and more. Still, hooked on the speed, glamour, and technology of their sport, multihull sailors continued to push the envelope, striving for new records and new thresholds. The multihull masters liked to think of themselves as a breed apart, the outlaw bikers of the sailing world, united in their disdain for plodding, safe monohulls. As Cam Lewis put it, "I'd rather sail fast boats fast than slow boats fast."

CHASING JULES VERNE

As transatlantic and transpacific crossing records fell with predictable regularity to the multihull enthusiasts, it was only a matter of time before they started looking for virgin waters and new records to shatter. Looming over all other goals was the holy grail of speed sailing: the nonstop round-the-world record. Going after it would mean somehow surviving the Southern Ocean for weeks at a time in the delicate machines. No matter, it was irresistible. Adding the Jules Verne angle only made it more so.

Even when they are racing, sailors sometimes find themselves on a slow watch with plenty of opportunity to let their minds ramble over the horizon. It is one of the most pleasant aspects of ocean voyaging, especially for anyone with an active, creative mind. Yves Le Cornec was a sailor and a dreamer, and also a fan of Jules Verne and *Around the World in Eighty Days*. During the 1984 transatlantic race from Quebec to St. Malo, Le Cornec speculated whether a multihull could travel around the world in eighty days without stopping. The question had obvious romantic appeal, and the answer, at least in theory, was yes. Many of the previous circumnavigators — both nonstop and one-stop — had sailed about thirty thousand miles over the course of their voyages. But a more direct route, particularly if a sailor did not stop in Sydney, as Chichester and Colas had, or wander all over the ocean, as Knox-Johnston had, certainly could be found. If a multihull could shave the sailing distance down to around twenty-six thousand miles, it would have to average just under 14 knots for the voyage. That was at least theoretically possible in a modern design, which could easily top 20 knots in the right conditions.

Looked at another way, however, Le Cornec's notion seemed absurd. In 1984 the nonstop record for a circumnavigation via the Southern Ocean stood at 292 days, set by Chay Blyth back in 1971. Blyth sailed single-handed and went westabout against prevailing winds — earning him the nickname "Wrong-Way Chay" — so his mark did not provide a good reference. If Tetley's *Victress* had held together in 1969, it would have been on course for a circumnavigation of about 256 days. But he had sailed solo as well, and in a cruising multihull. A better benchmark was Colas's 1973–74 voyage, which, although single-handed, at least was in a racing multihull. If Colas could have maintained his 7.41-knot average over a shorter nonstop route of twenty-eight thousand miles, he would have made the trip in 144 days. Obviously, *Manureva* would have averaged higher speeds with a full crew. At the same time, it was hard to know how to factor in the benefits of the long layover in Sydney. Regardless of how it was analyzed, Le Cornec was contemplating almost halving *Manureva*'s time, a bold proposition.

With each passing year, Le Cornec's project looked more and more reasonable. In 1987 French sailor Philippe Monnet single-handed a seventy-seven-foot trimaran around the world, with a stop in Cape Town, in 129 days. In 1988 Monnet's countryman Olivier de Kersauson, a cantankerous Tabarly protégé fast establishing himself as the *enfant terrible* of French sailing, lowered the record to 125 days, with two stops. These voyages shrank the world a little more and reflected the growing interest in racing multihulls around the globe. Yet Le Cornec's Verne-inspired idea bounced around until 1992 before the Trophée Jules Verne was formally announced. Le Cornec's collaborators included, among others, Bruno Peyron and his brother Loïck, Florence Arthaud (France's most famous woman sailor and a transatlantic record holder), and Titouan Lamazou, the current nonstop world record holder. In 1989, sailing in the inaugural single-handed Vendée Globe, the first nonstop round-the-world race since the Golden Globe, Lamazou had lowered the record to just over 109 days. That was a marked improvement over the reference times of 1984, but Le Cornec and the newly minted Association Jules Verne were still proposing a circumnavigation target that would require a performance jump of almost 30 percent.

Even powered vessels had never broken the eighty-day barrier. Up to that time, the fastest nonstop circumnavigation by any vessel had been posted by the nuclear submarine USS *Triton*. In 1960 the *Triton*, after starting from the eastern seaboard of the United States and picking up Magellan's sixteenth-century west-about route, completed a lap of the globe in eighty-three days, nine hours, and fifty-four minutes. The multihullers were now proposing to outpace one of the U.S. Navy's most sophisticated warships, exceeding nuclear power with wind power alone.

The rules were straightforward. To win the Trophée Jules Verne, a boat had to start and finish on an imaginary line that stretched across the English Channel between the Lizard and Ouessant, off Brest. The course left the Cape of Good Hope, Cape Leeuwin in southwest Australia, and Cape Horn to port, taking boats in an easterly direction that was favored by the prevailing westerly winds. Any crew that could beat Phileas Fogg home in eighty days or less would win the trophy and bragging rights to the fastest circumnavigation in history.

The Jules Verne Trophy excited the interest of many of the world's top racers, including Arthaud, Robin Knox-Johnston, and New Zealand's Peter Blake, the 1989–90 Whitbread winner. In order to traverse the Southern Ocean and round Cape Horn during the more benign Southern Hemisphere summer, boats would have to depart from the English Channel sometime in early 1993. Finding or building the right boat and raising the money to outfit it properly was a challenge. By January 1993 only three campaigns were far enough along to vie for the Jules Verne title that year. Bruno Peyron, with Cam Lewis aboard, was preparing to set off in *Commodore Explorer*. Olivier de Kersauson was readying his ninety-foot trimaran *Charal* but had declared he would sail outside the Jules Verne format (he did not want to pay the $16,000 entry fee). And Robin Knox-Johnston and Peter Blake had teamed up for an Anglo-Saxon bid they hoped would deny the French a major sailing honor. To this end, they had purchased an eighty-foot catamaran built in 1984 called *Formula Tag*. They lengthened it to eighty-five feet and re-named it *Enza* in honor of their principal sponsor, the New Zealand Apple and Pear Marketing Board (*Enza* stood for "Eat New Zealand Apples!"). The first Jules Verne fleet was complete.

Commodore Explorer and *Enza* set out together on January 31, a rainy, blustery day in the English Channel, catching the same weather window and fulfilling a gentlemen's agreement to stage an informal race to make the whole exploit more exciting. De Kersauson, typically, had set off in *Charal* more than a week earlier. "I will comply with nothing," he declared before he left. *Commodore* and *Enza* soon fell into a routine of regular radio contact, which included an exchange of positions. De Kersauson preferred radio silence, leaving everyone to wonder for days at a time where he was and what progress he was making. *Commodore* and *Enza* flew southwest, skimming over the waves at 20-plus knots and riding the favorable northerly winds of the depression they had set out in. Just over a week later, they were already approaching the equator, both boats ahead of their 14-knot average speed targets and sailing hard.

A nonstop circumnavigation, however, is as much about attrition as it is about speed. And this first assault on Jules Verne soon proved that chance is as much a factor as weather in determining if a record will fall. About two weeks into February came word that *Charal*, deep into the Southern Ocean and southeast of Cape Town, had struck ice and damaged her starboard float. De Kersauson had pulled out and was limping back to South Africa. Ten days later it was *Enza*'s turn. Still chasing *Commodore*, clicking off the Southern Ocean miles at a pace that produced one day's run of 476.5 miles, *Enza*'s crew discovered that the starboard hull had started to flood. Frantic bailing and a desperate search for the source of the leak revealed a crack right through the hull. Although they were almost a third of the way between South Africa and Australia and comfortably ahead of their average target speed, Blake and Knox-Johnston had no choice but to quit and head for Cape Town too. Less than thirty days into her Jules Verne run, *Commodore Explorer* had the Southern Ocean track to herself.

Bruno Peyron and his small, hardy crew had not been favored to succeed when this first Jules Verne attempt had begun. But Peyron and Lewis were resolutely keeping the cat at a record pace. It had taken Chichester 106 days to reach Sydney, and the fastest clipper had managed it in just under 70 days. *Commodore Explorer* covered the distance in 39, and by the crew's reckoning had passed the halfway mark in their voyage with a few days in the bank. Every day or two something broke on the boat, but the crew persevered. In the long descent to the deep latitude of Cape Horn, they sailed through snow and sleet and endured the chill, the damp, and the cutting winds of the Roaring Forties as *Commodore* continued to break records with every seamark passed. Cape Horn greeted the crew with predictable disdain, battering them with hurricane-force winds gusting up to 85 knots. Peyron was forced to take the sails down and "park," to ride out the blast.

Commodore survived, and after fifty-three days of sailing began her final sprint up the Atlantic. The storm had its cost; there was precious little time to spare to navigate the calms and headwinds of the Atlantic. Disaster threatened on day sixty-nine when *Commodore Explorer* collided with two whales at a speed of 14 knots. Whale blood and innards welled up around the boat. Fortunately, the damage was mostly cosmetic (the wounded whales chased the boat for a short time, then disappeared, their ultimate fate unknown). Five days later, in the home stretch, *Commodore* smacked into a twenty-foot log but again escaped without serious damage. At last, on April 20, with the sun setting behind them, Peyron, Lewis, and their three crewmates sailed *Commodore Explorer* across the finish line, holding red flares aloft in celebration. They had sailed 27,732 nautical miles at an average speed of 14.6 knots. Their time to circle the globe: seventy-nine days, six hours, fifteen minutes, and fifty-six seconds. The first Jules Verne Trophy had been won, barely.

Commodore Explorer had stolen the glory from *Enza* and *Charal,* but she had not extinguished their desire to sail nonstop at a record pace. In January 1994, while Peyron stayed ashore to raise the money and organization he would need to stage The Race, both *Enza* (after a refit that added seven additional feet to her length, to make her faster and better able to handle rough seas) and *Charal* (renamed *Lyonnaise des Eaux–Dumez* for a new sponsor) were at the starting line again. On January 16 the two boats — catamaran versus trimaran — set off again, out to take the Jules Verne Trophy from Bruno Peyron.

This time *Enza* completed her circumnavigation, setting a new twenty-four-hour distance record (520.9 miles) and one by one eclipsing most of *Commodore*'s marks. The crew of eight had thirteen circumnavigations among them. During the voyage *Enza* went farther south than any multihull had ever been, enduring eleven days below 60° south. In the maelstrom of the South, being inside the hulls sounded like being in a hurtling subway train. It was so rough that crew were repeatedly ejected from their berths, and Blake cracked his ribs so hard after being thrown across the nav station he was confined to a bunk for eight days. After seventy-four days, *Enza* was running up the English Channel in a full storm, on the way to a new record of seventy-four days, twenty-two hours, and seventeen minutes. She had knocked more than four days off *Commodore*'s reference time. De Kersauson and *Lyonnaise* followed just over two days behind, the third boat to beat Phileas Fogg, but failed to win any real glory. When Knox-Johnston approached him after he finished, de Kersauson said, "I 'ate you," then grinned and stuck out his hand.

De Kersauson, whose wife, Caroline, was a descendant of Jules Verne himself, was not to be denied, though. He was as persistent as he was provocative, and in 1995 he set out twice in pursuit of the record, only to return twice to the start because he judged the weather conditions unfavorable. He tried again in 1997 in the same trimaran, now under the banner of *Sport Elec.* This time he succeeded spectacularly, sailing around the world in a new record time of seventy-one days, fourteen hours, and twenty-two minutes.

The Jules Verne record had been set and lowered twice in the space of five years, with each successive record holder knocking a few days off the reference time. De Kersauson proved the capability of a trimaran on the global course, but he had not actually sailed faster than *Enza*. His time resulted instead from good weather and a short route, which brought *Sport Elec* home with fewer miles sailed. De Kersauson's record was vulnerable to a faster boat, yet it was hard to see how the multihulls then afloat could do much more than nibble away at the new record time. To take nonstop racing around the world to another level would require a new generation of multihull monsters, the sort of 120-footer Bruno Peyron had drawn up while in the depths of the Southern Ocean during his Jules Verne run. That's what The Race was about to produce.

5

A NEW BREED OF CAT

> I suspect that . . . the love of the sea, to which some men
> and nations confess so readily, is a complex sentiment
> wherein pride enters for much, necessity not a little, and
> the love of ships — the untiring servants of our hopes and
> our self-esteem — for the best and most genuine part.
>
> — Joseph Conrad

*B*RUNO PEYRON'S concept for The Race was both simple and compelling. There had never been an organized non-stop race around the world for crewed boats. The glory — and agony — of nonstop racing had been the sole preserve of single-handers. More important, Peyron was adamant that it should be an open-design contest, to both inspire and goad designers into conceiving multihulls larger and faster than any that had ever been built.

The largest ocean-racing multihulls on the water — the *Enza*s, the *Commodore Explorer*s — had been conjured and built in the 1980s. At the time, in the eighty-foot range and capable of speeds into the twenties, they seemed extreme. But interest in the class had dwindled, and new boats weren't being ordered. Instead, smaller, sixty-foot trimarans, specially constructed for transatlantic racing and the French inshore circuit, had become the hot boat class, drawing attention and sponsorship dollars. These trimarans, which looked like high-tech waterbugs, could hit speeds of 30 knots in the right conditions, but they were too small, delicate, and weight sensitive to reasonably take on a non-stop circumnavigation. The Jules Verne briefly gave new life to the older generation of multihulls, yet there was only so much that refits and hull extensions could do to make these boats sail faster in the Southern Ocean. They had not really been designed to make nonstop circumnavigations either. As Bruno Peyron and his crew had discovered when they set the first Jules Verne record, this generation was cramped, low to the water, and very wet.

Promoting The Race as a no-limits contest was a sure-fire way of injecting a shot of adrenaline into multihull design and creating a round-the-world venue suited to much bigger multihulls. Most of the world's great yacht races, from the Whitbread to the single-handed contests to the America's Cup, were subject to a variety of complex design rules aimed at close competition and safety. Peyron strongly believed in minimizing the dangers. The Race, in fact, required a long list of safety equipment, including engines on the boats (to assist in the pickup of any crew that might fall overboard), as well as survival training. But he wasn't particularly concerned about fielding a fleet with similar performance characteristics. He wanted The Race to be a design free-for-all in which designers and sailors, not the organizing committee, would be the arbiters of almost every aspect of the boats, from size to sail area to number of hulls to hull shape. If the boats looked radically different, so much the better. The Race would help determine which designs should be sailed into the future.

Ultimately, only one real design rule was adopted. The sailing systems aboard the boats had to be driven the old-fashioned way, with muscle power. No winches were to have electric motors, an increasingly common labor-saving feature of modern superyachts. In Peyron's race the sailors, and the sailors alone, had to be able to handle the boat. Aside from that restriction, Peyron was thrusting a blank sheet of paper at yacht designers and daring them to cut loose their creative powers, to produce boats fast enough to win The Race yet durable enough to sur-

vive it. The dawn of the new millennium seemed an appropri-
ate moment to launch what Peyron viewed as a millennial race.
A start date of December 31, 2000, about six years away, was
eventually chosen. The race to The Race was on.

Peyron and his fledgling race concept intrigued the world's
elite sailors. In the years leading up to the start, he received one
hundred inquiries from potential entrants in twenty-five coun-
tries. In 1997, with just under four years to go, more than sixty
syndicates and many of the world's top offshore sailors were still
declaring themselves in the hunt. But designing, building, and
supporting a cutting-edge boat for a competition like The Race
was a multimillion-dollar proposition, and a well-funded campaign might consume $8 to $10 million. That wasn't a bad deal
in the realm of modern sailing, where an America's Cup campaign could easily top $50 million and some Whitbread entrants
spent in the neighborhood of $20 million.

Nevertheless, the price tag was high enough to winnow the
fleet for a first-time event that had no obvious name recognition
to draw sponsors. Before the sailing even started, The Race became a competition among a handful of multihull designers. In
the end, three high-tech creations came off their drawing boards,
all more than a hundred feet in length. As Peyron had hoped,
each one reflected quite different ideas about how to build a
boat that could sail the most challenging seas at speeds that
might hit 40 knots or more.

THE GIANT

For a designer, a blank piece of paper is both a fantasy and a
daunting challenge. On the one hand, everything is possible. On
the other hand, everything is possible. The Race required highly
specialized boats, just as the clipper era had, boats that would
take full advantage of the latest composite materials and design
technology. The fundamental challenge for the designers could
be boiled down to one simple question: what is the biggest, most

powerful multihull that can be safely handled by a human crew? They would have only one chance to get the answer right. The Race boats would be prototypes with a limited window of time for development and refinement before the start. And getting it right on any boat that was headed for the howling Southern Ocean was crucial. As one designer told his crew, "If I screw up, you die."

The first design team to sit down in earnest with Bruno Peyron's blank sheet of paper could be found nestled among the marine businesses in the surfing town of Newport Beach, California. Morrelli & Melvin was a formal name for two affable and informal engineers who shared a love for fast multihulls and a knack for designing them. Gino Morrelli, who had the glasses and studious demeanor of a man comfortable with algorithms and blueprints, had been drawing multihulls for a living since 1975. In 1983 he earned his ticket into the brotherhood of race boat designers by moving to France, the epicenter of the world's growing infatuation with multihull racing, and turning out some winning designs. He went on to work as a lead designer of the innovative *Stars & Stripes* catamaran, used by San Diego sailor Dennis Conner in 1988 to defend the America's Cup from a rogue New Zealand challenger that skirted the established America's Cup design format. While Morrelli was building a reputation for drawing formidable multihulls, Pete Melvin was out racing them. An aerospace engineer by training, Melvin had the boyish, tanned look of the surfer he was. In 1988 he campaigned a twenty-foot Tornado catamaran in the Seoul Olympics. When he wasn't out on the water he was working on military and commercial aircraft designs at McDonnell Douglas.

Melvin first teamed up with Morrelli in 1990, in an effort to win the Little America's Cup, a top catamaran championship. Morrelli was in charge of the design and Melvin ran the sailing side and helped engineer the innovative wing sail. They lost to an Australian team in the finals, but in 1992 decided to merge their talents. They opened their own design shop alongside a sail loft in a converted warehouse. It was an informal office and a thoroughly modern one. A few computer workstations provided the only design medium they needed; there wasn't a drawing board in the place. Not long after they settled in, Morrelli and Melvin were contacted by a fifty-year-old Chicago multimillionaire named Steve Fossett. He had just bought a sixty-foot racing trimaran from Florence Arthaud (one of the Jules Verne Trophy founders) and needed help preparing it for racing in the United States. Morrelli and Melvin happily obliged. In 1994 Fossett had another request: he wanted them to design him the fastest sailboat the world had ever seen.

Coming from Fossett, the commission was not all that surprising. Steve Fossett had made his pile through shrewd, hardnosed trading in the zero-sum jungle of Chicago options. For most people, making split-second million-dollar decisions would provide more than enough stress, excitement, and validation for one lifetime. Fossett was wired for more action. His real pleasure in life — his obsession, even — was testing his physical endurance and setting records. Fossett was stocky, with a wide moon face and a shy smile. He had none of the gaunt air or corded musculature of a person built for absurd physical extremes. But whatever he lacked in physical gifts he made up for with methodical preparation and dogged determination.

Fossett grew up in California. He went rock climbing with the Sierra Club and was challenging the Matterhorn and the Eiger before he was out of college. The Eiger came close to killing him when he nearly slid over an abyss, but it did nothing to dissuade him from going on to attempt every major endurance adventure that might be found on a men's magazine Top 10 list. He swam the English Channel (failing the first three tries, succeeding on the fourth, clocking one of the slowest recorded times and putting himself in the hospital with hypothermia). He mushed in the Iditarod dogsled race. He completed the Ironman Triathlon in Hawaii and drove a racecar at Le Mans. He climbed the highest mountains on six continents. Only Everest eluded him. Twice.

In 1990 Fossett surveyed his life and decided it was time to put adventure first and the pursuit of money second. With characteristic deliberation he analyzed the sporting scene and came up with two goals that most interested him: becoming the first person to balloon nonstop around the world and sailing across the Atlantic single-handed. Fossett was not the kind of person to devote his time to the romance of the quest; his gratification came with success. Like Chichester, he was painstaking and stubborn. And he had the money and the organizational skills to vault immediately to the elite level. Between 1994 and 1998 he made five of the six longest balloon flights in history (although he failed in his quest to become the first to circle the globe) and racked up ten speed-sailing world records, along with eight race records.

That was pretty good work considering Fossett had done little sailing, and no serious offshore sailing, before snapping up one of the fastest trimarans, renaming it *Lakota*. The disciplines of sailing — patience, physical stamina, risk analysis, understanding weather and aerodynamics — appealed to him. Slogging around offshore for weeks on end in monohulls might have seemed a more natural fit for Fossett's stoic nature, but from the start he was addicted to speed sailing, and that, naturally, meant multihulls.

Just weeks after taking over *Lakota,* Fossett won the 1993 Round Britain and Ireland Race in near-record time. He then sailed *Lakota* in the 1994 transatlantic Route du Rhum, compensating for his lack of experience with a 150-page briefing book compiled by Ben Wright, a professional Australian sailor who would start managing Fossett's racing boats. Fossett finished fifth in the race and went on with *Lakota* to set a series of passage-making records, sailing solo and with crew. It was the single-handed records — such as crossing the Pacific from Yokohama to San Francisco in under twenty-one days — that were particularly important to him. He did not want to be perceived in the small confines of the sailing world as a novice who simply used his fat wallet to buy his way into the record books with cutting-edge boats and professional crew. "I like to do a single-hander about once a year just to show people I can do it," he explained. "I want to be thought of as a sailor."

Fossett's early successes helped establish his credibility in his new sport. But the three most prestigious sailing records — the transatlantic, the twenty-four-hour, and the Jules Verne — were the marks he coveted most. There was also The Race, which intrigued Fossett if it succeeded in becoming the ultimate proving ground for the latest high-tech yachts. To upgrade his record-breaking hardware for this ambitious program, he first contacted a leading British multihull designer named Nigel Irens, who had designed Blake and Knox-Johnston's Jules Verne cat *Enza*. Irens was already busy working on a Race design and couldn't accept the project. So Fossett turned to Morrelli and Melvin, his collaborators on *Lakota*.

Morrelli and Melvin were of course delighted to take on a high-profile commission to design the world's fastest multihull, and it first required them to address a fundamental question: two hulls or three? The debate over the relative performance of multihulls versus monohulls had long ago been resolved in the minds of top sailors and designers, but the relative merits of trimarans versus catamarans were still hotly argued, although there was loose consensus on a few points.

Generally speaking, a race between a catamaran and a trimaran of equal length will favor the trimaran. That's because a trimaran can be wider for a given length, which means it can carry more sail without capsizing. A catamaran's width is constrained by the fact that as the span between the hulls gets wider, the connecting beams must be made stronger and will at some point become too heavy; with three hulls, a trimaran can achieve greater width with shorter spans. Many designers also assumed that in flat water, in light air, or going to weather — that is, sailing in the direction the wind is blowing from — a trimaran would perform better. But take away a limit on length and throw in the rough sailing conditions of a round-the-world course through the Southern Ocean and suddenly the equation gets a lot more complex. Moreover, a trimaran, with its three hulls, is more expensive to build than a catamaran of the same length. So for a given amount of money, a designer could provide either a smaller trimaran or a larger catamaran.

When it comes to sailboats, size does matter. Length on the waterline contributes to a higher theoretical top speed, and big boats handle big seas better than small boats. So in a race between a smaller trimaran and a longer catamaran, it was far from clear which boat would win. Many designers suspected that the boats would be roughly equal when heading south through the Atlantic to the Roaring Forties, which usually involves sailing with the wind coming from behind the boat, but that the catamaran could be sailed harder and faster through the roiling seas of the Southern Ocean. On the other hand, it also seemed likely that the trimaran might hold the edge on the return leg north through the Atlantic, which involves a lot of light-air sailing and sailing into the wind. The only real test to date, the Jules Verne experience, didn't offer conclusive answers. In 1994 *Enza,* a catamaran, had sailed around the world faster than *Lyonnaise des Eaux–Dumez,* a trimaran. But three years later, *Lyonnaise* sailed around the world again as *Sport Elec* and lowered *Enza*'s record. During each circumnavigation the boats had sailed different distances in different weather systems, so it was difficult to make reliable comparisons.

In the days before powerful desktop computers, yacht designers had to make decisions based on experience and instinct. Their judgments could be tested with small-scale hull models towed through a tank of water to predict performance, but it was a labor-intensive process that limited the number of hull shapes that could be compared. Nathaniel Herreshoff, the designer of *Amaryllis,* didn't even have tank testing. He simply cut a small hull model out of wood, using his formidable eye and intuitive grasp of boat design to tell him the optimum shape. Once he was happy, construction plans based on his half model would be drawn.

On the eve of the twenty-first century, Morrelli and Melvin

didn't have to get out any woodworking tools. They could turn to something much more powerful, the Velocity Prediction Program. The VPP is a computer modeling tool that can conjure a virtual boat from a welter of design parameters, including measurements such as length, beam, and displacement. It can then be used to predict how fast the virtual boat will sail across a range of wind strengths and angles. Weather data, such as wind speeds and directions likely to be encountered over a specific route, can also be added to the mix, allowing the VPP to predict how long it will take the virtual design to sail a virtual route. All the design parameters can then be tweaked to see how performance is affected. The speed and power of computers in harness with the VPP made for a quantum leap in the art of creating sailboats. Instead of just a few painstakingly produced hulls to compare in a towing tank, hundreds of designs could be raced against one another with just a few clicks of a mouse.

VPPs tend to be highly proprietary programs, with different designers developing their own versions and constantly updating them based on how boats really perform once they are built. For their cat-versus-tri analysis, Morrelli and Melvin turned to a VPP that had been developed over ten years by an American designer named Clay Oliver, who had done extensive America's Cup work. Steve Fossett was most interested in pocketing the nonstop round-the-world record, so Morrelli and Melvin created four circumnavigation courses using wind speed and direction data collected from previous Jules Verne attempts, Whitbread races, and generic weather information sources such as Pilot Charts. They then refined the VPP further by plugging the design parameters for *Enza* and *Sport Elec* into the program and running them over the routes the boats sailed to see whether their predicted finishing times matched their actual finishing times.

Once the VPP was tuned up, it was time to see whether a trimaran or a longer catamaran was faster in a virtual race around the world. Morrelli and Melvin created three virtual trimarans and three corresponding catamarans, the largest well over one hundred feet, and ran them through the four circumnavigations, fiddling with the design parameters as they did so in an effort to squeeze more speed out of each boat. By the time the field was narrowed to just a couple of promising designs, they had their answer. According to the computer, in a nonstop race a longer catamaran should get home faster than a shorter trimaran. Thanks to the VPP, one fundamental question — cat or tri? — had been answered without ever leaving the confines of a desk chair. Now Morrelli and Melvin could use the computer's predictive power to help solve the next puzzle: how to design the fastest catamaran a human crew could race without killing themselves.

No designer had ever built a modern racing catamaran longer than one hundred feet, so Morrelli and Melvin, as well as the other designers that would work on Race boats, had to start from scratch. They could use computer power to scale up existing designs in the eighty-foot range to get a feel for what a new maxi-cat might look like, how fast it might sail, and what its working loads would be. But there was no existing design database to provide real numbers based on real boats sailing on real seas. Other than cost, only one fixed design parameter could be used to help establish the size and power of the new boat: it had to be manageable with muscle power alone. There was no point in building a two-hundred-foot catamaran with a theoretical top speed in excess of 50 knots if the mechanical hardware — the blocks (pulleys) and winches used to handle the lines controlling the sails — sufficient to withstand the loads didn't exist, or if the sails were so large and heavy the crew couldn't hump them around the boat to put them up.

Even if a crew could outmuscle the loads of a really big boat, custom manufacturing all the hardware for it would drive the building cost through the roof. So Morrelli and Melvin had at least one solid set of parameters they could cling to amid the infinite design choices facing them. The huge loads generated by the sails and speed of the boat they were designing had to fall within the working capability of the largest winches and racing hardware on the market. In a sense, they selected massively powerful winches — made by Lewmar, a leading manufacturer — and started designing a boat around them.

To get a better idea of costs, sailing speeds, and loads, Morrelli and Melvin turned again to the VPP. They designed a series of virtual catamarans from 105 to 120 feet in length, in five-foot increments, and with between 60 and 65 feet of beam between the hulls. This allowed them to see how fast, how expensive, and how difficult to control each boat would be and compare them. Fossett wanted a boat that a crew could comfortably sail, but he didn't want a boat that was so conservative that his future competitors would be fielding bigger, more powerful boats after he was already in the water. He wasn't the sort of businessman to invest his money in fleeting glory.

Initially, this logic inclined Morrelli and Melvin toward the 120-footer, which according to the VPP would be about 5 percent faster than the 105-footer and capable of an astounding circumnavigation. If the VPP was accurate, the boat might obliterate the Jules Verne record, knocking it down from just over seventy days to under sixty. But when the designers started crunching the numbers on the structure of the boat, its weight, and its rig and sails, they realized that the thing taking shape on their computer screens was a beast. It might indeed be 5 percent faster, but how often could the crew sail it at its full potential if they couldn't control it? Not often enough, Morrelli, Melvin, and Fossett concluded. The designers continued to run analyses on the 105- and 110-foot boats and were inclined to favor the 110-footer as the best balance between speed and manageability. Fossett, who had both his checkbook and his safety to consider, backed them off one more notch. "Let's just build this 105-footer," he told Morrelli and Melvin. "It's within our known range. And we're not getting too stretched out there as far as technology and what's been done before."

Once this key choice was made, Morrelli and Melvin faced another design dilemma. The goal with any race boat is to build it as light as humanly possible, but not so light it disintegrates in midocean. (An America's Cup joke defines the perfect race boat as one that falls apart just after it crosses the finish line; if it survives longer, it's overbuilt.) The more a boat weighs, the more water it has to push aside to move forward. More boat in the water also means more "wetted surface," which translates into additional drag. All other things being equal, a lighter boat will have a faster top-end speed and will be quicker to accelerate. Build too light, however, and you end up with an expensive hole in the water that can't complete the course. Fossett wanted the world's fastest multihull. He also wanted a boat that could endure the cross-seas, breaking waves, and slamming of multiple record attempts and circumnavigations.

Today's racing boats are literally baked from carbon fiber, an ultrastrong, ultralight composite material used extensively in the aircraft industry. Carbon fiber starts out as a cloth woven from threads, each consisting of thousands of strands of carbon. The cloth is impregnated with a resin and layered around a honeycomb core that is usually fashioned from a light, cardboardlike material called Nomex (for Fossett's boat, Morrelli and Melvin decided on a stiffer core made from aluminum). Layers of cloth and the core are placed in a hull mold and heated in enormous ovens at temperatures of $85°C$ or more. The resin liquefies and permeates the carbon fiber and the core. When it cools and hardens, the result is an incredibly stiff, light laminate skin that is matte black and easy to paint to a glossy finish. The stiffness or strength of the skin is determined by how much carbon fiber is used. Stronger means heavier. But even at its beefiest, a carbon-fiber hull is a miracle of weight to strength, matching the stiffness of steel at about one tenth the weight. Carbon fiber used to be exotic and prohibitively expensive, but in the early 1990s the cost dropped by almost two thirds as it became a standard material in everything from tennis rackets to bicycles. In the end, Fossett's carbon-fiber sailing machine would cost around $5 million.

There is an old adage in sailing: "To finish first, first you have to finish." That meant Morrelli and Melvin had to take a stab at predicting all the different forces their boat would endure as it raced across the seas and make sure there was enough carbon fiber in all the right places to keep it in one piece. This sent them back to the realm of computer simulation. With the help of a structural engineer, they created a virtual boat made from the minimal amounts and thicknesses of carbon fiber they thought they could safely get away with. And then they "sailed" the boat through a range of conditions to try to break it. If something broke, they strengthened it. If it didn't, they could sometimes shave away a layer or two of carbon fiber and save a little more weight.

It was impossible to guess every way in which the boat would be stressed in the real world, so Morrelli and Melvin double-checked their work by subjecting the virtual boat to a number of extreme situations, figuring if it could survive those, it could survive everything normal sailing would do to it. In one virtual scenario, they sailed the boat upwind on one hull and launched it off a wave, so that when it came crashing back into the ocean, the weight of the entire boat was absorbed by one bow. The bow was pushed three meters out of line, graphically illustrating the radical movement that would occur between the two hulls on a boat as big and fast as the one they were building. In another scenario, they slammed their virtual boat so hard into a wave they stuffed the bows forty feet underwater. It was like driving into a pile of wet sand, an experience no sailor in his or her right mind would ever want to go through. The maxi-cat was almost vertical in the sea, with water lapping around the main crossbeam. It was a useful exercise, because it was important to see what water pressure did to hulls that could submarine to depths no hulls had ever seen before, short of sinking.

These scenarios were critical to refining the engineering and determining how much carbon fiber was needed, but it was also important to avoid getting carried away. If they built their 105-footer to survive every drastic situation a boat sailing at close to 40 knots could get into, Morrelli and Melvin would end up with a boat so heavy it would never break a record or win a race.

They had to assume good judgment and seamanship would be exercised by the crew. Yes, the boat could probably be sailed at 30 knots in nasty seas, racking up ridiculous shock loads. But no human crew could — or would want to — endure the physical abuse of repeatedly launching off waves or stuffing the bows. A new-generation maxi-catamaran could reach automobile speeds on the oceans; however, the oceans are not flat like a road. In certain conditions, at certain speeds, it would simply be impossible for the crew to function — to stand, to work the sails, to steer, to cook, to sleep — because they would be thrown around with such force. Morrelli and Melvin could design a boat that might survive those conditions, but there was no sense building a boat that broke long after the people did. To Robert Perry, a noted American yacht designer, the design and materials technology in Morrelli and Melvin's catamaran had crossed an interesting threshold. "These things have almost reached the stage of modern jet fighters, where technology has produced planes human beings physically can't control," he said. "Historically the boat was not as important as the guy. Now the boat is everything and the guy is just a flea."

Morrelli and Melvin slowly refined the structure and details of the boat — where all the lines would be led, how the living areas would set up, where the galley would go. The most important remaining decision was what type of rig their baby should have. A standard mast consists of a single carbon-fiber tube held in position by rigging made from strong synthetic fibers. But over recent decades, designers have devised a more efficient alternative: a rotating wing mast.

As the name implies, the wing mast is shaped like a very narrow airplane wing stood on end, and it swivels on a ball-and-socket joint instead of being solidly anchored in the deck or hull. That allows it to be turned for maximum aerodynamic efficiency as the mainsail is let out or pulled in according to the wind angle. Sails drive boats forward not because the wind pushes them, but because air flow over them produces lift, just as it does for an airplane. In effect, the boat is sucked forward. A wing mast helps keep the flow of wind over the sail smooth and free of lift-sapping vortexes and, unlike a standard mast, provides additional lift of its own, so a boat with a rotating wing mast can get the same horsepower with a shorter mast. That lowers the boat's center of gravity, which improves stability. Smaller sails also weigh less and are easier to handle.

French designers for years had been using wing masts to great effect on their ocean racing designs, and Morrelli and Melvin themselves had built a wing mast for *Stars & Stripes.* But they worried that a rotating wing mast might be more prone to failure at sea than a traditional mast. They hesitated to stick one on a boat whose power and size had already taken them into unknown territory. Ultimately, Fossett opted for the simplicity and presumed reliability of a conventional mast. A wing mast could always be substituted after the rest of the boat design had been proven.

Morrelli and Melvin's maxi-cat was no ordinary piece of design work. By the time they shipped blueprints to the builder, Cookson Boats in New Zealand, in 1997, they had invested five thousand man-hours in the project, more than triple the time required for a standard racing multihull. For all their effort, there were still so many unknowns and so many subjective decisions in the design process, neither Californian could be sure how the boat was going to work out. It would be up to the oceans — the ultimate test tank — to pass that judgment. "There are no books that tell you how to design one of these boats," Pete Melvin observed. Six thousand miles away, in a small town on the Brittany coast, another team of designers was writing its own book.

THE OLLIER SISTERS

The village of Vannes is an attractive seaside community with a walled old city and a harbor that is crammed with sailboats only their owners could love. Not far down a canal that leads from the village center to the Gulf of Morbihan is a shipyard that turns out some of the most advanced racing sailboats in the world. Chantier Multiplast was started in 1981 by a French naval architect, Gilles Ollier, at a time when composite materials such as Kevlar and carbon fiber were just beginning to transform the boat-building industry.

Ollier was a compact, bookish man with watchful eyes and a reserved demeanor. He started out as a monohull designer, but in the late 1970s was increasingly bewitched, like most French sailing enthusiasts, by the superior speed of the multihulls carving up the transatlantic racecourses. As a young man Ollier had left home for his tour of military service loaded down with articles on carbon fiber. Now, with Multiplast, he wanted to use composites to design and build the world's lightest, fastest multihulls.

Ollier and Multiplast built the first all-carbon racing multihull, a sixty-footer called *Crédit Agricole II,* which took the lead in the 1984 OSTAR and then capsized (the skipper was rescued). In the same year Multiplast turned out the eighty-five-footer *Jet Services IV,* pushing Ollier's expertise into bigger designs. Unfortunately, this boat also ended up upside down, off Spain, killing a sailor.

Ollier's growing facility with fast hull shapes and sleek wing masts led to one of the most successful racing catamarans ever built, *Jet Services V,* launched in 1987. At seventy-five feet, she was not as large as some of his earlier multihulls, but she was rugged, simple, and very quick. She won the 1987 Round Europe Race soon after hitting the water, and went on to win the transatlantic Quebec–St. Malo race in 1988 by a full three days. In 1990 *Jet Services V* set a new transatlantic record, covering the 2,925 miles between New York and the Lizard in just six days and thirteen hours, at an average speed of 18.62 knots. This extraordinary record, which knocked seventeen hours off the existing reference time, remained unbroken for more than a decade. Eventually, *Jet Services V* ended up in Bruno Peyron's hands, where she was lengthened, renamed *Commodore Explorer,* and sailed on Peyron's record-breaking Jules Verne circumnavigation. That milestone confirmed Ollier as one of the best in his profession. With his love of bigger and faster, and his association with Peyron, it was only natural that he would jump into the thick of the design competition for The Race.

When Ollier first generated design ideas for The Race in 1995, there were no firm customers for a Multiplast boat. Still, the no-limits concept of The Race had hooked him, and on spec he and his team of three designers set about the same evaluation process that was consuming Morrelli and Melvin. They stuffed a VPP full of round-the-world weather information and trimaran-versus-catamaran designs. And it spat out the same results. Over the range of conditions boats in The Race were likely to experience, their computer agreed, a catamaran would probably be faster. It seemed to confirm that the catamaran would be disadvantaged in light winds, but also indicated the cat would have a 2 to 3 percent advantage over the trimaran in winds above 10 knots, particularly when the wind was blowing from behind. Average wind speeds during a circumnavigation were believed to be about 12 knots, giving the catamaran the edge. Ollier also suspected that a big catamaran would be more stable in the rough seas of the Southern Ocean, a point that preoccupied him.

The Ollier team then moved into the same iterative design sequence that was producing the Morrelli and Melvin Race bid. They took powerful stock winches (Lewmar again) and calculated the size of the sails that could reasonably be handled by ordinary mortals grinding those winches. They then, in effect, designed a boat to fit those sails, testing different hull lengths and beams to come up with the basic dimensions. To keep the loads on the sheets and rigging within reason, Ollier and his team aimed to no more than double the loads Multiplast had already mastered with *Commodore Explorer* and their other multihulls.

When all the number crunching was done, they were looking at a catamaran about 105 feet long and 57 feet wide. Ollier considered these dimensions, then added another five feet to the hulls, mostly because he suspected sponsors would be more interested in a boat that was longer than the Fossett cat. The computers also ran through the fluid dynamics of thirty-four different hull shapes to find the right balance between speed and sea-kindliness. The best candidates were then tested in large towing tanks, with one-eighth scale models, to verify the results. Once the hull's basic structure and shape were resolved, those parameters were plugged back into the computer and fourteen different sail plans were tested, again using the almighty VPP. This produced a 136-foot wing mast — tall enough to power the boat at speeds of 40 knots, but not so tall that its large surface area would threaten to capsize the boat in winds of less than hurricane force.

The maxi-cat represented in the Ollier team's final blueprints was the product of more than three years of analysis and study. It was dubbed Code Zero until a sponsor could be announced, and construction began at the Multiplast yard in the spring of 1999. In December of that year, Club Med stepped forward to buy the boat and sponsor its run in The Race. To lead the campaign, Club Med selected New Zealand sailor Grant Dalton, one of the most experienced ocean racers on the planet. Two additional orders for the Ollier design followed. Bruno Peyron could not break away from organizing The Race without threatening the collapse of the whole competition. Loïck Peyron, his younger brother, was therefore named as the skipper of the second boat, which was to be called *Innovation Explorer*. The third, to be called *Team Adventure,* was sold to Cam Lewis.

Lewis had been present at the conception of The Race down in the Southern Ocean, and he was determined to be a part of it. He faced a difficult struggle to raise the $6 million he had budgeted for the campaign because sailing in the United States was never an easy sell. But he loved the no-limits, nonstop format Peyron had created, and believed The Race could change the way the world looked at big-time sailing. "It should be a heck of a lot more interesting than the Wonderbread race," he said, poking fun at the Whitbread, "where you basically sprint from hotel room to hotel room." As for the America's Cup, Lewis revealed the true disdain of a speed junkie. "An America's Cup campaign will spend thirty-five million dollars for a boat that sails ten knots and never really goes anywhere," he scoffed. "And if it blows over twenty knots the crews go sit in the bar."

The Race was also a perfect match for Lewis's bold personality. Standing over six feet tall, he had boyish good looks and a former model for a wife. He grew up in a wealthy Massachusetts family whose forebears included governors and a senator. Lewis could also claim the polar explorer Richard Byrd as a distant relation, and he was animated as a child by the spirit of adventure and exploration. He had no interest in the family specialty, finance, and had found in sailing a physical, intensely competitive sport that took him all over the world. He started in small boats, racing around buoys, but had been converted to the multihull faith thanks to Bruno Peyron and *Commodore Explorer*. The Ollier catamarans were at the cutting edge of multihull design, and that's where he knew he was meant to be. For Lewis, The Race was the prelude to what he hoped would be a multiyear program of bold record-breaking sailing.

First, though, he had to lay his hands on the boat. Each Ollier cat required tens of thousands of man-hours to construct, and they finally started hitting the water one after another in the year 2000, with *Club Med* first to launch in May, and *Innovation Explorer* and *Team Adventure* following in October and November, just scant weeks before The Race. The latter two boats would be largely untested and unfamiliar to their crews, a big handicap. But The Race was an adventure, and all adventures require more than a little improvisation. Once the boats were racing, anything could happen.

THE WAVE PIERCER

Gilles Ollier and Morrelli and Melvin were pushing catamaran design to brave new limits, but they weren't reinventing it. That role was played by an iconoclastic designer named Adrian Thompson and a freethinking English sailor named Pete Goss.

When he was three years old, Pete Goss watched Blondie
Hasler set out on the 1964 OSTAR transatlantic race. From that
young age Goss was a confirmed sailing addict, throughout his
childhood building rickety vessels out of cardboard and any
other useful debris he could lay his hands on. Like Hasler, Goss
embarked on a career in the Royal Marines, but in 1990, at the
age of twenty-nine, he retired from the service so he could devote his life to his chosen sport. With mostly empty pockets, a
few hard-won donations, and plenty of help from his friends
Goss scraped together a campaign for the 1996 Vendée Globe
single-handed race. In part to compensate for his limited funds,
and in part because he liked to be different, Goss turned for his
boat design to Adrian Thompson, a self-taught naval architect.

Thompson was an unusual figure in the world of design, a
former farmer and furniture maker with a shaggy head of hair
and no formal university training. He might never have gone
near a drafting board but for the travails of Francis Chichester
in his cranky *Gipsy Moth IV*. Thompson figured that if a professional yacht designer like John Illingworth could turn out
such a lemon, there was no reason a nonprofessional couldn't do
better.

Thompson decided to build a boat and enter it in the 1982
Round Britain and Ireland Race. As a first step, he went into
seclusion to devour the canons of naval architecture. The result
was a thirty-foot monohull called *Alice's Mirror,* which had ballast tanks under the side decks that could be filled with water for
increased stability and sail-carrying power. At this time water
ballast was far from a standard design trick, and *Alice's Mirror*
won her class, beating many larger boats around the course. She
launched Thompson on a productive racing-boat design career,
although he still dabbled elsewhere, turning out a carbon-fiber
bike that won a stage of the Tour de France and an aerodynamic
carbon-fiber golf club that was banned from professional events
because it hit the ball too far.

For Goss's Vendée Globe bid, Thompson and Goss came up
with a fifty-foot boat that they hoped would outsail many of the

elite sixty-footers in the race. Although it was theoretically slower, they reasoned that a smaller boat would weigh less and be easier to handle, allowing Goss to sail it closer to its full potential than the single-handers struggling with their larger, more demanding machines. Thompson's major innovation on this boat, the *Aqua Quorum,* was a keel that could be moved from side to side, to better counteract the heeling force of the wind in the sails. The swing keel would allow Goss to carry more sail than he could have with a less efficient fixed keel. During construction, the bare hull of *Aqua Quorum* was so light it could be picked up by six men. Still, as Goss discovered during the race, size does indeed matter. He was fifth out of six finishers, although that in itself was an achievement in a race in which ten starters failed to complete the course.

More important for his sailing career, Goss returned home a hero after his Southern Ocean rescue of Raphael Dinelli — Dinelli's boat had been rolled and sunk in a fierce storm. When the request for assistance came from race headquarters, Goss barely hesitated, even though he was 160 miles downwind, trying to survive the same winds and seas. He knew he was Dinelli's only hope, and turned back into the hurricane-strength gusts, knowing his boat might not survive the pounding. *Aqua Quorum* was knocked flat to the water every half hour, and after more than twenty-four hours fighting his way into the maelstrom, Goss somehow managed to find Dinelli, who was hypothermic and clinging to his life raft. Goss was almost as spent as Dinelli: he had lost seven pounds in the effort to reach him. Dinelli clambered on board and was offered a bottle of warm tea. When Goss reached the finish line at Les Sables d'Olonne, he was greeted by 150,000 cheering fans and the news that French President Jacques Chirac had decided to present him with the Legion of Honor.

Goss knew from the moment of Peyron's announcement of The Race that he wanted to launch a campaign. Before he even set forth in the Vendée Globe, he turned Thompson loose on the design of a giant catamaran. Goss loved the notion of a race that set no design limits at all, and Adrian Thompson, who was then forty-five, was just the designer to take full advantage of the freedom. Together they intended to exploit the no-limits concept with a potentially revolutionary design. The faster a conventional multihull sails, the harder it slams into the seas. The resulting impact is brutal on the boat and wearing on the crew. When the forces become extreme, they either limit the speed of the boat or start breaking it into pieces. This was the sort of elemental problem that Thompson loved to attack with radical innovation. For Goss's maxi-cat his approach was elegant and direct. Instead of building a catamaran that pounded across the oceans, which Thompson compared to trying to skip a rock across a choppy pond, he proposed one that sliced through the waves.

This deviant concept was not wholly without basis in practical experience. Thompson had already explored the "wave-piercing" idea in high-speed military attack craft, known as very slender vessels (VSVs), which he had designed for U.S., British, and German special forces. The needle-like bows of the fifty-foot VSVs, with their reduced buoyancy and narrow profile, were shaped to cut through waves, not launch off them, resulting in a smoother high-speed ride for troops who needed to be well rested when they reached their destination. Thompson had doubts about the durability and comfort of a conventional catamaran scaled up to more than one hundred feet and saw no reason why the wave-piercing concept should not work if it was engineered correctly.

This line of thinking produced a 120-foot cat that was straight off the pages of a Jules Verne novel. It had strikingly slender hulls, which looked a bit like enormous pencils, set seventy feet apart. Their midsections were connected by two beams that supported a fifty-foot-long pod in which the crew would eat, sleep, and navigate (at one point, Thompson considered making the pod detachable so it could be used as an escape craft in an emergency). There was no front beam to stabilize the bows, because a front beam would only impede the boat's passage through the waves. During normal sailing the bows were expected to submerge to depths of fourteen feet or more. As buoyancy increased in the hulls as waves moved bow to stern, the boat would lift with a smooth surging motion. It was a catamaran designed to sail both over and under the water.

Without a front beam to anchor rigging, Thompson and Goss had to come up with an alternative to the standard single mast mounted in the middle of a central beam. After studying the possibilities, they decided to place a 130-foot wing mast in each hull. Here they took the opportunity to address another fundamental problem: the risk of capsizing. Catamarans get blown over when they have too much sail up. On the conventional cats being built for The Race, the sheer size and weight of the sails would make reducing sail a time-consuming, tiring chore. If the crews waited too long to take sail down, or got caught by a sudden squall, they might quickly find themselves in a fight for survival. At a minimum, they would have to sail conservatively, always trying to shorten sail in advance of any danger. Thompson and Goss opted to make their masts freestanding, and stood each mast on a ball-and-socket joint on the floor of the hull so it could be rotated almost 360 degrees. Each spar would fly a single mainsail, to be controlled by a "wishbone rig."

In other words, Thompson and Goss outfitted their $6 million maxi-cat, to be named *Team Philips* after its principal sponsor, with two giant windsurfer sails. The beauty of the system was that it allowed the crew to take the pressure of the wind out of the sails almost instantly, merely by letting the wishbone rigs rotate into the wind. It would be like having a fast-acting emergency brake while the other catamarans sailed with a five-second delay. In theory, *Team Philips* would be able to be driven harder with a greater margin for error.

This novel rig design had another benefit that appealed to Goss, who, like Hasler, was always looking for ways to make boats lighter and simpler. It would demand fewer crew. The rotation of the wishbones and the set of the sails would, in essence, be controlled by just two lines. And by splitting the total sail area between two masts, the sails themselves would be smaller and relatively easy to raise and lower compared to the larger mainsails on the other maxi-cats. Goss figured that every additional sailor in a sixty-to-seventy-day race would require hundreds of pounds in additional stores, gear, and living space. So if he could race around the world with just five or six, while Fossett, Peyron, and Lewis sailed with crews of thirteen or fourteen, *Team Philips* might save a ton or more on crew-related weight.

Goss and Thompson were a captivating pair. Their otherworldly craft attracted plenty of skepticism from the professional sailing world. But Goss, soft-spoken, handsome, and relentlessly logical, sold his project with an evangelical zeal. From the build site in the tiny Devon town of Totnes, he transformed *Team Philips* into a national event. Television and newspaper reporters dropped by to see what was happening with his crazy boat. Goss invited the rest of the public to stop in as well. Before long, crowds were traipsing through his cavernous warehouse, poring over the interactive displays explaining *Team Philips* and The Race and eating scones in the visitors' café. Letters from well-wishers and schoolchildren covered the walls. Thousands of supporters sent £25 donations in return for having their names inscribed on the hulls taking form. One Granny Barney, a truly inspired *Team Philips* fan, celebrated her sixtieth birthday by walking the length of Cornwall with her golden retriever to raise money. She netted £10,000 and gave half to a church and half to *Team Philips*. The donation was used to equip the small kitchen on the boat, henceforth referred to as Granny Barney's Galley. Even Queen Elizabeth took note of the phenomenon and agreed to christen *Team Philips* in a ceremony on the London docks (the only other private vessel the queen had ever christened was her namesake, the Cunard Line's *Queen Elizabeth II*).

Goss and Thompson freely admitted that their design looked "wacky," but they also predicted it would race across the oceans at speeds up to 40 knots. The accuracy of that prediction, of course, would only be demonstrated on the water. But no one, not even the experts, could rule out the possibility that Goss and Thompson might be about to change multihull design forever. Nigel Irens, the designer Steve Fossett had first turned to, compared the debate over *Team Philips* to the controversy over the transition from sturdy biplanes to more efficient, but seemingly more fragile, monoplanes. "That must have sounded as crazy then as this does now," he said. "Progress never happens unless someone is willing to take a risk."

No matter what *Team Philips*'s fate, Thompson and Goss had created just the sort of suspense and anticipation that Bruno Peyron had been hoping for when he first conceived of a race without design limitations. Thompson was acutely aware that his friends' lives would be riding on the soundness of his boat and its engineering. Nevertheless, the iconoclastic designer was enjoying the uncertainty. "It would be boring if all the boats looked the same," he said. "Only one of us will be proved right."

6

SPEED AND CARNAGE

> The cure for everything is salt water — sweat, tears, or the sea.
>
> — Isak Dinesen

AT 5 P.M. local time on December 21, 1998, Christine Fletcher, the mayor of Auckland, New Zealand, and a crowd of the curious gathered at Auckland's America's Cup Village for the launching of a new era in ocean racing. For the past twenty-one months, the swarm of workers at Cookson Boats had referred to Steve Fossett's behemoth simply as the BFB, as in "big fucking boat." Now, with a flick of Fletcher's wrist and the crack of a champagne bottle on a sleek carbon-fiber bow, the BFB officially came to life as *PlayStation,* named for the popular video-game system of her principal sponsor, Sony.

She was the largest and most powerful ocean-racing multihull ever to take to the water, a machine designed to do only one thing: break speed-sailing records. Every effort had been made to save weight. The two hulls contained no interior paint — leaving them a gloomy matte black — because paint would have added a couple of hundred pounds. Each hull contained only four berths, which would have to be shared by the crew of ten to fourteen in a practice known as "hot-bunking." There were no large tanks to store drinking water. Instead, *PlayStation* was fitted with a machine that could filter salt and impurities from seawater, making just enough drinking water for each day's use.

The port hull contained a simple galley with a propane stove to heat lightweight freeze-dried meals. In the starboard hull, the navigation station was packed with instruments and readouts that monitored every aspect of the catamaran's performance and position. Both hulls had large circular ports halfway between the waterline and the deck which let some light into the tomblike interior. More important, the ports could be opened and used to get in and out of the hulls whether the catamaran was right side up or upside down.

With her bold yellow, black, and red graphics and futuristic styling, the big catamaran looked as if she had beamed into Auckland Harbor from the screen of one of Sony's video games. But the days of computer simulations were over. Fossett himself was thousands of miles away, and thousands of feet above the earth, trying yet again to balloon nonstop around the world, this time with British tycoon Richard Branson. He and Branson would be forced by bad weather to splash down in the Pacific off Oahu on Christmas morning. Early in the new year, Fossett would fly to New Zealand to rendezvous with his latest record-breaking toy. It was time for Morrelli and Melvin's virtual creation to go sailing.

The launch of *PlayStation* took preparations for The Race into a suspenseful new phase. Engineers and designers could crunch and tweak all the numbers they wanted, but it was only when boats started sailing that their true nature could be evaluated and understood. What did the unprecedented power and speeds of these new multihulls portend? Could they be controlled? Would they hold together under the incredible stresses they would be subjected to?

PlayStation's early training runs, in the blustery March winds of the Southern Hemisphere fall, established just how close to the edge Morrelli and Melvin had pushed the design. Take the mainsheet controlling the boom, for example. When the full mainsail was spread before the wind, the tension on that critical line and the fittings attached to it could spike up to fifteen tons. On conventional sailboats the mainsheet can be trimmed within seconds to adjust to changing winds. On *PlayStation*, even with all her winch power and four crew grunting away on the winch handles, that simple process could take a minute or more. Raising and lowering the giant 1,700-pound sail or changing any of the heavy headsails required tremendous physical exertion. Simply put, *PlayStation* was a beast to sail. Every maneuver had to be well thought out and precisely coordinated. Every maneuver was tiring. Almost nothing could be done quickly. The crew, in essence, had to learn to sail as if in slow motion. That meant when wind speed started to increase, sail reductions had to be made early, before the power of the wind in the sails made them close to impossible to handle. "With current technology, this boat is at the limit of human capability," Pete Melvin acknowledged.

This was just the problem that Goss and Thompson were trying to address with the simplified rotating wishbone rigs on *Team Philips*. The enormous loads on *PlayStation* were not merely hard to manage, they were potentially lethal. Sheets and lines were like steel bars when the boat was sailing. Any extremity accidentally caught in a winch or block could easily be mangled. If a fitting or connection failed, thousands of pounds of tension could send a line or piece of hardware scything through the air with enough power to injure or kill a sailor in its path. The crew were forced to be aware at all times of where they were standing, and tried to minimize time spent in any of the danger zones around the highly loaded fittings.

The perils were dramatically emphasized when Fossett and his team set out to sail *PlayStation* at full throttle for the first time, targeting the twenty-four-hour distance record of 540 miles (set in 1994 by a trimaran). Early in the speed run Ben Wright, Fossett's boat manager, was up on the back of the boom leading the crew in the procedure to reef, or lower slightly, the mainsail. As the boat pitched through the waves, Wright grabbed a reef control line with his right hand to steady himself on the swinging boom. The line ran through a nearby block. It would be wound in during the reefing procedure, so Wright made sure to grab the line on the safe side — where the line would be exiting the block. The crew handling the reefing lines got confused, however, and let the line out a few inches.

It was a small mistake. But no mistakes were minor on a boat with such dangerous loads, and it was just enough to run Wright's little finger into the nearby block. Wright gasped in pain as the finger was crushed by the ton of pressure between the line and the wheel in the block. He managed to yell for the crew to wind the line back in so he could extricate his mangled finger, but they were at the base of the mast, nearly sixty feet away. The noise of wind and water muffled his cries for help, and some of the crew didn't seem to realize what had happened. Wright faced a brutal and instantaneous choice. He could keep yelling and hope he would be understood before his whole hand was pulled into the block and crushed, or he could take action himself. He jerked his hand away from the block with all the force his pain and desperation could muster. It pulled free, leaving the fingertip behind. *PlayStation* immediately returned to Auckland so her first victim could get treatment.

If the accident was a graphic lesson in the high cost of errors aboard a maxi-cat, *PlayStation* followed it with a lesson in power performance. With Wright recuperating on shore, she set out the next day to make another run at the twenty-four-hour record. As soon as she hit the open ocean, she found 25-knot winds from the northeast and accelerated away from New Zealand at speeds that exceeded 30 knots in the gusts. Twenty-four hours later, *PlayStation* had covered just over 580 nautical miles, breaking the record by 40 miles. During the course of the run she averaged 24 knots and hit a top speed of 36 knots. Conditions for the record run hadn't even been very favorable, with rough seas and 40-knot squalls that had required time-wasting sail changes. Even so, Fossett's new toy shattered a record that had stood for almost five years. And with improved crew work, a better understanding of how to wring maximum speed out of the new boat, and better weather conditions, the target of six hundred miles in a day seemed feasible. Only nine other multihulls had ever cracked the five-hundred-mile barrier. Now, with the arrival of the maxi-cats, sailors started talking about the possibility of seven hundred miles in a day, a ridiculous proposition just a few years earlier.

PlayStation had delivered the twenty-four-hour record Fossett craved, but he and the sailing team still barely had an inkling of the boat's potential or how to sail her safely. In the fall of 1999, following a freak electrical fire that required extensive repairs, *PlayStation* was shipped by freighter to Philadelphia. Fossett and the crew would resume working the boat up, but this time they would take a crack at the second item on Fossett's hit list: the transatlantic record from Ambrose Light to the Lizard.

The key to this record was finding solid, steady breezes over the length of the 2,925-mile course and keeping *PlayStation* in one piece. Fossett had commissioned a study of North Atlantic weather over the previous ten years and knew that it was easy to find strong winds at the start but much harder to find a weather pattern that would keep the winds blowing all the way to the finish. *Jet Services V* had ideal conditions in 1990, strong following winds that never petered out and that allowed her to sail an almost direct course to the English Channel (which was why her record of six days and thirteen hours had been so hard to beat). Many of the boats that had tried to surpass her record in the nine years since had simply run out of wind at some point in the passage.

For six weeks Fossett and *PlayStation* patiently waited for a likely-looking weather pattern to carry them across the Atlantic. Finally, in mid-December a strong front was forecast to move off the East Coast of the United States. Fossett issued a "Code Green" summons to his crew, gathering them in New York for the record attempt. In the early afternoon of December 16, *PlayStation* rocketed past Ambrose Light in building winds and headed toward Nantucket and the Atlantic beyond.

The ten-man crew pushed the boat hard, eager to clear Nantucket Shoals and bear up toward Newfoundland, which would put them on the most direct line to the English Channel. The wind overnight was forecast to peak at 35 knots — which could be safely managed in a boat *PlayStation*'s size with the right amount of sail set. But at 4 P.M., an hour before dark, *Play-Station* sent a little warning that she might be running a mite fast for the choppy sea state, digging her bows into a wave and lifting a hull and rudder out of the water. She lurched and came back down, but still Fossett and his crew pressed on at top speed.

By 7 P.M. the wind was blowing the forecast 35 knots. *Play-Station* was ripping along at almost the same speed, with black, frigid water flying everywhere. Gino Morrelli, who planned to sail with Fossett in The Race, was at the helm, squinting to read the instrument readouts in front of him. Without warning, the wind piped up to 45 knots and the big cat was carrying too much sail. Only a handful of crew were on deck, and although Ben Wright and some others moved quickly to roll up the head-sail on its furling drum to slow the boat down, the pressure of the wind in the sail made it very slow going. Before any off-watch crew could get suited up to come on deck and help, a 62-knot gust slammed into *PlayStation* and hurtled her into the seas ahead. Morrelli struggled to keep her pointed dead down-wind — to turn across the wind would have meant instant cap-size — and her bows and front beam started submerging.

This was the classic prelude to pitchpoling, and *PlayStation* seemed to be following the script. Her stern and rudders lifted out of the water as her bows were driven down. Wright, work-ing at the base of the mast, looked aft and saw the trampoline between the two hulls rising above him. In a flash he realized that if *PlayStation* somersaulted, he and the others at the base of the mast might be trapped under the boat. Getting free would require a thirty-foot underwater swim through icy water and a rat's nest of lines. Wright unclipped his safety harness and sprinted toward the side of the catamaran. That way he would at least be able to jump clear if she went over. His mates were not far behind him. *PlayStation* teetered on the verge of flipping, then crashed back down onto her hulls. The wind slammed the mainsail across the boat and back, breaking four of the long rods, or battens, that help hold its shape.

The broken battens effectively depowered the sail and the crisis was over. Without enough spare battens, so was the record run. The crew in any case was deeply shaken, and rushed to take the mainsail down. As they did so, Wright was struck by the fact that the giant catamaran was rewriting standard safety procedure. On most boats, the worst thing that could happen was to go overboard without a safety tether. On *PlayStation,* Wright now thought, the worst thing that could happen was for the boat to flip over while you were still attached to a tether. He went about the work of cleaning up the mess on deck without clipping his safety tether to the boat, shaking off a lifetime of training and habit. A few others followed suit. Fossett decided to head for nearby Newport as he absorbed the lessons of the near catastrophe. "There are no prizes for carrying too much sail when it is howling," he later observed. "Depowering must be done early, because once loads spiral out of control on a boat this powerful there is nothing ten men can do except hold on. And hope."

Fossett was mildly relieved that *PlayStation* had been pushed well into the red zone and survived relatively unscathed, but he and the rest of the crew were slightly unsettled that the red zone had been so easy to find. The conditions that had almost somersaulted the boat weren't extraordinary, particularly in the Southern Ocean. Fossett had planned to use the transatlantic run as a delivery to Europe to set up for a Jules Verne record run in the winter months. With questions about the boat and crew's state of preparation for the South, however, he decided to take her to Bermuda for the winter instead (pocketing the Newport–Bermuda record on the way). There, Fossett ordered the secret installation of ballast tanks in the back ends of *PlayStation's* hulls. If the boat threatened to stuff her bows underwater again, the tanks could be pumped full of water to weight the sterns down and raise the bows. Theoretically, adding weight is never good for performance, but in the real world of unruly oceans, the ballast tanks would give *PlayStation* a margin of error that would ultimately allow her to be sailed faster.

The modifications did not end there. After two more transatlantic runs (neither yielded a record), *PlayStation* was sent to a boatyard in England to have her bows extended by fifteen feet and her sterns extended by five feet. The ocean miles had given Fossett and Morrelli an important insight into maxi-cat sailing: sea state was often a greater limitation on speed than sail power — especially when the boat was sailing upwind — because in rough seas the boat frequently had to sail slower than its potential simply to prevent the beams and bows from digging into the waves. Training had proved that *PlayStation* had a surplus of sail power. Putting more boat underneath the towering rig and enormous sail plan, they decided, would create a more balanced machine, one that would be able to sail closer to her potential in wavy conditions.

Morrelli began making sketches of what the modifications might look like, and back in Newport Beach Pete Melvin crunched the numbers. It would be a massive project. The bow extensions would have to be grafted onto the existing hulls from a point well aft of the front beam. Each extension would be the equivalent of a new fifty-foot carbon-fiber hull. The modified *PlayStation*, at 125 feet, would be relaunched in late November, after nine weeks of work. "Now we have probably put the proper-size chassis underneath the motor," Morrelli said of the impressive upswept destroyer bows that emerged from the build shed. "I think we've really come into scale."

THE FRENCH FLOTILLA

PlayStation would need all the refinements Fossett could afford, because from the day *Club Med* was launched, in May 2000, it was apparent that Gilles Ollier had crafted a well-rounded speedster that would be tough to beat. The new Ollier design was a significant leap from *Jet Services V:* about thirty feet longer, twice as heavy, and much more powerful. *Club Med*'s 3,767-square-foot mainsail was 50 percent larger than the mainsail on *Jet Services V* and weighed more than twelve hundred pounds. Overall, *Club Med*'s rough dimensions were similar to those of *PlayStation*. But if *PlayStation* was a muscle car, with enormous power to blast her across the seas, *Club Med* was a Ferrari, with a slightly narrower beam and a smaller, more efficient sail plan, thanks to the wing mast. On paper she was just as fast, but easier to handle. The sail plan would still test the crew's stamina at times, but the Multiplast team was confident it was within reasonable working limits.

They did have one safety concern, though, and that was the surface area of the wing mast, which was like a sail that could never be furled. The mast had to be tall enough to carry sails that could drive *Club Med* at high speeds in normal weather, but not so tall that powerful winds would capsize her even if she had no sail up. Multiplast had settled on a 136-foot wing mast that had an exposed surface area of almost 500 square feet. According to Ollier's calculations, it would not threaten to flip the boat unless she was unlucky enough to run into the 80-plus-knot winds of the sort Bruno Peyron and *Commodore Explorer* had endured off Cape Horn. In those conditions, skipper Grant Dalton wryly noted, *Club Med* would be "tumbleweed."

To minimize the tumbleweed potential, Ollier gave the new catamaran water ballast tanks in each hull to help glue the hulls to the surface of the sea in extreme conditions (the largest, about halfway along the hull, could hold two thousand liters and came to be known aboard *Club Med* as the "oh shit!" tank). Just in case that wasn't enough, *Club Med* was designed with watertight bulkheads so the crew could survive in the overturned hull while waiting for rescue. The generators were rigged so that they could be run while the boat was upside down, providing power for the communications equipment. Emergency antennas could be pushed through openings in the upside-down hull, just as Alain Colas had planned on *Manureva* almost thirty years earlier.

Club Med had a fine French pedigree but only a scant seven months to prepare for The Race. Figuring out how to sail her safely at maximum speed and determining whether her construction was strong enough to withstand the Southern Ocean was up to Dalton. Dalton had been eager to be on the starting line ever since Peyron announced the concept of The Race. Yet in a way, he was an odd choice to skipper a prototype catamaran that was to be thrown on short notice into a nonstop race around the world: he had virtually no multihull sailing experience.

What he did have, and what his *Club Med* sponsors were banking on, were tremendous leadership skills, the know-how to rapidly assemble a topnotch sailing team, and sound sailing sense, all accumulated over the course of five Whitbread races and 300,000 ocean-racing miles. Dalton, who was forty-two when *Club Med* first hit the water, had started out, improbably, as an accountant in Auckland. But his tastes ran to more adventurous pursuits, including motorcycle racing, weightlifting, endurance sports, and sailing. In 1977 he skipped his university classes to watch the Whitbread fleet arrive in Auckland; then and there he knew what he wanted to be doing. None of his friends were surprised when the 1980–81 Whitbread race found Dalton aboard the eventual winner. He hadn't missed a Whitbread since — sailing once with a broken collarbone — and the only numbers he had crunched were sailing campaign budgets and handicap ratings.

To get *Club Med* race ready, Dalton, with the help of Bruno Peyron, put together a sailing team that matched many of his old Whitbread crewmates with some of the best European multihull sailors available. From his Whitbread days, Dalton recruited his favorite navigator, Mike Quilter, also a New Zealander, who over a long sailing career had managed to earn the nickname "Lowlife" — "for where he sits on the boat and how he has

behaved," as Roger Badham, retained by Dalton as *Club Med*'s
shoreside weather router, joked. Dalton added Neal McDonald,
a top English Whitbread and ocean racer, and Ed Danby, who in
addition to sailing with Dalton in the 1989–90 Whitbread had
sailed with Blake and Knox-Johnston aboard *Enza* during their
record-breaking Jules Verne voyage. For multihull depth, Dalton turned to French racer Fred Le Peutrec and Spaniard Guillermo Altadill, both Olympic-caliber small-catamaran sailors.
Later, Hervé Jan, a sailmaker and veteran of Olivier de Kersauson's Jules Verne record, was signed on. Franck Proffit, a
multiple winner on the French multihull circuit, arrived to take
up the slot of cocaptain. It was a formidable cast. Taken together, Dalton's crew had more than twenty racing circumnavigations among them.

The real challenge, however, was figuring out what kind of
boat they had underneath them. When Dalton first visited *Club
Med* while she was being assembled at Multiplast, he was blown
away by her sheer scale. "How the fuck are we going to control
this thing?" he wondered. He noticed the same reaction in his
crew when they gathered at the boat for the first time. "Well,
what do we do next? This thing is an elephant that just goes
where it wants," he could see them thinking. The only answer
was to start sailing the thing and hope it got smaller through
training and repetition.

One nuance of the catamaran that Dalton grasped immediately was that communication among the crew was going to be
more difficult than on any boat he had ever sailed. Sailors would
be fifty or sixty feet from one another, and when the boat was
sailing at 30 knots the roar of wind and water was going to
overwhelm even shouted instructions. The only solution was to
use as many hand signals as possible, such as a twirling finger
to indicate "hoist," or a raised, clenched fist to indicate "stop."
Dalton also firmly swept aside potential language barriers in
this multinational crew. All spoken communication was to be
in English. On a boat as powerful and dangerous as *Club Med*,
he wasn't going to risk any confusion. He was characteristic-

ally blunt about his expectations: giving sailing instructions in French, Italian, or Spanish could be grounds for dismissal from the crew.

Club Med hit the water with a racy blue Formula 1–style paint job that featured a bikini-clad swimmer on each bow. On her first sea trials she powered across Quiberon Bay, off the western coast of France, at 30 knots, topping out at 34 knots in flat seas and 18 knots of wind. By early June, Dalton pointed her bows toward the open sea for the first time with a fast delivery to Cádiz, Spain. In moderate conditions the boat was amazing. For hours at a time *Club Med* loped along over the blue sea at average speeds of 30 knots. It was a good omen for what lay ahead. Cádiz would be the staging port for an east-to-west transatlantic crossing and record attempt. The course, which ran thirty-five hundred miles to the Bahamas, was known as the Discovery Route, because Columbus had traversed it in 1492. The current record had been set by Ollier's *Jet Services V* in 1988, at twelve days and twelve hours (Columbus took sixty-nine days). Although Bruno Peyron would not be sailing in The Race, he managed to escape from his organizational obligations to get a feel for the big catamarans his concept was producing. He was not disappointed.

Three days into the crossing, *Club Med* sailed past the Canary Islands into 20-to-30-knot winds and progressively flatter seas. Dalton and Peyron had been working the catamaran up slowly, sailing fast but keeping her a notch or two below top speed as the crew adapted to her size and learned how to handle the sails smoothly. Now they were ready to press her a little harder, and the drivers rotating through the steering position every few hours now maintained speeds close to 30 knots, once hitting a peak of 37 knots. Twenty-four hours after the run began, *Club Med* decisively usurped *PlayStation* as the twenty-four-hour record holder, sailing almost 626 miles to *PlayStation*'s 580 miles. She was the first sailboat in history to break the 600-mile barrier.

Dalton, at least in his own mind, had settled any doubts about whether he could make a successful jump to multihulls. "A lot of people would have you believe that sailing multihulls is a black art, and I certainly think sailing small ones is a highly skilled, specialist-type job," he said. "But *Club Med* is a lot easier to sail than a monohull. It's just like driving a coffee table, because until you get into the death zone (and we have no idea where that is yet), there's a whole lot more latitude for just driving it. In a Whitbread monohull which is cranked with a full-masted chute you get ten degrees out of shape and you are going for a swim. In this thing you get way out of shape and all you do is go a little slower." After just ten days and fifteen hours at sea, *Club Med* sailed into port, claiming *Jet Services*'s crossing record as well. In one transatlantic run, Dalton and *Club Med* had confirmed the performance potential of the Ollier design. The only open question remaining was that of reliability.

Dalton was used to preparing Whitbread boats, which would be trashed at sea then repaired at the end of every leg. The Race was a new challenge because it was meant to be sailed nonstop, and any boat that put in to port for repairs was assessed a prohibitive time penalty. *Club Med*'s designers and engineers had done all they could to accurately model and predict the stresses she might endure over twenty-eight thousand miles. But Dalton had only a few short months to verify their calculations on the water. He was sure that *Club Med* would have to be beefed up before The Race; he just didn't know where and how yet. The only way to find out was to sail the boat hard and try to overtax it — a crude but effective way to improve the design. "We've got to break something," Dalton would sometimes shout as the crew put *Club Med* through her paces during test sails.

This brute philosophy got results when *Club Med* set out across the Atlantic in late July to return to Europe. The weather had not set up well for a good run at *Jet Services*'s elusive west–east transatlantic record, but Dalton intended to find some rough North Atlantic weather and run the boat roughshod. One day into the delivery, *Club Med* had motored through a patch of light winds to hook into a windy low-pressure system moving east off the coast. Up went the main, with one reef, and the stay-sail (the smaller of *Club Med*'s working jibs). The cat surged ahead at 25 to 30 knots, in a 27-knot wind and an agitated cross-sea that continually slapped against her hulls. Dalton himself was at the wheel when he heard a loud crack. The port bow in front of the forward beam had ripped clean off.

Racing multihulls are built with a false bow, known as the "crash box," that is designed to break away on impact with any large objects in the water. The crash box acts like a car's crumple zone, absorbing the blow and protecting the rest of the structure from damage. There is a watertight bulkhead behind the crash box, so a boat that loses it cleanly can sail on, albeit less efficiently (*Jet Services V* set a 1988 transatlantic record despite splitting her bow open on a growler). Dalton and the crew quickly lowered *Club Med*'s sails to assess the damage. No one had heard or felt any impact before the bow tore away, and the piece had disappeared. There were no major leaks, but the fracture had extended beyond the crash box itself to the main structure of the bow. *Club Med* reversed course and headed back to Newport, less than five hundred miles away. There she was loaded onto a ship, to be delivered back to Multiplast in Vannes for repairs.

The broken bow was exactly the sort of structural weakness Dalton had been probing for, and half expecting. Without the broken chunk, however, it was impossible to know for sure what had caused the failure. Ollier and his team suspected a collision. Dalton wasn't so sure. Nor was he prepared to race around the world with the risk that water alone might tear off one of his bows. In the miles she had accumulated since her launch, *Club Med* had also experienced some delamination of the hull skin on the underside of the main beam. The constant abrasion of water at 30 knots had caused the hull to peel open, exposing the Nomex core. Dalton's instincts were telling him that the boat had been too lightly built to survive a nonstop race around the world. Coming across the Atlantic, he had prowled around the cat looking for weaknesses. Inside the bow he had leaned against the hull as it knifed through the water and could feel it flexing. "If it pants like this during normal sailing," he had thought, "it's only a matter of time before we hit a big enough wave and this thing is coming in."

Dalton felt he was working against the natural inclination of designers to underbuild their boats because they want them to be light enough to win. When the boats break, revealing where they are underbuilt, they are patched up, refitted, and sent out to race again. Through a cycle of breakage and repair, sometimes over a period of years, the structure is refined to the point where it is adequate for the stresses being placed on it. But Dalton didn't have time to go through this normal workup cycle and was starting to realize that designers didn't have any idea how to accurately anticipate the radical forces the maxi-cats would experience at sea. He would have only one shot at The Race. If *Club Med* wasn't right when she arrived on the starting line in Barcelona, he and his crew would be risking more than a chance at first place. "Guys, this is a fuckup," Dalton told the Ollier team. "This boat ain't gonna make it." He wanted a second opinion on *Club Med*'s engineering and put in a call to High Modulus, an engineering firm in New Zealand that specialized in racing boats and had worked on most of Dalton's boats. "Get your asses over here," he said. "I need a complete structural analysis of this boat from bow to stern."

Gilles Ollier was none too pleased to have a team of engineers from New Zealand second-guessing his work. His designs were proprietary and at first he resisted handing over the architectural drawings for the boat. Dalton hadn't accomplished five circumnavigations at sea by backing off when faced with adversity, however. Lean and fit for his age, with thinning, bleached hair, he was built like a rugby back, with broad shoulders and an aggressive set to his jaw. He had brought in some of the most trustworthy, experienced engineers in the business, and to his way of thinking Ollier's attempt to give them the brush-off was unacceptable. "The Ollier folks believed that as Kiwis we didn't have a fucking clue, that the power of multihull sailing — structure, design, build, sails — all belonged in France," he recounted later. "And they thought we were trying to change the balance of power." Dalton just wanted to be sure his catamaran would stay in one piece for this one race and didn't give a damn about cultural sensitivities. In a showdown meeting at Multiplast he hammered away at Ollier.

"I want the drawings."

"You can't have the drawings."

"I own the fucking boat — what do you mean I can't have the drawings!"

"We think the structure is fine."

"I don't think the structure is fine. It's not your fucking boat, it's my boat."

For fourteen hours they went back and forth, and one by one the drawings were handed over. The last one, showing the design of the crucial front beam, was relinquished only after a final shouting match. Bruised egos and bitter feelings resulted, but Dalton got what he needed to evaluate the structure of the boat. Over a period of three weeks the engineers from High Modulus examined every piece of the maxi-cat — which was sitting on blocks in the Multiplast yard with no bows — and came back with recommendations for structural modifications to strengthen the hulls and beams. Dalton calculated the weight of each suggestion before deciding whether to include it or not. "In the end my philosophy was pretty simple," he said. "I thought we were prepared enough to win The Race, so what was going to stop us? Not finishing. So we did whatever we had to do to make sure we finished."

Ultimately, that meant reinforcing *Club Med*'s main beam and adding bulkheads to the interior of the hulls. The reengineering added about one thousand pounds to the boat and cost Club Med $200,000, but Dalton was convinced it was necessary. Without the modifications, he believed, *Club Med* "would not have made it past the Canaries." Eventually even Multiplast agreed: many of the changes were incorporated into the two other catamarans being built.

Over the course of six weeks, Dalton closely supervised the rebuild work from a trailer in Multiplast's yard. He also took the opportunity to remove the galley in the port hull. The original design had included a galley in both hulls, for redundancy in case of an emergency (you could find yourself stuck in either hull when the boat flipped) and because Ollier and his designers figured that carrying food across the trampoline in the Southern Ocean would test a team of acrobats. Dalton knew that his crew was up to the challenge and wanted to jettison any excess weight he could find. Work on the boat went on almost nonstop. It cut drastically into the planned sail-training time. At least Dalton was gaining confidence that *Club Med* could handle a battle with the Southern Ocean.

In late September *Club Med* was craned back into the water to resume her pre-race workup. One week later she was back in the headlines, this time for racing at 20 knots the wrong way up a shipping lane in the English Channel in the dead of night, scattering freighters and earning Dalton a $24,000 fine. From England, he and his crew went to Portugal for a final round of training and sail design refinements. *Club Med* would arrive in Barcelona for the start of The Race with a well-thought-out wardrobe, featuring a new mainsail that was almost one hundred pounds lighter than the original and a huge, six-thousand-square-foot headsail designed for very light winds, made from Cuben Fiber. The material alone cost $75,000.

On October 12, *Innovation Explorer* was finally launched from Multiplast, followed by *Team Adventure* about a month later. *Innovation Explorer* was almost identical to *Club Med*, and *Team Adventure* differed only slightly, with greater winch power, sterns that were cropped to save weight, an interior layout that put the nav station forward of the living area in the port hull (on the other two boats it was located aft in the starboard hull), and steering positions in the front of the cockpit so the driver could have a clearer view ahead and communicate more easily with the crew below. Peyron and Lewis also took mercy on their crews by letting Multiplast install splash guards along the outside wall of the cockpits. These had been part of the original Ollier design and were intended to help protect the sailors from the flying water and wave tops that would slop into the cockpit at high speeds. Dalton, never one to trade speed for comfort, had declined the splash guards and their additional four hundred pounds.

Normally, it would be foolish to expect that two brand-new boats could race around the world with just six to eight weeks of preparation. But many of the structural refinements made to *Club Med* had been incorporated into these newer craft in the final stages of their build-out. Dalton had managed to keep some modifications secret, but he reckoned that almost three quarters of what he'd learned by sailing *Club Med* had been picked up by the others, saving Loïck Peyron and Cam Lewis months of testing. Peyron and Lewis still had to organize their crews and learn how to sail their boats for maximum performance, but both men were highly skilled sailors who would quickly learn the subtleties of making a maxi-cat fly. Peyron had the assistance of American coskipper Skip Novak, a forty-eight-year-old adventurer who had survived four Whitbread races and 300,000 ocean miles in a sailing career that included two ocean-crossing records with Bruno Peyron on *Commodore Explorer*. And Lewis had the help of Randy Smyth and his sails. *Team Adventure* was pushing 40 knots shortly after she hit the water.

Innovation Explorer and *Team Adventure* spent the weeks before the start training, scrambling for additional sponsorship money, and trying to avoid being swamped by the enormous logistical problems of getting ready. Neither had time to refine their crews, as *Club Med* had been doing with tryouts held during training. Lewis and Peyron just recruited the best sailors they could and hoped they would perform well and get along. *Explorer* and *Team Adventure* would eventually make their way to Barcelona in a state of barely controlled chaos. But make it they did.

7

THE TRIALS OF TEAM PHILIPS

Optimism is a moral virtue.
— Sir Ernest Shackleton

ON MARCH 5, 2000, while Steve Fossett and the crew of *PlayStation* were struggling with the foibles of a massively scaled-up conventional catamaran, Pete Goss's radical, wave-piercing machine was craned into the water for the first time. To extricate the enormous cat from the build shed, workers had to knock down an entire wall. It seemed a small inconvenience for the launch of a brash experiment in boat design. Forty thousand spectators crammed the little town of Totnes to witness the long-awaited debut. In a final frantic sprint to get the boat fully ready, Goss and the build team had worked twenty-four hours a day for three straight days, a triumph in itself. But an inescapable question loomed over the festivities: how would *Team Philips* perform?

The two 130-foot masts were lowered into place in the hulls, and she set off for London. In the rush to make the naming ceremony, there hadn't been enough time to work out all the minor bugs in the masts and wishbones, which left the sails looking like "a sack of spuds," as Goss put it. *Team Philips,* still without her engines, was pushed clear of the docks by motorized inflatable dinghies. A hint of breeze ruffled across the water and *Team Philips* suddenly accelerated away. Goss and the five-man crew were amazed to see that their catamaran was slipping along at about 8 knots in just 3 to 4 knots of wind. *Team Philips* was creating her own wind with forward movement. Added to the true wind, it was enough to propel the powerful, light craft at a velocity greater than the wind speed. All the new maxi-catamarans, in fact, were capable of sailing at almost twice the true wind speed in light breezes.

The crew, suspended twelve feet above the water, was struck by the eerie lack of noise. *Team Philips* had no rigging to whisper in the wind. "Rigging is like air conditioning," Goss said. "You don't really notice the noise until it's turned off." Hours later, when he woke up from a nap in the accommodations pod, he thought the boat was motionless in a calm. He was pleased to learn that she was sailing along at 23 knots, in just 14 knots of wind. In contrast to the Herculean labors required of the crew on *PlayStation,* Goss and his team discovered that just two people on deck could easily handle *Team Philips* in normal sailing trim, and that three crew, drinking tea if they liked, could pull off intricate maneuvers like jibing (in which the boat's sterns are turned through the wind, flipping the sails from one side to the other). The trip to London confirmed that *Team Philips* was relatively easy on the crew and fast, even in light air. But exploring her true nature and performance limits would require a lot heavier weather than she was getting just then in the English Channel.

Goss was eager to conduct serious sea trials in hopes of tuning up the boat in time to take a crack at the Jules Verne record late in the spring. Immediately after the naming ceremony in London, *Team Philips* was sailed back to Dartmouth, on England's south coast, so she could be readied for a voyage out into the Atlantic. A little more than a week later she put to sea again. This time the wind was blowing hard, at 24 knots from the northeast.

The entire crew was exhausted from crossing hundreds of jobs, big and little, off the long list needed to transform *Team Philips* from an unrefined catamaran into a racing machine.

Goss decided they would hoist no sails and meander through the night to get some rest. The bare wing masts were trimmed to the proper angle to the wind, creating lift. Within minutes *Team Philips* was sailing at almost 17 knots with no sails up. "Have a beer," the proud skipper told the crew. The comfortable passage in rough seas confirmed the fact that Adrian Thompson's narrow, wave-piercing hulls were easily driven. But the speed *Team Philips* achieved under wing masts alone also suggested she might be hard to slow down in a real blow. That could be a problem in the Southern Ocean, where slowing down — to minimize the danger of pitchpoling or capsizing — was sometimes as important as speeding up.

Goss continued to work the boat up gradually in the daylight, raising the sails to the third reef, so they were only about one third of the way up the mast. *Team Philips* forged ahead at whatever speed the wind happened to be blowing. Once clear of the English Channel, he pointed the bows toward the southwest tip of Ireland, and the crew settled into their seagoing routine. Three watches of two men each rotated in two-hour shifts, with one off-watch crew always in full gear on standby. The boat tracked effortlessly and smoothly across the Irish Sea. "You could steer with your hands in your pockets," Goss commented later.

By Wednesday morning, March 29, *Team Philips* was headed back to the English Channel, to rendezvous with a helicopter for a photo shoot off the Scilly Isles. The sun had just come up and Mike Calvin, a sports journalist, and Andy Hindley, Goss's second-in-command, were on watch. The catamaran remained under reduced sail, slicing through the seas at about 16 knots in a moderate 20-knot northeasterly. Suddenly there was a loud crack, and the forward third of the port hull started to work back and forth. Calvin compared it to a tire blowout on the highway — he knew something was very wrong, he just couldn't see how bad it was. Goss and the rest of the crew tumbled out of the accommodations pod, sleepy, confused, and at first suspecting that a mast or wishbone had collapsed. They were wholly unprepared for the sight that greeted them. Looking forward, the port bow was waggling in the swells and looking as if it were about to break off.

Goss's world was fracturing before his eyes, but he displayed the cool that had saved Raphael Dinelli's life in the Southern Ocean. His immediate concern was that if forty-five feet of the port bow did indeed break away, *Team Philips* might roll over and even sink, leaving her crew at the mercy of the Atlantic waters. He tersely ordered everyone into survival suits, which are designed to ward off hypothermia. The grim crew initiated the abandon-ship drill, mustering "grab bags" that held water and food, and readying the life rafts for launch. Goss got on the satellite telephone and called the Maritime Rescue Coordination Centre at Falmouth. "Hallo, Pete," came a jovial voice. "I suppose you've called to tell us you're sinking." "Well, get your pens out, because we bloody well are," Goss shot back.

With that, the rescue services swung into action, sending out a lifeboat from St. Mary's in the Scilly Isles, luckily just thirty miles away, and scrambling a helicopter from the mainland. Goss next called Adrian Thompson, at home on the Isle of Man and about to begin what he described as "the worst twenty-four hours of my life." Goss explained the situation and asked Thompson whether *Team Philips* would roll over or sink if she lost her port bow. Thompson reassured him the light honeycomb core and multiple watertight compartments would keep her afloat. Relieved, Goss and the crew secured *Team Philips* as best they could, pointed her toward St. Mary's Island, made some tea, and settled in to wait for the lifeboat.

When it arrived, *Team Philips* could still sail under her own power. But as the convoy closed on St. Mary's, there was a hideous shriek of tearing carbon fiber and the port bow finally broke clean away. The lifeboat tried to set up a tow for both the valuable bow and *Team Philips,* but lost its line to the bow. The helicopter that had been hired to get dramatic footage of *Team Philips* slicing through the rough tidal race off the Isles of Scilly instead captured the sad image of the stricken cat's port bow, emblazoned with the slogan LET'S MAKE THINGS BETTER in bold white letters, drifting away. Seeing waves lap at the names of supporters on the side of the hull almost brought Goss to tears.

Team Philips made it safely to port, where she was pumped out and buoyed by flotation bags. Andy Hindley, flying in a plane volunteered by a *Team Philips* supporter, raced local salvagers to locate the lost hull, and found it floating twenty-five miles southwest of the Scillies. The broken catamaran was then towed backward to Dartmouth and up the Dart River to Totnes.

Newspapers and sailing pundits had a field day with the catastrophe. Britain's Sky TV covered the events live throughout the day. Grant Dalton, preparing for the launch of *Club Med* in a month, concisely captured the widespread skepticism toward a catamaran design in which the bows were unsupported by a front beam. "You almost put a black line on there which says 'tear here,'" he cracked. The public, however, wasn't ready to give up on *Team Philips*. Letters of support and advice poured in — one schoolchild recommended stronger glue.

Goss, too, was far from ready to give up. He believed passionately in *Team Philips*'s design concept and was prepared to fight to the last minute and the last dollar to get the boat ready for The Race. Along with Thompson and the engineers who had run the original numbers on the boat, he undertook a crash investigation into the hull failure. Thompson suspected a manufacturing problem, since the bows had been engineered to withstand side forces up to seventy tons and had failed at about 10 percent of that load. In a little over a week they concluded that carbon strakes that ran the length of the hulls to stiffen them hadn't bonded properly with the Nomex honeycomb core inside the hulls' skin. This could be remedied by stripping the layers of carbon fiber in the skin back to the strakes from the outside and repairing the hull from the inside out. But a closer look at the data originally used to determine the required strength of *Team Philips*'s hulls suggested that even if the strakes had bonded properly, the hulls could have used some additional stiffening.

Goss and the build team decided to add lightweight frames throughout the hulls to increase their rigidity. "Next time, this boat has got to be bulletproof," Thompson said.

The repairs would take six months and add another 1.6 tons to *Team Philips*. When engines were installed, the new weight in the boat would total about 3 tons. That would slow her down in light winds because she would be heavier and sit an inch or two deeper in the water. Goss tried to pass this off as trivial — "like throwing a suitcase into the trunk of a car" — but no extra weight was trivial on a boat in which the crew would be eating out of dog bowls with Kevlar utensils to save a pound or two. Still, no one was interested in sailing an underbuilt cat into the Southern Ocean, where there would be no rescue services within a thousand miles.

The heartbreaking crack-up and long repair job, along with the derision of second-guessers, could easily have broken the spirits of Goss's team. "None of them deserved to endure this," Goss said. "It's like asking a marathon runner to start all over again when he is enjoying a cup of tea, exhausted near the finishing line." So before the resurrection of *Team Philips* began in earnest, he gathered everyone at the build site and told them that anyone who wanted to walk was free to do so, with no hard feelings. To his five-man crew, whose lives would be on the line, he conveyed an even more direct message. "The Southern Ocean is no playground," he wrote in a memo. "I would like each of you to give your answer the gravity it deserves." That Goss offered anyone who had lost faith an easy out was a reflection of his compassion. That no one accepted his offer was a reflection of his ability to inspire. After months of round-the-clock labor, on September 23 *Team Philips* finally began her second life in the waters of the River Dart. There was no longer time to go around the world before The Race. Two quick runs across the Atlantic would have to serve as a final shakedown.

On October 5 *Team Philips* sailed out of Dartmouth into an 18-knot breeze. Again she had a chance to show what she could do, and Goss and the crew braced themselves as she jumped from a standing start to 20 knots in just ten seconds. After so many months on land, it took them a few hours to relax, settle into the watch routine, and get used to the mesmerizing sight of her thin bows slicing the lumpy swells with barely a hitch. Goss, Alex Bennett, the crew's youngest member at twenty-four, and Paul Larsen, an Australian multihull sailor, lingered in the cockpit enjoying the experience of being at sea after so much stress and disappointment. But breaking in a radical design once more proved a cruel business. As Bennett watched the two-and-a-half-ton freestanding masts flex with the motion of the boat, there was a hitch in the port mast and the motion grew excessive, with the mast tip scribing circles in the sky. Again there was the horrible sound of carbon fiber fracturing.

Goss, his heart sinking, called all hands for the second time in *Team Philips*'s brief seagoing career. Nine feet below deck level, the ball-and-socket joint supporting the mast had failed. The ball consisted of a melon-sized casting of titanium. Somehow it was creating unexpected friction as it rubbed against the bronze cup in the bottom of the mast. The friction had wrenched the cup loose, and the mast had dropped down onto the floor of the hull, around the ball. There it started moving around, like a pen stirring an inkwell, and banging into the carbon-fiber bulkheads in the compartment. Goss and the morose crew once again went into emergency mode, stabilizing the wandering mast with a web of lines.

Team Philips turned around to make another ignominious return to Dartmouth. The problem this time was relatively minor, and a fix involving slightly different metals in the cup, a grease injection system, and greater reinforcement at the base of the mast was quickly sketched out. But repairing anything structural on a boat *Team Philips*'s size, particularly when it meant removing the masts, was a matter of weeks, not days.

More important, both Goss and the boat were running out of time and credibility. The *Independent* newspaper suggested he was on the verge of becoming either of two favorite English stereotypes: the radical innovator who succeeds against all odds, or the spectacular and romantic failure, in the mold of the doomed polar explorer Robert Falcon Scott. Goss's own team was beginning to show the strain too. Mike Calvin, the onboard journalist, wrote in the *Mail on Sunday*, "We have to decide whether, after two narrow escapes, we are prepared to remain true to Goss's dream."

Calvin had known and respected Goss for ten years. They had raced together in the Southern Ocean in the 1992 British Steel Challenge, a race for paying amateurs in which Goss was a skipper. They built such a close friendship that Goss was godfather to Calvin's youngest son. But that son, and his three other children, made it hard for Calvin to convince himself that sailing *Team Philips* in The Race would be anything short of reckless. Three weeks later Calvin quit. "Goss selected his crew because he believed we had the mentality of test pilots, not kamikaze pilots," he wrote. "Having survived two calamities at sea this year I could not countenance giving the boat a third chance to kill me by sailing it into the Southern Ocean without undergoing a realistic test of its strength."

On November 20, with just forty days before The Race, *Team Philips* was ready to go one last time. Her instruments were calibrated during a series of short sails. The new mast steps appeared to be working well. On December 2 Goss took her to sea. It was the last chance to put the boat through her paces, to see if she could live up to the promise of her design. If she did, the plan was to continue on to Barcelona for the start of The Race.

December in the English Channel and the North Atlantic brings some of the worst weather of the year, with frequent gales whistling in from the west with strong winds and vicious seas. As Goss prepared for *Team Philips*'s make-or-break sail, several storms were blasting the channel and another massive depression, stretching from Ireland to Africa, was moving in. It was a very ugly picture, but with so little time Goss had no alternative but to get the boat out and sailing. On board to replace Mike Calvin was Richard Tudor, a professional sailor who had already been in two round-the-world races. Phil Aikenhead, a member of the build team who could help with any structural glitches, was recruited as well, bringing the total crew to seven.

In consultation with Lee Bruce, a weather router based in Wolfeboro, New Hampshire, Goss decided to take *Team Philips* up England's east coast and counterclockwise around the British Isles. That would give her favorable following winds as she tried to sail north and up over the top of the depression. Once the storm blew through, she would be able to sail south on its back side and, with luck, head for the Mediterranean. Racing around a massive weather depression hundreds of miles in diameter was an audacious plan, but if *Team Philips* was going to sail in The Race and was going to get a stern beating to evaluate her mettle for the Southern Ocean, this was the chance. If she couldn't sail her way around or through the storm, she wasn't ready.

Initially, the strategy worked beautifully. *Team Philips* turned east up the English Channel and with strong favorable winds was soon rocketing along at 35 knots. Two days later she had raced up the east side of England and Scotland and was approaching 60° north latitude. If she'd been trying to sail around the British Isles in record time, she would have been right on pace.

For once, the boat appeared to be performing as Goss had hoped she would, coping with winds that ranged from below 10 knots to more than 30 knots in gale-force conditions. At one point seas were so rough that the accommodations pod, twelve feet above the water, plowed into a wave. Still, for the first time Goss felt a growing confidence that the boat was a safe haven in large seas. The ability to weathercock the rigs to take the wind out of a sail made reefing a straightforward, undramatic procedure. This was exactly what Goss and Thompson had intended. *PlayStation*'s inability to get sail down quickly had almost caused her to flip during her transatlantic run. Goss now felt he could allow his crew to keep sail up longer and push the boat harder. The wave-piercing concept was also performing as expected in the heavy seas. The catamaran plunged down the steep waves and the bows submerged until there was enough buoyancy to smoothly lift them free. *Team Philips* showed no tendency to stop suddenly and throw her crew around. Goss felt as if he were racing a car with superior suspension.

The innovative cat was flaunting her design but still had to prove herself in the extreme conditions she might encounter during The Race. On December 4, as she turned west into the Atlantic north of the Orkney Islands, at the top of Scotland, she got her chance. With the weather picture growing more complicated by the hour, the immediate forecast called for winds up to 40 knots, seas that would build to more than twenty feet, and sleet and frigid temperatures to rival the Southern Ocean. A series of subsequent depressions, set to sweep east from the American continent, was close behind. The North Atlantic seemed intent on gilding its fearsome winter reputation.

Team Philips had an escape route if she could sail south through the gap between the current storm and those that followed it. If Goss and his crew missed this opportunity, however, the next storm would pile in with stiff winds from the south, blocking the boat's path to the calmer latitudes of the Mediterranean. To make the escape south even trickier, there was an area of light winds lurking in the region.

The early hours of December 6 found *Team Philips* more than four hundred miles west of the Outer Hebrides, off the coast of Scotland, sailing at about 22 knots in easterly winds blowing 35 knots and gusting over 40. A slow turn toward the south was feasible, but Lee Bruce, scanning the weather information splashed across his multiple computer screens back in Wolfeboro, worried that a premature turn would send the boat into the pocket of light winds, wasting precious hours in the race to get safely south. Bruce wanted Goss and his crew to make sure they got far enough west to clear the bubble before making the course change. He advised maintaining a heading that dipped no farther than west-southwest for the time being. Bruce would later castigate himself for not being more explicit on this point, since he was working with the Goss crew for the first time. A few hours later, he got a disheartening message from *Team Philips:*

the catamaran had cut the corner too early. In an Atlantic Ocean whipped by heavy winds over most of its surface, Goss and his crew were almost becalmed.

It was a cruel trap. Just twenty miles to the southwest, a commercial ship was reporting northwest winds of 20 knots — exactly the escape winds *Team Philips* had been hunting for. Bruce could see that *Team Philips* had only a short time to get to those winds before they evaporated. The easiest solution was to start the engines and motor out of the calm patch. But here more bad luck arrived: one engine had a leaky seal and was out of commission. The crew tried to start the second engine. It refused to catch.

With no power, the cat spent most of the day drifting in a sloppy sea. By the time *Team Philips* had found enough wind to sail fast again, the northwest winds needed to get south had passed by. Instead, a new depression was reaching out from the west. *Team Philips* was now truly on her own, five hundred miles west of Scotland and more than four hundred miles south of Iceland. Storm systems scattered throughout the Atlantic created powerful swells of twenty feet and higher. A building 30-knot wind knocked the tops off, concocting a confused, dangerous melee of white water that battered *Team Philips* from all sides.

The ocean has a relentless way of probing a boat for defects, and after almost a week of hard sailing, the continual wash of waves inexorably found a new weakness to exploit. Cracks started to appear around the edges of the accommodations and crew pod. They seemed more cosmetic than structural, yet they indicated that the pod was being stressed in a way that hadn't been anticipated by the engineers. Goss began to worry that the heavy winds on the way might do more catastrophic damage.

He discussed his options with Bruce. "What happens if we stay close to the shipping lanes?" he asked the weather router. "What happens if we sail away?" The answers weren't encouraging. *Team Philips* could try to dodge the new storm tracking her down by sailing north and west to stay in the gale system's lighter winds while waiting for it to weaken. But that would take her away from assistance if she needed it. In any case, Bruce predicted *Team Philips* would still be facing severe winds of 40 to 50 knots and potentially boat-breaking seas. The alternative was to continue into the depression, which would at least keep *Team Philips* near any commercial traffic. Goss decided the boat would simply have to survive yet another blast of winds and heavy seas, and sailed toward the storm, staying near the shipping lanes. Bruce sensed he was starting to worry more about his crew's safety than about the future of the boat.

Weather has no agenda, no emotion. It is a purely physical process, chaos theory in action. Nevertheless, when you are at sea in a vulnerable sailboat, it is sometimes difficult to resist the feeling that the spinning systems are somehow reacting to your presence, reducing options, closing doors, setting you up. Pete Goss was a military man and a practical sailor, capable of keeping irrational feelings and fears at bay in extraordinarily adverse circumstances. He was doing everything he could to respond to the deteriorating situation — to look after his boat and crew — with logic and calculation as he worked tirelessly to find an escape to the Mediterranean. Yet the North Atlantic would not relent. As if hurling yet another gale in *Team Philips*'s direction weren't enough, the barometer in the nav station started plummeting beyond anything indicated in the forecasts. That announced a more immediate problem, a rapidly intensifying area of low pressure — a storm — right in *Team Philips*'s vicinity. Bruce did a double take when he saw how fast the Atlantic was forecast to pounce on *Team Philips* and went back to the weather models to verify there wasn't some glitch. The computers weren't lying. The boat and crew were now confronting their own personal weather bomb, with winds that would build to hurricane force of more than seventy-five miles an hour and seas that would top out around sixty feet.

What had been a rough test sail was now becoming a fight for survival. The storm was as bad as any that Goss, even with all his Southern Ocean miles, had experienced. The crew kept reducing sail as the winds increased, until *Team Philips* was flying no sail at all. Even then, the wind on the bare masts kept hurtling her through the surf. Long lines and a parachutelike drogue were pitched over the stern to try to slow the runaway catamaran down to navigable, safer speeds. The added drag reduced the cat's mad rush to under 20 knots. Still, *Team Philips* was sailing on the edge, at times accelerating to 29 knots despite all the gear dragging behind her.

The catamaran was almost perfectly centered in the North Atlantic, equidistant from Iceland, Greenland, and Ireland. In that lonely purgatory the mountainous waves grew steeper, colliding with leftover swells from previous gales to create a churning seaway that chipped away at the carbon-fiber structure. There was so much flying spray in the air that it was sometimes difficult to distinguish the huge seas racing at them from clouds. The most vertical waves drove *Team Philips* forward with a surge that would bury the bows until the underside of the central pod slammed into the water and the sterns and rudders lifted out of the water. At other times the sterns were pushed under twenty feet of hissing white water. Now and then Goss could see a bow wave being thrown off by the pod, which was supposed to fly clear of the seas. Somehow the catamaran seemed to be holding together — until over a period of minutes three misshapen waves caught her from astern and tons of water exploded against the crew pod from behind and below.

It wasn't designed to withstand that particular assault. Carbon fiber snapped and disintegrated. Fissures opened up along the underside, panting open and closed as the angry ocean continued to hammer at the catamaran. The damage threatened the hydraulic pumps and linkages controlling the twin rudders. As long as *Team Philips* had steerage, she had a chance. Without it, the 120-foot boat would be at the mercy of the winds and seas, which would try to throw her broadside and flip her. Fearing for the crew, Goss ordered everyone but Andy Hindley into a watertight compartment in the starboard hull. Hindley remained on deck, manning the communications gear and ferrying hot tea to Goss on the wheel. He got in touch with Bruce. "It's not good, we're in trouble here," he told him, asking when the winds might start to abate. There was no panic, but Bruce could hear the stress in Hindley's voice over the crackling satellite relay. In the background he could hear the jet-engine roar of the storm and a series of horrendous bangs. "Hold on a minute," Hindley interrupted after one almighty crash. He was back in a minute. "We're all right for the moment," he said.

It was obvious that Goss and Hindley felt their lives were in danger. The satellite phone connected Bruce directly to the unfolding drama, yet there was little he could do to help. It was a terrible feeling. He sat alone in his quiet office, providing information when called, none of it reassuring. Then he would hang up, wait, and wonder.

Out in the middle of the Atlantic, *Team Philips* was barely holding together and another enormous depression, expected to stretch from Newfoundland to the Canary Islands, was rumbling their way. Ten hours earlier, the crew had been worried that they might be late to the start of The Race in Barcelona. Now they worried about staying alive. The fifty-foot pod on which their steering, communications, and shelter depended was in bad shape, flexing so much that the access hatch to the interior was visibly changing shape. A couple of the men sat with their backs to one wall of the crew cockpit and stretched their legs to the other side. There was so much movement there, too, they couldn't lock their knees without risking injury.

How to proceed would be Goss's decision, and he gathered the crew together to discuss the options. Emotionally, everyone wanted to stay with the boat and try to nurse her through the coming storm. It would be a high-stakes gamble. *Team Philips* would be forced to run with the winds, away to the northeast and away from the shipping lanes. If the pod and steering disintegrated entirely, Goss and the crew would find themselves in a brutish North Atlantic winter netherworld where assistance might be a long time coming, if it came at all.

As he had so many times before, Goss made the tough deci-

sion. Nothing mattered more than the crew's lives. The moment
had come to abandon the radical boat he had spent the past
three years working so hard to perfect. He called his friends
at the Maritime Rescue Coordination Centre in Falmouth and
issued a heartbreaking mayday. The German container ship
Hoescht Express was 150 miles away. Goss and the crew settled
in overnight to endure the hours it would take for the ship to
arrive.

At 7 A.M., with the cold blackness still upon them, the 965-
foot *Hoescht Express* hove into view, lights blazing, and set up
to drift downwind alongside *Team Philips*. In the heavy seas it
was difficult to keep the boats alongside each other for long. The
crew of the container ship, with no time to deploy a heavy cargo
net, threw a narrow rope ladder over the side. Goss struggled at
the wheel to keep *Team Philips* in synch with the huge ship,
communicating with the bridge via radio. Hindley and Larsen
lined up the rest of the crew on the side deck. A safety line was
attached to each man as he prepared to make the jump across.
A slip, a mistimed jump, or a missed grab at the ladder would
mean a plunge into the Atlantic between the two slamming hulls.
To prevent that from happening, Larsen and Hindley grabbed
each man's harness as he stepped forward to the edge. They released it only when they judged that *Team Philips* had reached
the top of her motion and the jumper was relaxed enough to
have a good chance of success. The release was the green light to
jump, but there were a number of reloads before everyone except Hindley and Goss were across. A Royal Air Force Nimrod
airplane circled overhead, with thermal imaging equipment to
help pinpoint anyone who disappeared into the inky swells. "I'm
not very happy about this," the RAF flight deck heard Goss say
as the banging between the two boats continued and he worried
that a mast would collapse.

Goss had good reason to fret. In the midst of the chaos,
Larsen and Hindley looked up to see a line swing from the head
of *Team Philips*'s mast and snag a container on the *Hoescht Ex-*

press as she rolled toward the catamaran. "It's not what we want right now, is it?" Larsen spat out as he and Hindley froze, praying that the container wouldn't be pulled free when the boats rolled apart. If it did, it would drop like a wrecking ball 130 feet to the catamaran's deck. For once, luck was with them. The container stayed put.

Before he made his jump to the *Hoescht Express,* Hindley walked back to the cockpit to shake Goss's hand. "See you in a minute," he said to his friend, standing lonely in the battered cockpit. When Hindley was safely across, Goss clipped his harness to a line thrown from the deck of the container ship, lined up *Team Philips* as best he could, and sprinted for the side. He leapt for the ladder and barely had to climb as his crew heaved him bodily up the side of the *Hoescht Express. Team Philips,* her port bow badly damaged from knocking into the rescue vessel, drifted slowly off into the spume, her masts passing close enough to allow one final touch.

Goss and his team stood on the deck of the enormous ship, tears in their eyes, until the *Hoescht Express* turned away to resume her course to Nova Scotia. They had done everything they could to prepare *Team Philips* to survive the Atlantic alone, leaving lines in the water to slow her drift, snugging the sails tight in the wishbones, and locking down the ports and openings. If it was humanly possible, they would return to reclaim her for yet another resurrection. But the innovative cat didn't have nine lives, only three. Just a week after she was left to drift, her emergency position transponder ceased emitting a signal. "Dare to Dream" had been the team slogan. Now the dream was over.

In May 2001, months after the end of the race *Team Philips* had been built to win, wreckage from her hulls was spotted off both the Irish and Icelandic coasts. The vast separation indicated that the boat had likely broken up shortly after she was left to fend for herself.

Goss returned to the quiet countryside of Devon, a sympathetic figure in a nation that is generous to its failed heroes. No

one truly knew the disappointment and pain he experienced except perhaps his wife and children. He kept a tight lid on his
emotions in public and did his best to endure the disappointment he faced in private. Piece by piece the elaborate visitors'
center and boat-building business he had created to support
Team Philips began to come apart. Goss spent his time behind
closed doors, dealing with creditors and insurers. It would have
been easy for pundits to mock him and the hubris of his Race
project. But somehow he was too nice a person, and too sincere
in what he had been trying to achieve, to make an easy target.

The Race challenged sailors and designers to reinvent multihulls and ocean racing. Pete Goss, more than anyone, had em-
braced the spirit of innovation that lay at the heart of Bruno Peyron's concept. Perhaps he pushed engineering and design a little
too far beyond established principles. *Team Philips* had been the
most radical, exciting sailboat the racing world had seen in
decades. It was hard to score Goss for that.

As *Team Philips* drifted to her sad fate, the rest of the fleet
slowly converged on Barcelona. By Christmas the old harbor
was dominated by soaring masts and a collection of the fastest
multihulls ever assembled. *Team Philips,* with her electric-blue
hulls, would have been the most stirring sight. Nevertheless, the
floating docks provided striking visual proof of the leap in scale
and design that The Race had set in motion. The venerable
Enza, lengthened to one hundred feet and being campaigned
by English sailor Tony Bullimore as *Team Legato,* was moored
alongside the worthy *Jet Services V/Commodore Explorer,* now
sailed as *Warta Polpharma* by a Polish crew. Bullimore, sixty
years old and the tubby, jowly personification of a British bull-
dog, had more than 250,000 sea miles to his credit, many in
multihulls. He was best known for stubbornly surviving his
overturned monohull in the 1996–97 Vendée Globe. His preparation of *Enza* for The Race had been disorganized, rushed, and
hampered by a chronic lack of money. Bullimore was good color,
but no one gave him much of a chance. *Warta Polpharma* was
also the longest of shots. She was skippered by Roman Pazske,

a professional racing sailor, and was the first Polish entry in a round-the-world sailboat race since the inaugural 1973 Whitbread. In their day, *Enza* and *Commodore Explorer* had dazzled all of sailing with their size and speed. Alongside *PlayStation, Club Med, Innovation Explorer,* and *Team Adventure,* they looked like toys.

8

TO THE ATLANTIC

The sea! the sea! the open sea!
The blue, the fresh, the ever free!
— Bryan Waller Procter

DECEMBER 31, 2000, brought a perfect blue sky to Barcelona and a beautiful northwesterly breeze that Bruno Peyron must have whistled for in his dreams. After seven years of planning, millions of dollars, and enough skepticism to sink a fleet of boats, The Race was about to get under way.

Boats were scheduled to depart Port Vell Marina at 11 A.M. in preparation for a 2 P.M. start off Barcelona's beaches. A warming sun climbed over the fluttering flags and sponsor tents in the race village that had been set up alongside the floating docks. For two weeks, thousands of sailing fans had wandered about the site, checking out the monster catamarans, drinking strong coffee, and buying up Race T-shirts, pullovers, and caps. Huge speakers and video screens pumped out rock music and images of the boats flying over the waves during training. Ocean racing in Europe was like the Grand Prix, and the race village had a slick, professional ambience.

Down on the docks, departure rituals were in full swing. The hours before a long voyage, particularly a dangerous one, are telescoped for any sailor. In the nineteenth century, the hard-bitten and wifeless would spend their time chasing ale and women.

Robin Knox-Johnston spent his last night in Falmouth's Marine Hotel, where the goodbye party went on until 5 A.M. and left him with a hangover to blight his first day at sea. He half jokingly put in an order for a steak dinner and lemon meringue pie, to be ready upon his return. (It was.) Most of the sailors in The Race spent an evening with friends and family. Many of them were married, and they were about to disappear from the lives of their wives and children for two or three months.

Professional sailing was voracious in its demands, so it was important to make the most of every minute ashore. A top sailor could easily spend most of the year at sea or in training, segueing from one sailing campaign to another with only brief intervals to catch up with family. In professional sailing there used to be a distinction between the inshore, round-the-buoys racers and the offshore madmen. But by the 1990s these two sailing realms were merging. Offshore races like the Whitbread, with the Southern Ocean experience and the Cape Horn rounding, were no longer seen as a bizarre form of masochism. Instead, round-the-world racing became a glamour sport that attracted America's Cup and Olympic sailors who wanted to be able to say they had done it all.

Part of the lure was money, of course. As race campaigns started to suck up millions of dollars, sponsors were increasingly willing to hire the talent to make their investments pay off with top finishes. Elite skippers and navigators like Grant Dalton and Mike Quilter might earn $20,000 or more a month over the course of an event. Watch captains could pull down $10,000, and even regular crew might earn $6,000 to $8,000 a month. That sort of money wasn't always there, but when it was, it made it easier for families to tolerate the long absences. In the early days of round-the-world racing, a sailor with a family might have a hard time justifying his zeal for adventure. Now, whatever the real motivation for spending half the year at sea, a sailor could at least say he was earning a living.

For The Race, whispers on the dock put the ordinary wages aboard *Team Adventure* at $6,000 to $10,000 a month, and on

Club Med at $5,000 to $6,000. Steve Fossett was no doubt paying his *PlayStation* crew good money too. The only maxi-cat team that was struggling along hand to mouth in early Whitbread style was the underfunded group aboard *Innovation Explorer.* Money was so tight that for most of the twelve sailors The Race was practically a volunteer effort, the only payoff being a chance to sail an extraordinary boat around the world at record speeds. For the younger crew members it was a worthwhile lark. For the sailors with wives and children, however, it wasn't as easy to justify the commitment. Skip Novak caught less grief than most. His wife, Elena Caputo-Novak, an Italian journalist, agreed to join the crew (becoming the only woman in The Race) to help produce onboard reports and deal with the media. The income gap affected morale and work habits, though, forcing Loïck Peyron and Novak, the two skippers, to scramble constantly to keep enough money flowing to hold the crew together and get the boat to the starting line.

If the maxi-catamarans lived up to their impressive VPPs, at least The Race would be mercifully brief. And in a sense the boats were not really disappearing over the horizon at all, thanks to the extensive communications array carried on each boat. The days of radio silence in ocean racing were long gone. Bernard Moitessier, who had refused to allow a long-range radio aboard *Joshua,* liked his solitude at sea, and when he felt like communicating with the rest of the world, he would slingshot messages in film canisters onto the decks of passing ships. Bruno Peyron, for his part, wanted the world to share in the experience of The Race. The enormous catamarans were excellent platforms for satellite domes and antennas that would give each crew radio, telephone, and e-mail capability. He encouraged the teams to send daily e-mails, digital photographs, even video. All of it would be posted on The Race's Web site, which was the modern way of transforming an essentially isolated experience into a global event.

The technology also transformed the experience on board the boats. The media station tucked into the back of the port hull on

Explorer would become such a popular hangout at sea it was dubbed JJ's Cyber Café. Novak sometimes had to push past a crowd of sailors e-mailing or calling home before he could retrieve an update on fleet positions. The scrum made him nostalgic for the 1977–78 Whitbread, when, shortly after leaving Cape Town in rough weather, flying water from the toilet shorted out the long-range radio, leaving the boat in a happy world of its own for the thirty-five-day voyage to New Zealand. The unprecedented degree to which the catamarans were linked to the global communications network did cause some glitches, however. The computers on *Club Med* and *Explorer* caught nasty e-mail–borne viruses, thanks to the ceaseless electronic traffic between the boats and civilization. The Race traveled a remote route, but never would racing sailors be less isolated while at sea.

That didn't slow the hugs, kisses, and tears on the docks as the final minutes to departure ticked off. Among the competing skippers and crews there was also a feeling of camaraderie, an acknowledgment of the fact that they were all about to share the same unquantifiable dangers, that any one of the boats might need to call on another for assistance — which could mean the difference between life and death in the Southern Ocean. *PlayStation* navigator Stan Honey and *Team Adventure* conavigator Larry Rosenfeld saluted each other on the dock. Crews shouted friendly gibes across the pontoons. Skip Novak walked over to wish both Cam Lewis and Rosenfeld a good journey. Bruno Peyron wandered the docks, wishing each boat good luck, and no doubt suppressing a bit of envy. "Maybe we'll see you in Marseilles . . . and maybe we won't," Lewis teased his old shipmate.

One by one the huge boats pulled away from the docks, to loud cheers and whistles from the spectators. First out was *Warta Polpharma*, her best chance to lead the pack. Next went *Club Med* and *Team Adventure*, their sponsors' flags snapping in the fresh breeze. Earlier that morning, *Team Adventure* had taken the time to have Lewis's aunt, a minister, bless the 110-foot boat. *PlayStation* chose a more raucous sendoff, easing away with the on-deck stereo speakers blaring "Who Let the Dogs Out." The last of the maxi-cats, *Explorer,* presently slipped her lines, bringing up the rear.

Only *Team Legato* stayed firmly moored to the dock, while Tony Bullimore wrestled with finalizing a crew and provisioning the boat. The race committee was also insisting that he complete some additional safety prerequisites, such as painting her rudders and daggerboards — which extended down from the hull and helped keep the boat tracking in a straight line — fluorescent orange. That way they would be more visible from the air if *Team Legato* flipped. They also wanted *Legato* to sail 150 more qualification miles. All boats were required to have sailed 2,500 miles, which she'd been unable to complete in the scramble to get to Barcelona on time. The exasperated Bullimore joked that if the current off Barcelona was strong enough, he would simply anchor outside the harbor and let the rush of water past his boat rack up the needed miles on his log. Ultimately, he would start twenty hours late and more than 200 miles behind the leaders. In such a long race that was not necessarily a death sentence. In any case, *Team Legato*'s only real chance of doing well in The Race depended on her larger, newer rivals' suffering breakdowns.

Out at the starting area, hundreds of spectator boats and seven hovering helicopters created a frenzied scene. A Goodyear blimp floated serenely above the bustling tableau, recording it with the omniscient eye of its television camera and broadcasting it live in France and Spain. Round-the-world yacht racing had come a long way since the amateur competitors in the Golden Globe slipped quietly to sea, observed by just a few boats carrying relatives, friends, and interested journalists.

Just beneath the glossy veneer of modern sport — the media center, the sponsorship tents, the publicity blitz — there remained a mild undercurrent of disbelief that The Race, so long in the making, was actually about to come off, that six crews were embarking on a nonstop circumnavigation in giant catamarans. Steve Fossett, ever the oddsmaker, had always harbored doubts that The Race would emerge intact from all the time pressures, breakdowns, and organizational challenges of any major event's inaugural run. In fact, he had seriously contemplated abandoning The Race in favor of a Jules Verne record attempt. The only thing that had stopped him was a near mutiny by his crew, many of whom were determined to compete in The Race and threatened to quit the boat if Fossett chose the solitary record run. (As *PlayStation* sailed south from the English Channel before the start, Grant Dalton jokingly e-mailed Fossett a reminder to turn left at the Strait of Gibraltar.) Before leaving the dock, the taciturn midwesterner, used to solo record-setting adventures, admitted his amazement. "David Scully" — one of *PlayStation*'s crew and a veteran of the French-dominated single-handed sailing scene — "told me all along that there is nothing more disorganized than a sailing regatta, except a French sailing regatta, but that they somehow all come together in the end," Fossett said.

Scully was right, and as 2 P.M. approached, five enormous multihulls picked their way cautiously around the starting line. In a short round-the-buoys fleet race, being at the head of the pack at the gun, where the wind is undisturbed by other boats and the tactical options are wide open, can be half the game. In a round-the-world race, hitting the line at speed is more a matter of vanity than of necessity. The best strategy is a simple one: stay on the correct side of the line until the gun fires, and don't hit anything.

Following that strategy isn't always easy, however, especially when state-of-the-art racing boats are powering at high speeds through the chop and confusion of a large and unpredictable spectator fleet. Roger Nilson, the navigator aboard *Explorer,* knew that lesson better than most. In the 1989–90 Whitbread race Nilson was the skipper of an eighty-one-foot, two-masted ketch called *The Card.* On the leg from Auckland, New Zealand, to Punta del Este, Uruguay, Nilson started well but dipped into the spectator fleet. Heeling slightly in the gentle breeze, *The Card* tried to slip past an anchored sailboat full of onlookers and snagged her rigging on the boat's mast. *The Card*'s forward momentum pulled the hapless boat over onto its side, forcing the startled race watchers to scramble for safety. Something had to give, and that something was *The Card*'s second, or mizzen, mast, which crashed to the deck. Nilson surveyed the damage, rapidly assessed his options, and ordered the crew to cut the felled mast away — after salvaging the radar and antennas — and dump it over the side. Just minutes after the start, *The Card*'s chances for a top placing on that leg were virtually wiped out. She sailed on with her mainmast alone, Nilson figuring that *The Card* would lose less time because of the suddenly reduced sail area than she would by returning to port for repairs.

At 2 P.M. a cannon launched the maxi-cats on their 23,000-mile drag race (the actual sailing distance would be much greater). The course would take them down to the Strait of Gibraltar, about 525 miles away, then out into the Atlantic. After that, race rules called for the boats to circle the globe from west to east — leaving South Africa's Cape of Good Hope, Australia's Cape Leeuwin, and South America's Cape Horn to port — and return to the Mediterranean to finish in Marseilles. There were no restrictions in picking the best route to complete the circumnavigation other than that the boats had to pass through the Cook Strait, separating the North and South Islands of New Zealand. That would force the catamarans to emerge briefly from the depths of the Southern Ocean, and it would lengthen the course. It would also provide an interesting tactical wrinkle, given the notoriously changeable winds of the strait, and create a media- and spectator-friendly "gate" at about the halfway mark, which would provide an unambiguous check on race positions.

The five maxi-cats managed to clear the starting area without incident, frantically waving overenthusiastic sailing fans out of their way as they sliced through the assembled fleet of small boats at more than 20 knots. *PlayStation* and *Explorer,* determined to avoid any disastrous mishaps at the outset, started with reduced sail. *Team Adventure,* to no one's surprise, powered quickly into the lead and headed west into the afternoon sun, flying a hull in the puffs. *Club Med* followed in hot pursuit. When *PlayStation* and *Explorer* were free of the spectator fleet, they shook out their mainsail reefs and went into full racing mode as well. The crews on deck drove and trimmed their big catamarans for maximum speed, and began to settle into the cyclical watch routines that would dictate their lives. Down below, navigators, surrounded by glowing numbers in their cramped stations, began the ceaseless monitoring of position, performance, and weather that would shape the head-to-head tactical battles about to unfold.

Sailing around the world is not just a matter of following a straight line that unravels cleanly across ocean after ocean. Wind velocity and direction have profound effects on any boat's speed. That's especially true for catamarans, which are highly sensitive to wind angle. They thrive on winds from behind or from the side, and can be sluggish and unmanageable when working into a headwind. Even a change in wind angle of just 5 or 10 degrees can mean a difference in boat speed of 5 knots or more. So an indirect route with favorable wind is often faster to the mark than a direct route with headwinds or less wind pressure. For this reason, accurate forecasts of weather and sea conditions are as critical to fast sailing as good boat design and an expert crew.

Matthew Maury's Wind and Current Charts popularized the notion that a longer course could actually result in a faster voyage than a more direct one. Beyond his charts, though, the clipper navigators and skippers of his day had only the crudest of tools to predict the weather. Most important was the barometer, which measures atmospheric pressure and can indicate the presence or approach of both high (light winds) and low (strong winds) pressure systems. Experience and conventional wisdom ("Red sky at night, sailor's delight; red sky in the morning, sailors take warning") also played a role. But right up until the era of the Golden Globe, ships didn't play the weather so much as they hoped to survive it. Robin Knox-Johnston and his com-

petitors had one advantage over their forebears: the occasional
high-seas weather reports and forecasts they received over their
long-range radio equipment — when it worked properly. Even
so, weather forecasting remained a fairly crude art that offered
few insights into ocean regions off the major shipping routes,
which is to say most of the Southern Ocean. Knox-Johnston did
not really begin to work out the best round-the-world route
until he was already racing. Over the course of the voyage, he estimated, weather anomalies, as well as simple errors of judgment
about the weather systems he encountered, kept him at sea a
month longer than necessary.

With its high-speed boats and their ability to communicate
continuously with shore-based weather forecasters — who could
make much more accurate predictions — The Race gave the
navigators and skippers an entirely different relationship with
the weather. It was no longer a mysterious, sometimes merciless
wild card. Although by no means perfectly predictable, it had
become a strategic weapon that a skilled navigator could use to
gain an advantage over the competition. The outcome of The
Race would be determined not so much by how the weather
played the boats but by how the boats played the weather. They
would be racing across the same oceans, but each would be
sailing its own personal racetrack, which would get longer or
shorter according to the local sea and wind conditions at any
given moment. Finding the shortest racetrack was the key to
victory.

Navigation for the clipper ships and in the Golden Globe era
meant, above all else, establishing and keeping track of the
boat's position, a time-consuming chore employing the traditional tools of the trade. Speed and heading were logged and
plotted many times a day to ascertain an estimated "dead reckoning" position. A sextant and chronometer were used to verify
or improve the accuracy of that position, which could rapidly
accumulate error owing to variations in current and imprecise
recording of boat speed and heading. Simply fixing a boat's position with sextant and chronometer — and a good fix could be

miles off — was an exercise that could take hours. Chichester understood the challenge of the process better than most. A few days after departing Plymouth he discovered he had forgotten the precalculated navigation tables used to convert sextant sights into a line on the chart. Luckily, he found in another book the required trigonometry formulas, so he could work out the math in longhand, just as the clipper captains he was chasing had done. Slocum would have been proud.

Navigators in The Race — in fact, navigators since the arrival of satellite positioning systems in the 1980s — no longer needed to worry much about calculating the boat's position. That vital information, so elusive throughout most of the history of sail, was automatically and continuously provided by a readout on a black box in the navigation station, and it was accurate to within tens of meters (though Stan Honey, *PlayStation*'s navigator, brought his trusty sextant aboard in case of electrical meltdown). Their primary and almost sole concern had become tactical: using weather forecasting information and the known performance parameters of the boat to try to find the fastest, or most wind- and sea-favored, track around the world. Bernard Moitessier had used his sextant, barometer, instincts, and powers of observation to steer *Joshua* clear of major storms, yet *Joshua* was repeatedly capsized by overpowering winds and seas. In The Race, Mike Quilter on *Club Med* and the other navigators could in no way afford to risk severe weather that would put their masts into the water, because the masts wouldn't be coming back up. Instead, they would be looking to use the great speed of their catamarans to precisely place the boats in moving weather systems, aiming to find winds coming from a specific direction at a specific strength. All the boats would in essence be trying to skip from weather system to weather system, dodging the worst of the weather and hopscotching their way across the oceans with a minimum loss of time.

Most ocean races required the navigators to use equipment they carried on board to make their own forecasts. By the late 1990s that included laptops and satellite links with Internet access — albeit somewhat slow and unreliable — on top of the older weather facsimile charts received via radio. Bruno Peyron wanted the entrants to sail the fastest possible route and show-case all the ways technology could transform ocean racing, so the boats in The Race were allowed to confer with shore-based weather routers while they were at sea. This practice originated as far back as the 1968 OSTAR, when an English competitor named Geoffrey Williams sailed courses recommended by a mainframe computer that was fed a series of weather maps. Williams won that OSTAR after avoiding a storm that slowed the rest of the fleet.

Shore-based routing was immediately and widely criticized as violating the self-sufficient spirit of that transatlantic race. But as forecasting and communications technology had improved, shore-based routing became an important tactical element in any race that permitted it. Jean-Yves Bernot, a pioneering French router and conavigator on *Team Adventure*, estimated that by the 1980s shore-based routing was shaving between 8 and 12 percent off transatlantic times. Another pioneer, considered by many to be the godfather of the discipline, was a retired U.S. Air Force forecaster named Bob Rice. In the 1970s, from a base in New Hampshire, Rice started helping adventurers of all kinds negotiate the weather. One of his eventual clients was a bal-loonist named Steve Fossett. Other than ballooning, no sport is as directly dependent on accurate weather forecasting as sailing. As Rice got more work, he recruited other forecasters into the business, including *Team Philips*'s Lee Bruce. With Bruce's help, Rice went on to route both *Enza* and *Sport Elec* to their record-breaking Jules Verne voyages.

By 2000 the routing game had produced a handful of top routing forecasters. Rice signed on with *PlayStation*. Roger Badham, an Australian — known far and wide as "Clouds" and also one of the best in the world — teamed up with his long-standing mates Grant Dalton and Mike Quilter. Pierre Lasnier, another of France's elite forecasters, was brought in to work with *Explorer*. And Bill Biewenga and Ken Campbell, two more

Americans, were hired to back up Jean-Yves Bernot on *Team Adventure*.

The intensity of the contact between the boats and the shore-based forecasters varied according to the complexities of the weather problems, but it was a relationship somewhat similar to that of a racecar driver and his pit crew. The forecasters constantly updated the weather prognosis and made routing recommendations; they were rarely out of touch for more than a few hours at a time. When new weather information arrived on board, the navigators filtered it through programs on their laptops that could analyze thousands of potential routes to a given waypoint and within minutes spit out the fastest predicted course. It was Matthew Maury taken to the technological edge. The symbiosis between boat and forecaster was so powerful that the forecasters were considered "virtual crew." By the end of The Race, for example, Badham had survived for two months on four hours of sleep a night. That wasn't bad considering he sent thirty or more e-mails and ten weather maps a day to *Club Med* and sometimes talked with Dalton and Quilter on the satellite phone as much as once an hour. (Dalton figured the intricacy of any given weather puzzle could be measured by the size of the phone bill.)

For the moment, Badham and his fellow forecasters were intent on helping the boats through the Strait of Gibraltar and out into the Atlantic. Every race, even a round-the-world race without stops, can be broken down into tactical legs that are separated by a geographical gate, such as the Cook Strait or Cape Horn, or a weather gate, like the light-air Doldrums that blanket the equator. The gates provide a measure of progress and a target for each boat to focus on. The Strait of Gibraltar was The Race's first because its winds and currents can change dramatically from hour to hour. The first boat through might break away if conditions around Gibraltar shut down for the trailing boats. Next up was the transit of the equator, where patches of calm could park unlucky boats for hours or days in baking heat.

Of all the gates, arrival in the Southern Ocean first was the most critical. The history of round-the-world racing offered one clear lesson: the first boat that made it through the South Atlantic and into the strong, reliable westerlies of the South usually won. In the high latitudes the relatively regular weather pattern, with one depression after another sweeping from west to east, favors lead boats because passing lanes are more often found in changing, unpredictable weather or windless holes. Of course any boat could lose a lead in the Southern Ocean if it suffered gear failure in the extreme conditions, but the first boat around Cape Horn often was first to finish. Though the return Atlantic leg was just as tricky as the outbound leg, ten thousand miles of Southern Ocean sailing had a tendency to spread fleets over hundreds, even thousands, of miles, requiring much more dramatic gains and losses to shuffle the order.

For all these reasons, Mike Quilter aboard *Club Med,* Stan Honey aboard *PlayStation,* Roger Nilson aboard *Explorer,* and Jean-Yves Bernot and Larry Rosenfeld aboard *Team Adventure* considered getting to the Southern Ocean first to be the most important strategic objective of The Race — Quilter and Dalton viewed it as 80 percent of the game, and no one would disagree.

The only hitch was that in the push to hit the gates first, it was equally important not to break the boat. On multihulls that might sail more than six hundred miles in a day, any downtime for repairs — even an hour or two — would be measured in dozens of miles lost. The maxi-catamarans were largely untested, which meant that reliability and caution — which is to say seamanship — would be as necessary as flat-out speed and tactics. Grant Dalton, the veteran, understood what was required, adopting five-time Formula 1 racing champion Juan Fangio as his strategic inspiration. Fangio used to say that he aimed to win races while going as slowly as possible, and Dalton fully intended to do the same in The Race.

Among the gates that lay ahead, the Strait of Gibraltar was the most gatelike. Just eight miles wide at the narrowest point, the strait cleaves between Europe and Africa to form the Mediterranean's only connection with the broader Atlantic. No previous round-the-world race had required boats and crews to run the gauntlet of the strait, which is thick with shipping at all hours. The prevailing currents flow westward as if the Mediterranean were draining into the Atlantic. The wind, however, can blow from either the east or the west. If it blows into the Mediterranean and against the current, it can kick up a punishing sea for boats punching their way into the Atlantic. For the catamarans of The Race, tacking back and forth against a headwind as the crews tried to find their sea legs and settle into watch routines was quite an unpleasant prospect. But that is exactly the scenario the weather gurus predicted for the fleet when it approached Gibraltar, followed by rapidly diminishing winds. Any boat that didn't get through the strait quickly could find itself trapped in the Mediterranean, losing miles as the leaders arced south toward the equator. "It's going to be a shitfight beat all the way," Mike Quilter predicted just before he climbed aboard.

Shitfight or not, Cam Lewis intended to lead the pack through it. His strategy to sail home first was aggressive and simple: get ahead and stay ahead. Blasting through Gibraltar in the lead would also be a big morale boost for his crew and serve notice that *Team Adventure* was a serious contender. And right from the start she was sailing slightly faster and closer to the wind than her rivals in a demonstration of pure performance that Skip Novak, aboard *Explorer,* found astonishing. *Team Adventure* had spent hundreds of thousands of dollars on a high-tech (although unproven) Cuben Fiber sail wardrobe, and the investment was delivering a speed bonus. Whether the fabric would hold up well over the entire race was yet to be determined. But for now *Team Adventure*'s rivals could only marvel — and fret — over her intimidating combination of superior sails and slick drivers.

Lewis had been confident that even without a lot of training *Team Adventure* would be as fast as or faster than the other boats. He and Randy Smyth were a well-honed team, the sails were the best money could buy, and speed was their specialty. Now he was watching it all come together as *Team Adventure*

opened up a six-minute lead after just fifty-three minutes of sailing. "Shit, he's quick," Quilter commented as he watched *Team
Adventure*'s progress on his radar screen. Dalton was less surprised. He had followed the building of all the boats very closely
and estimated that in terms of structure alone *Team Adventure*
was about five hundred kilograms lighter than *Club Med*, thanks
to better building technique.

A little over twelve hours into the sailing, Lewis showed that
he was also willing to take chances. *Team Adventure* was clinging to a four-mile cushion as all four maxi-catamarans (the
smaller, older *Polpharma* was steadily falling behind) sailed
south in a cluster that took them between the Balearic islands of
Ibiza and Majorca. With the wind shifting into the southwest
and blowing from the direction of Gibraltar, it was time for the
navigators to make a decision. *Club Med, PlayStation,* and *Explorer* all tacked — changed course — to head back toward the
Spanish coast. Aboard *Team Adventure,* however, Jean-Yves
Bernot and Larry Rosenfeld advised Lewis to keep sailing toward Africa.

If you think you are faster than the other boats, as Lewis suspected, it's often safer to stay with them so you are sailing in the
same weather and can work your speed. But Lewis was by nature a gambler, and had a flair for the dramatic. In what he later
termed a "great call" by his navigators, *Team Adventure* continued south for three more hours before tacking. By splitting
from the fleet, *Team Adventure* risked an early setback if Bernot
and Rosenfeld were wrong. At first she lost ground, falling
twenty-two miles behind *Club Med* in the race to Gibraltar. But
when Lewis and his crew finally converged with the other boats,
almost exactly twenty-four hours into the racing, it became clear
that Rosenfeld and "the Wizard" had found better wind angles.
Team Adventure crossed in front of the fleet and opened up a
lead of twenty-five miles. "Our cat is loping across the Mediterranean and chewing up the miles in grand style," Lewis exulted.
"With the wind quartering across our bows at sixteen knots,
we're flying a hull and doing twenty knots." Dalton, pursuing

doggedly, could only shake his head and give Lewis credit. "*Team Adventure* is on fire," he admitted as the boats started to close in on Gibraltar. "They are going quick and they are sailing smart."

The Kiwi skipper was impressed, yet unperturbed. He knew that getting to sea and settling into peak racing mode is never easy after all the stress and frenzy leading up to a departure. The ill-fated Donald Crowhurst set out with his rigging in knots and his cabin and bunk so strewn with gear that he had to spend his first night on the floor, using a rubber frogman's suit as a mattress. Robin Knox-Johnston embarked with completely untested self-steering gear. Dalton's *Club Med* campaign, the fourth round-the-world racing program he had led, was much more professional. With millions of dollars in sponsorship and a good shore-support crew, *Club Med* was as ready as an expert organizer could make her in a matter of months and a favorite to win. The day before the start, as all the teams were desperately trying to complete their preparations, Dalton had publicly joked that the only item on his schedule was a nap. But no matter how well prepared a boat is, it takes the crew a few days to adjust to the constant motion, the separation from life ashore, and the wholesale reordering of daily rhythms that comes with a watch routine.

The rising wind from the southwest, gusting to 30 knots, was making *Club Med*'s transition more difficult than usual. The crew was kept hard at work reducing and changing sails to keep the catamaran moving at her best, safe speed. Down below, where the off watch tried to snatch some sleep in the lulls between sail changes, the boat creaked and groaned in the short, sharp seas as she raced westward. Even after months of training, some of the sailors had not quite adapted to the jerky motion of the light, powerful boats as they constantly decelerated and accelerated. In Barcelona, some of the Whitbread club, including multiple circumnavigators Roger Nilson and Mike Quilter, had admitted to each other that sailing the cats sometimes made them seasick. The unusual movement caused other novel problems. It was hard to sleep, for example. A body in a bunk would slide forward as *Club Med* punched into a wave and slowed, only to slide backward, headfirst into the bulkhead behind, as she leaped forward again on the other side of the wave. The only solution was to pile any available loose bedding or clothing between skull and bulkhead to cushion the blow.

Club Med's violent motion made working on deck difficult too. Moving from hull to hull on the giant catamaran meant crossing the expanse of spongy netting laced between them. In harbor, the net was irresistible to children, who happily bounced around on the largest trampoline they had ever encountered. At sea, however, that same trampoline forced the sailors to master an exaggerated, cartoonish running style to attain decent speeds. When the trampoline was really heaving, it was hard to stay upright. Random waves would shoot up through the netting with enough force to knock a crewman flat. On *Club Med* this fate became known as "getting mugged," and the crew soon learned that some anomaly of design made the couple of meters in front of the aft beam a high-crime area. Cam Lewis first confronted this oddity of large catamaran sailing with Bruno Peyron on *Commodore Explorer.* He responded with typical exuberance, puzzling his French crewmates by sprinting across the netting, then skidding into the cockpit and shouting "Safe!"

Franck Proffit, coskipper of *Club Med,* was first to fall victim to the catamaran's bucking motion. He was surprised by one particularly abrupt leap off a wave and smashed his head against the sharp tip of a winch handle at one of the grinding pedestals, opening up a bloody gash above his eye. It was the kind of unexpected, but not unusual, injury that seems to be a part of going to sea. Round-the-world racers, particularly single-handers, had proved most susceptible thanks to the sleepless hours and risk-taking required to keep pushing a boat toward top speed. Robin Knox-Johnston, while puttering about his cabin nude in the Tropics, accidentally sat on a scalding-hot pressure cooker full of stew he had just removed from the stove. He reported no "important" damage (although he could not sit for three days), but it is easy to imagine more serious consequences, including dangerous infection. Later, in the Southern Ocean, Knox-Johnston managed to squirt himself in the left eye with battery acid when *Suhaili* was thrown on her side while he was checking the amount of charge in the batteries. He ran on deck and immediately splashed seawater in the stinging eye. Armed only with a text called *The Ship Captain's Medical Guide,* Knox-Johnston worried that he might lose sight in the eye. He considered abandoning the Golden Globe and heading for South Africa. In the end he decided winning the race would be worth an eye. (Luckily, it healed completely on its own.)

At least Proffit didn't have to endure the stress and danger of treating his own injury. Each boat in The Race had a designated medic and a well-stocked medical pack. On *Club Med* thirty-seven-year-old Alexis de Cenival, a dentist by trade, was the official sawbones.* De Cenival realized immediately that Proffit's wound required stitches, and he set about sewing him up — without anesthetic. Doing delicate work with a needle just above an eye on a boat sailing at 15 to 20 knots and pitching wildly isn't part of the curriculum in dental school. He improvised well, though, timing each pass of the needle with the passing of the waves, and somehow managed to preserve Proffit's handsome visage.

Ship-to-shore communications had also transformed medicine at sea since Knox-Johnston's scalding. The Race directors kept an experienced doctor named Jean-Yves Chauve on standby throughout the competition, to offer diagnoses and advice in emergencies. Chauve had for years been devising techniques to assist offshore racers and single-handed sailors with the weird medical crises characteristic of the sport — for example, he once helped a Vendée Globe sailor stitch up his own tongue.

One of his projects was to write a medical booklet that took sailors step by step through a diagnostic tree, the results of

---

*Francis Chichester would have been happy to have had his services. He broke a tooth during his one-stop circumnavigation, and when epoxy failed to cement the pieces together he grabbed a file from his tool kit and ground the stump down.

which could be relayed back to doctors on shore. In the 1996–97 Vendée Globe race, Chauve had, by fax and e-mail, helped Pete Goss tend to the hypothermic Raphael Dinelli after his Southern Ocean rescue. Later, he directed Goss through the bloody process of lancing an abscess. This form of "telemedicine" for round-the-world racers gained real prominence in 1998 when a Boston doctor, Dan Carlin, talked Russian racer Viktor Yazykov through similar self-surgery on an elbow as he raced in the South Atlantic during the Around Alone contest.

Yazykov had banged his arm and developed a large abscess, which had to be opened and drained. Carlin e-mailed him a detailed, ten-step procedure. Yazykov, a fifty-year-old retired Soviet paratrooper, put on a headlamp, started his video camera, and cut into himself.

Telemedicine had its flaws, however. Yazykov had failed to mention to Carlin that he had been taking about a dozen aspirin a day for arthritis pain. Aspirin thins the blood and inhibits clotting. After the operation Yazykov's arm continued to bleed, covering him and the cabin in blood. Yazykov couldn't contact Carlin immediately because his boat's batteries were low, so he improvised a tourniquet from a bungee cord. When he finally got through to Carlin the next day, his arm had turned white and lost all feeling. Carlin told him to cut the bungee cord loose or he would lose the arm. Yazykov just managed to get to Cape Town without becoming, as he morbidly joked, truly "singlehanded."

Telemedicine could only treat injuries; it couldn't prevent them. In addition to the damage to Proffit's eye, Hervé Jan, a sailmaker and one of *Club Med*'s most experienced drivers, got mugged crossing the trampoline, spraining his ankle badly enough to take him out of the watch rotation for two days. "It is really bumpy, none of the crew have settled in yet, we haven't been able to eat properly," Dalton reported. "Frankly, it's been a tough start to the race. Even though we are in a watch system it is impossible to sleep and everyone is pretty tired."

Aboard *PlayStation,* Steve Fossett and Stan Honey were more upbeat. They had been closely monitoring performance from the start, and even with the added weight of the hull extensions, *PlayStation* seemed a fraction of a knot faster than her Ollier rivals.

Their satisfaction lasted only a few hours into the first evening, though. The wind was blowing a moderate 20 knots and *PlayStation* was powering across a fairly flat sea when there was a bang, and the Solent jib, the basic working headsail, slid down the headstay. The head, or top corner, of the new Cuben Fiber sail had ripped clean away. The surprised crew quickly rolled up the damaged sail and replaced it with the smaller staysail. The wind had been steadily building, so *PlayStation* did not slow down much, but the unexpected failure of a primary sail on the first day of the race was a demoralizing shock. Damian Foxall, a gritty Irishman who had raced everything from single-handed designs to America's Cup boats, had just been heading for his bunk. When he realized what had happened he felt queasy, knowing that if one Cuben Fiber sail failed, others might fail as well.

The next morning, Stu Wilson and Nick Moloney, *PlayStation*'s onboard sailmakers, spread the failed sail across the trampoline and began the arduous task of sewing it back together. Off-watch crew stopped by whenever they could to help push the needle through the stiff material. After working through the day, the sailmakers declared the sail fit for action again. No one was relieved, however. Even as the Solent was being repaired, it was apparent the fabric of the mainsail was suffering too, stretching at the seams and losing shape. Clearly, something was amiss in the engineering of the new Cuben Fiber sails. *PlayStation* raced on, a sense of foreboding building with each sharp gust of wind.

They didn't have to wait long. The following morning, in 27 knots of breeze, there was another heart-stopping bang. The clew of the main — the corner that is fixed to the end of the boom — had surrendered to the huge load and torn free from the sail. There were four clews, or attachment points, climbing the trailing edge of the main which allowed the sail to be set at full hoist or lowered to one of three successive reef points when the wind got up. At the time, *PlayStation* had been sailing with one reef in the main, meaning that it had been lowered to the first of the three reefing clews. It was that first clew that had ripped, and it was immediately apparent that needle, thread, and patching material would never be enough to make the repair.

Losing the head of the Solent was bad; losing a reefing clew on the mainsail was disastrous. The mainsail was the boat's primary engine, and each reef point was like a different gear that *PlayStation* could shift into according to wind strength. Without the first reef clew, the crew would be forced, in certain winds, to choose between carrying too much sail with the main at full hoist (which would be dangerous) and carrying too little sail with the main lowered to the second reef point (which would be slow). Aside from this impossible performance dilemma, everyone had lost faith in the new sails.

"You hear that bang and you just go, 'Fuck. That's it. It's all over, boys,'" Foxall said, recalling the disappointment. The crew went into autopilot, dropping the flapping main to the second reef point. After the swearing ended, there was silence. Foxall and some others gathered in the cockpit and glumly watched as *PlayStation* slowly bled miles to the opposition. *Explorer* crossed close by and then disappeared into the sea smoke. That was the last they would see of her.

For a boat that had been one of the favorites to win because its crew had had the most time to work the kinks out, the serial failure of the sails was a bitter and ironic twist. *PlayStation* had been building a reputation for reliability, but in the final months before The Race Fossett had taken two gambles in hopes of boosting performance. The first was to lengthen the boat, which took her off the water for crucial weeks that the team could have used for sail-testing. The second was to invest in Cuben Fiber sails.

Cuben Fiber had been developed during the 1992 America's

Cup by the winning syndicate, *America³* (which was known as "America Cubed," hence the name Cuben Fiber). It was not so much a new fiber as a novel form of sail construction that produced a stronger and lighter sail. It was very expensive (a mainsail for *PlayStation* cost more than $200,000), and it had never been used in a nonstop round-the-world race, so it wasn't clear how it would hold up. Nevertheless, every reduction in weight, particularly weight carried high up the mast, which induced pitching, meant a small boost in performance. More important, Fossett had concluded that the sheer weight of *PlayStation*'s original mainsail was costing the boat minutes and miles every time the crew struggled to reef or unreef the sail. That mainsail, built from a more conventional cloth called Spectra, weighed almost a ton and would gain weight in the Southern Ocean as it absorbed moisture. A Cuben Fiber main would weigh five to six hundred pounds less and resist taking on water weight.

Steve Fossett was always eager to have an edge and generally willing to spend the money needed to get it. The only hitch was that *PlayStation*'s rebuild would give the crew just one month to test and fine-tune the new sails before The Race. When they were delivered as *PlayStation* returned to the water in late November, they didn't fit quite right and had to be sent back for a recut. *PlayStation* sailed from England to the Mediterranean with her old sails, leaving just a week in Barcelona to fit the Cuben Fiber main and jibs. That made Nick Moloney very nervous.

Moloney, a thirty-two-year-old Australian, was not averse to risk. He had sailed the Southern Ocean, raced for the America's Cup, and windsurfed across the stormy Bass Strait from Australia to Tasmania. But he'd been around race boats enough to be skeptical of unproven sails, and was beginning to lose sleep over Fossett's attachment to the new Cuben Fiber set. Before they were sent back for a recut, Moloney suspected they were slightly underbuilt and might not be up to the abuse they were in for. Just before the start, driven by instinct, experience, and the guts to speak his mind, he went to Fossett and recommended that *PlayStation* race with her old Spectra mainsail. He also urged his skipper to carry the old Spectra jibs as backups if he decided to sail with the new sets.

Fossett was used to analyzing variable risks, but he was in a bind. Moloney might be having doubts about the durability of the Cuben Fiber sails, but the old Spectra mainsail already had fifteen thousand miles of sailing on it and might not prove any more durable. In fact, Fossett doubted it. If both mainsails were questionable, he might as well opt for the main that offered the greatest performance gain and hope for the best.

Now Moloney had been proven prescient and Fossett had lost his wager. With a blown mainsail that couldn't be repaired, Fossett and *PlayStation* had only one hope to stay in the running. They could scramble the shore team to put the old mainsail and jibs on a truck and rendezvous in Gibraltar, just sixty miles and a few hours' sail away. *PlayStation* would have to absorb a stiff penalty, because according to the rules, any boat that stopped had to remain in port for forty-eight hours. But Stan Honey analyzed the weather ahead and advised that the leaders might be slowed by light winds when they cleared the Mediterranean. If *PlayStation* was lucky, she might be able to pick up her old sails in Gibraltar and put to sea again after her forty-eight-hour penance with fewer than five hundred miles to make up. Even so, this was a huge blow so early in the competition, and *PlayStation*'s chances to recoup her losses would depend on great luck with the weather or bad luck aboard the other boats. Her race was not over, but she had been forced to play the expensive assistance card depressingly early in the game. It was a quiet boat that sailed toward port.

If spirits were sinking on *PlayStation*, they were soaring aboard *Team Adventure*. Just forty-eight hours after the start, Cam Lewis and his crew sped between the Pillars of Hercules guarding the entrance to the Mediterranean, sailing at 20 knots and still flying a hull. According to myth, the two promontories that form the Pillars — the Rock of Gibraltar in Europe and Jebel Musa in Africa — had been left by Hercules during his travels. For *Team Adventure* they marked the escape into the wide expanse of the Atlantic and victory in the first mini-leg of The Race. Both *Club Med* and *Explorer* were chasing hard. Still, they were more than thirty miles back, even after Lewis paused near Gibraltar to drop off a television crew he had invited on board to film the first few days. "We sent them home before we started to smell bad," Lewis joked. But the truth was that with the Mediterranean behind, there would be few chances for a camera crew to make an escape as *Team Adventure* dove toward the Southern Ocean. "We are out in the Atlantic, shredding the big blue planet," Lewis crowed as *Team Adventure* turned south toward the coast of Morocco in an attempt to find the best winds to launch the boat to the equator. "I am looking through the office escape hatch at two-time Olympic silver medalist Randy Smyth, who is across the cat on the other hull, driving the machine with a big smile on his face."

Neither Smyth nor Lewis would be smiling for long. Instead of steady ocean breezes, a glutinous high-pressure system was settling over the area (just as Stan Honey had predicted), bringing the sort of light, variable winds guaranteed to drive a sailor mad. *Club Med* and *Explorer* were still in the breeze back in the Mediterranean, but tiring of the battle into headwinds. As *Club Med* finally approached the Strait of Gibraltar, two hours after *Team Adventure* had made her escape, Dalton surveyed his crew — worn out by all the sail changes required to keep pace with Lewis in the blustery conditions — and lamented, "Cam is going a bit fast. I don't think we are sailing badly, they are just very quick at the moment."

Dalton had been hoping to sail as slow as possible while winning, but already it was clear that winning meant sailing very hard and very fast. The lighter winds and easier motion waiting in the Atlantic would allow the *Club Med* team to catch up on some sleep, yet Dalton himself was already battling another problem: a nasty flu that before long would knock off other crew members in *Club Med*'s cramped, infectious living quarters. On top of the flu bug stalking the boat, Guillermo Altadill,

the Spanish Olympic sailor, had sprained his ankle while working at the mast. *Club Med* was in the thick of the race, but she
was still out of synch.

Another twenty miles back, *Explorer* had no flu aboard but
had discovered an unwanted stowaway of a different sort. In the
early hours of the race, skipper Loïck Peyron and navigator
Roger Nilson had been puzzled by a seeming performance handicap. Their cat was just slightly off the pace, which was odd
given the almost identical design of her sister ships. It was not
until the approach to Gibraltar that an explanation presented itself. Skip Novak was down in the starboard hull and heard
water sloshing around. Curious, he checked the ballast tanks —
which were built with valves that would scoop up seawater
when opened — and discovered that the center tank in the starboard hull was half full of water. That meant *Explorer* was carrying an extra thousand pounds. Peyron speculated that the
valve handle must have been inadvertently pushed open during
the frenzied preparations in port.

It was a stupid mistake, yet Peyron managed to keep both his
sense of humor and his perspective, joking to his older brother,
Bruno, at race headquarters that "it was all part of a long-term
strategy." Ironically, Peyron was right. The center ballast tank
proved to have a faulty valve, which the crew isolated to prevent
water from leaking in. Then the starboard aft tank also developed a leak, which defied every effort at repair. Its valve was isolated too, but somehow water still seemed to find a way in. The
only solution was to set up a schedule in which the tank was
checked on every watch and pumped dry. The problem plagued
Explorer all the way around the world.

Peyron's lighthearted attitude was characteristic of his leadership style. Instead of losing his cool over the extra weight, he
tried to defuse everyone's annoyance with a joke. The jokes
came easily because Loïck Peyron had loved sailing since he was
a young boy, when he would stay out late on the water with
Bruno. Together they would sail into the freezing winter months,
sometimes having to pee on their hands to warm them enough

State of the art, 1854: the clipper ship *Lightning*.
Mystic Seaport, Mystic, CT

Captain Joshua Slocum, the first solo circumnavigator, at breakfast. Slocum's thirty-seven-foot *Spray* could be steered with the trim of her sails. *Courtesy of the Joshua Slocum Society*

The pioneers: Blondie Hasler (second from left) with 1960 OSTAR entrants. *PPL*

England's modern sea hero: Sir Francis Chichester. *Chichester Archive/PPL*

"*Muy hombre*": Chichester and *Gipsy Moth IV* battle Cape Horn. *Chichester Archive/PPL*

First nonstop: Knox-Johnston and *Suhaili* approach the finish.
Bill Rowntree/Knox-Johnston Archive/PPL

Knox-Johnston, ready to eat his way around the globe. *Bill Rowntree/Knox-Johnston Archive/PPL*

The Golden Globe's tragic figure: Donald Crowhurst (inset). Crowhurst's abandoned *Teignmouth Electron* in mid-Atlantic. *PPL*

The Golden Globe's mystic figure: Bernard Moitessier. *NI Group*

Vendée Glober Raphael Dinelli facing death in the South. *Sportshoot/PPL*

The Southern Ocean: a day at the office. *Adrian Rayson/PPL*

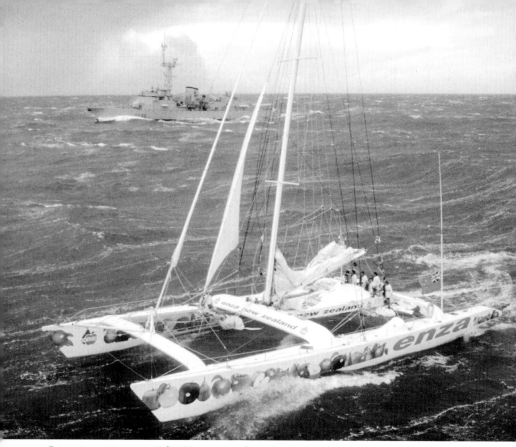

Enza storms to a new Jules Verne record. *Mark Pepper/PPL*

Mugger wave: crossing the trampoline can be dangerous. *Team Adventure/DPPI*

The visionary: Bruno Peyron.
Gilles Martin-Raget

The veteran: *Club Med*'s Grant Dalton.
© *Jacques Caraës/Club Med*

The high flyer: *Team Adventure*'s Cam Lewis. *Jacques Vapillon/DPPI*

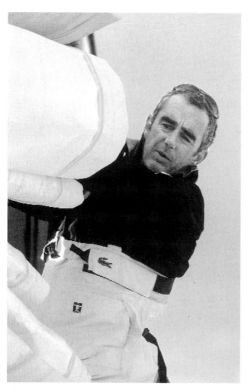

The technician: *Innovation Explorer*'s Loïck Peyron. *Jean-Marie Liot/DPPI*

The multimillionaire: *PlayStation*'s Steve Fossett. *www.fossettchallenge.com*

The dreamer: *Team Philips*'s Pete Goss. *Rick Tomlinson*

The concept: *Team Philips* under way. *Henri Thibault/DPPI*

The nightmare: the wave piercer loses a bow. *Rick Tomlinson*

Ollier pedigree: *Club Med* at speed. *Carlo Borlenghi/Sea & See*

The art of maxi-cat sailing: *Team Adventure* flies a hull.
Jacques Vapillon

The Race begins, December 2000.
Jacques Vapillon

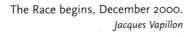

The giant: *PlayStation* and her upswept destroyer bows. *Henri Thibault/DPPI*

Round-the-clock maintenance: *Club Med*'s Jan Dekker replaces a pad eye.
© *Jacques Caraës/Club Med*

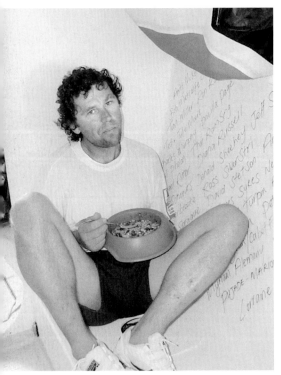

Mealtime on *Team Adventure:* a dog bowl and a few moments of rest. *Team Adventure/DPPI*

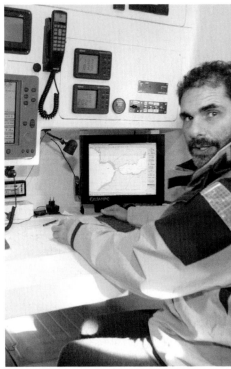

The puzzle palace: Larry Rosenfeld in the nav station. *Jacques Vapillon/DPPI*

Honoring Neptune: the *Team Adventure* crew does it in style. *Team Adventure/DPPI*

Broken boat: Yann Penfornis surveys *Team Adventure*'s main beam in Cape Town. *Team Adventure/DPPI*

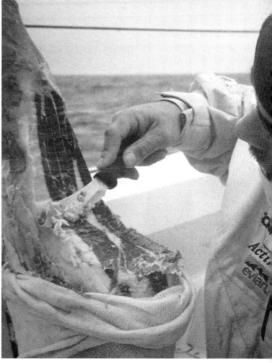

Contraband ham: one way to spice up a bland diet. © *Jacques Caraës/Club Med*

Southern Ocean roller: surfing conditions aboard *Club Med*. © *Jacques Caraës/Club Med*

Bad habit: *Club Med* sticks a bow into a wave. © *Jacques Caraës/Club Med*

Southern Ocean shooting gallery: *Team Adventure* leaves an iceberg behind.
Team Adventure/DPPI

Rounding the Horn: Cam Lewis and *Team Adventure* find snow but no storms.
Team Adventure/DPPI

Sixty-two days: the *Club Med* crew celebrates the fastest circumnavigation ever.
Carlo Borlenghi/Sea & See

to grasp the tiller or a line. Loïck went on to become a superb sailor and, later, a champion and charismatic national hero in France, with millions in sponsorship money for his Formula 60 trimaran. Now forty-two, he had been across the Atlantic thirty-four times and had sailed the world nonstop in the 1989–90 Vendée Globe. He was wiry, energetic, and whip-smart, with a head of close-cropped graying hair, and Skip Novak had never sailed with anyone who had such an instinctive feel for steering and trimming a racing multihull. Loïck would come up on deck at all hours and, with a few subtle adjustments, find that fraction of a knot of additional speed. Behind the wheel he had an ability to take the big catamaran right to the edge of control and keep her there, in a zone that the other drivers and sailors on board found unnerving. "Nobody could match him. He was at a level so far above us it was like night and day," Novak said. "He was comfortable with amounts of sail that had the rest of us struggling and panicking that we wouldn't be able to hang on."

With her ballast tanks empty for the moment, *Explorer* followed her sisters out to the Atlantic. A tight one-design race was now under way among the Ollier boats. No one knew whether *PlayStation* would get back in touch with the fleet. But *Warta Polpharma* and *Team Legato* were clearly outclassed by the maxi-catamarans. Both were more than three hundred miles behind the leaders, and *Team Legato* would soon head for Gibraltar for repairs as well.

With scarcely six hundred miles sailed, The Race was effectively down to three identical catamarans. None of them had made a decisive break in the escape from the Mediterranean. The next objective was to get across the equator.

9

TO THE EQUATOR

Yea, slimy things did crawl with legs
Upon the slimy sea.

— Samuel Taylor Coleridge

Team Adventure bounced and rolled in sluggish seas, struggling in the light winds and determined to keep *Club Med* behind her. On the big catamarans these conditions were just as abusive as heavy weather. The sails slatted freely back and forth without a press of wind to steady them, tugging violently on the sheets and snatching at the fittings. Psyches were tested too, by a frustration that could be relieved only by steady forward acceleration and the slap of water pushed aside by the bows. A few of the crew took advantage of the warm sunshine to stretch out on the expanse of the trampoline. Down below, Jean-Yves Bernot, his face creased in concentration, his hair an unruly cap, pored over the Atlantic weather maps for the fastest route to the equator. It was a problem he and Larry Rosenfeld had been analyzing since well before the start.

The Atlantic leg of any race around the world is the most tactically challenging. To get quickly from the North Atlantic to the South Atlantic is not a matter of simply steering south, as early sailors headed for Cape Town and the Indian Ocean might have done. The Atlantic is like a giant pinball machine, with spinning weather systems and weather holes that can easily trap an unwary or unlucky navigator. The most prominent features are two vast bubbles of high pressure that dominate the centers of the North and South Atlantic. In the north, winds swirl clockwise around the periphery of highs, and in the south counterclockwise. Toward the center of both systems, sometimes known as the Azores High and the St. Helena High for the island groups they encompass, there is often little or no breeze at all.

In the days of the square-riggers, any ship that ventured too close to these breathless zones might spend weeks chasing zephyrs in the effort to escape. If there was no wind, men were sent out in small rowing boats to tow the ship free of the calms. Sailors called these regions the Horse Latitudes. The popular explanation for the name is that Spanish and Portuguese ships transporting men and horses to the New World were sometimes forced by the light winds to throw horses overboard to save on food and water. The more likely explanation is that it sometimes took British ships a month or more to get past these latitudes, by which time the seamen had worked off the advance pay they had been given for signing on. That period of debt was known as the "dead horse." Its completion was a cause for celebration, which included hoisting an effigy of a horse stuffed with straw to the yardarm and cutting it loose to fall into the sea while the crew sang, "Old man, your horse must die."

To skirt the Horse Latitudes, ships heading south wanted to stay to the east of the Azores High and to the west of the St. Helena High, to take advantage of the clockwise and counterclockwise wind rotation and keep the wind behind them. Next up was a zone that extends from roughly 30° north to 30° south latitude, where they would find the famous trade winds. At the equator, heated air rises into the atmosphere, creating a vacuum that the trades rush to fill. As they blow toward the equator, the earth's rotation to the east bends the winds to the west. This is known as the Coriolis effect, and it means that in the Northern Hemisphere the trades blow from the northeast, and in the Southern Hemisphere they blow from the southeast.

The trade winds are warm, reliable breezes that blow anywhere from 15 to 25 knots. They produce some of the most pleasant sailing on earth, high daily average runs, and earned their name over the centuries by speedily and efficiently moving commerce from the Old World to the New. Matthew Maury studied these beneficent winds and wrote that they "blow perpetually, and are as steady and as constant as the currents of the Mississippi River." It was in the trade winds that *Enza* recorded a record-breaking 520-mile twenty-four-hour run during her 1994 Jules Verne voyage. It was also in the trades that Donald Crowhurst believed he could get away with claiming a single-handed twenty-four-hour record, the first outright deception of his final, fatal journey.

Everyone in the fleet was well aware of the exhilarating speeds that lay ahead, but to catch the trades the catamarans had to get some four hundred miles south, to the Canary Islands off the coast of Africa. When the Azores High is strong, that passage is normally a downwind run. As it happened, the progression of winter storms across the North Atlantic had disrupted the usual pattern. "The boats made it to Barcelona [sailing] to windward. They have now left and are still sailing to windward," observed Bruno Peyron from race headquarters in Paris. "It's crazy."

The craziness put a special burden on navigators and weather routers to get the tactical choices right. The first boat to break into the steady trade winds to the south might get a big jump on the rest of the fleet. "It's a cat-and-mouse game out here, searching for wind and second-guessing the tactics aboard the other boats," *Team Adventure* conavigator Larry Rosenfeld reported. Navigators and onshore weather routers were in constant contact, analyzing the smallest changes in the forecast. There were two basic choices: head south along the African coast, which was the direct route to the equator but probably subject to lighter winds, or go west toward a weather front approaching from the central Atlantic. The route west would mean extra miles, but the front was packing strong northwest winds that would deliver higher sailing speeds.

The choice hinged on how fast the front would move east. If

it was slow, boats headed directly south would suffer and those that went west would make out. If it moved swiftly to the east, any boat in the west would have sailed extra miles without gaining a big advantage. Other tactical considerations complicated this decision. The farther from the competition any boat strayed, the greater its potential gains — or losses — as the weather changed.

The choices in the clipper ship and Golden Globe eras were in a way much simpler. All a skipper could do was sail the best route indicated by historical data and his own experience, and take advantage of every wind shift available. The Race fleet, in contrast, had a wealth of weather and position information to weigh. Blondie Hasler and the purists who had given round-the-world racing its start might have scorned the level of outside assistance streaming into the nav station of each boat. Technology had, in effect, transformed a round-the-world race into the equivalent of a close inshore race in which all the competitors could see one another and peek into the future besides. At times all the variables could be overwhelming. Still, Grant Dalton, who had sailed five Whitbread races without outside forecasting, was one sailor who was glad to have all the input. "I think it is more fun," he explained. "We are able to do a more clinical job on the route we choose . . . This is after all a mechanized sport. Technology and everything is here to stay."

"We're really running a twenty-four-hour round-the-clock weather station here," Cam Lewis observed from *Team Adventure* as the cat clawed her way clear of the Strait of Gibraltar. All the technology could not manufacture a breeze, though. About the only crew happy with the slow pace was aboard *PlayStation*, serving their penalty time in Gibraltar and readying the boat for sea again with the old mainsail and Solent. For once, light winds were a gift, practically gluing the three lead boats in place and reducing the probable loss to about four hundred miles. Spirits on Fossett's boat, so low after the horrific sail failures, were climbing. The crew believed *PlayStation* was a fast boat. With thousands of miles of racing still to come, no one was ready to write her off just yet. "*PlayStation* points high and is impressively fast," Loïck Peyron acknowledged. "The boat is quick."

Before the start, Fossett and Honey had been keen to get into the lead, where they could try to control the fleet by staying between the pursuing boats and the finish. Now they would be forced to press hard from behind, taking even greater risks with the weather and gear failure than the lead boats. But *PlayStation* had proved reliable up to the start, and her hefty hulls and raised bows were well suited for heavy-weather running in the big seas of the Southern Ocean. If *PlayStation*'s luck with the weather held, she might be able to close some of the gap during the passage across the equator. The ten thousand miles of rough ocean around Antarctica would also be a chance to grind down the boats ahead or perhaps just catch a good break. During the 1994 Jules Verne matchup between *Enza* and *Sport Elec*, *Enza* opened up a lead of more than fourteen hundred miles early in the Southern Ocean. Yet by the time she cleared Cape Horn, that lead was down to around three hundred miles. The light winds of an unusual high-pressure system had caught *Enza* between New Zealand and South America, proving once again that the weather gods will have their fun. Fossett and the crew hoped to see that joke again.

Off the coast of Morocco, however, no one was contemplating the Southern Ocean. Tack to starboard, wind shift, tack to port. Struggle against the fitful southwesterly breeze. Since the start, boat speeds had averaged less than 10 knots — more suitable for a fast monohull and well below the 20-to-25-knot average speeds the boats could make in the right conditions. Even Grant Dalton, who had logged more round-the-world miles than anyone in The Race, had had enough. "Whoever said that sailing round the world was downwind," he grumbled. "It's beginning to get on one's nerves." Loïck Peyron agreed. Desperate for new wind from a better direction, all three Ollier catamarans decided to work their way west, *Team Adventure* leading the way. "The game right now is to drag race to the cold front coming across the Atlantic from the west," Cam Lewis explained. The choice made a sort of sense, but that didn't make it any easier to stomach. "You can't believe the weather conditions we've got," Peyron complained from *Explorer*. "We are forced to tack in the opposite direction to our route."

The skippers wanted more breeze, and they soon got it. As they approached the island of Madeira, the winds in advance of the coming front picked up and restored the double-digit speeds the crews had signed on for. Higher speeds had the boats pounding into the waves. Peyron urged his crew to preserve the cat by sailing a little slower. As the wind and seas continued to build, *Explorer* became the first to bail out, tacking south toward the Moroccan coast. Dalton was down in the nav station talking with Quilter and Badham about whether *Club Med* should keep sailing toward the front. Badham was firm. "No way are we going to do that," he told Dalton, predicting winds of 30 to 35 knots. "I'm happy with twenty-five," Dalton responded. So *Club Med* also turned south toward the equator, sailing into lighter winds to wait for the front and cannily taking up a position between *Explorer* to the east and *Team Adventure* to the west. "There's probably a bit more pressure [wind] to the west," Dalton said. "But you can't take too much of a hit to get there."

This simple tactical choice was a good illustration of Dalton and Quilter's straightforward racing philosophy. Hundreds of thousands of racing miles had convinced them it rarely paid to stray too far from the direct route. Multihull sailors were more inclined to chase after wind in their constant quest for more boat speed. The multihull world had wondered whether Dalton and Quilter would adapt their routing philosophy to the big, fast catamarans (and some of the French experts on *Club Med* weren't happy with Dalton's decision to turn south). Apparently they wouldn't, preferring to sail more directly at the mark, even if it meant going a little slower. "It doesn't feel any different," Dalton commented. "There's me and Lowie in the nav station. Me losing the rest of my hair and Lowie going grayer. And it's just like we've done the last eight years."

Despite the fact that his two adversaries had turned south,

Lewis kept steaming west. Bernot and Rosenfeld had done a great job of getting *Team Adventure* out of the Mediterranean in the lead, and now they were convinced that west was best. The route would take the cat on an unorthodox path to the north of Madeira. No matter. It wasn't always easy to anticipate what the chasing fleet was going to do, and to Lewis it seemed obvious that getting to the new wind first would pay off. Lewis and his brain trust touched all the bases. They talked with their onshore forecasters. They analyzed infrared satellite images and the barometer — "and even consulted the curly hair on the back of my neck," Lewis e-mailed. "Jean-Yves (our crack navigator) says, 'Go for it.'" So they did.

Now there was nothing for the three crews to do but sail hard for twenty-four hours and see what the winds would bring. The wait was most difficult for the crew of *Team Adventure*. They had led The Race for most of the first four days. Now they had to endure a succession of position reports showing them dropping behind the competition as they opted for position over the direct route. "We think it is one step back for two steps forward," conavigator Larry Rosenfeld said. "It's a gamble, but Jean-Yves Bernot and I think it is an informed one." Grant Dalton wasn't so sure. "This could be the first real break of the race," he predicted. "*Team Adventure* may be okay, but they may have gone too far."

The cold front swept over *Team Adventure* almost twelve hours after the other catamarans had tacked south. Her speed quickly climbed to more than 20 knots, but she was now a good 130 miles behind *Club Med* and *Explorer*. Bernot and Rosenfeld had been right about the increased wind speeds and favorable wind angle, but they hadn't fully anticipated the price of getting there in rough seas. With every mile sailed aboard the maxi-catamarans, it was becoming clear that sailing upwind in any real breeze was both slow and very taxing for the boat and crew.

Team Adventure had been in battle, changing headsails, reefing and unreefing the mainsail, and coping with gear failure as vicious rain squalls blasted through in advance of the front. By the time she was past Madeira and could head south, she had broken some mainsail battens, the long, thin rods that give the mainsail its shape. "We wanted to avoid the ridge of high pressure over the Canaries," Jean-Yves Bernot, a much-chastened weather "Wizard," admitted. "This was a mistake because we had real trouble moving westward . . . We also pushed the boat a little harder than we should have done. We still have much to learn about this boat." Worse, the front had swept east faster than expected, delivering the better breeze to the two lead boats. "They were able to cut the corner on us," Lewis acknowledged later. Racing is a game that requires one educated guess after another. Every skipper and navigator guesses wrong sometimes. The key is to make fewer bad guesses than the competition.

With two battens splintered and in danger of doing damage to the mainsail, getting the mainsail lowered and the battens repaired became an urgent problem. By the time the battens had been replaced and all the sails set properly, *Team Adventure* had spent some twelve hours at reduced speeds. That cost the former leader another seventy-five miles to the competition, further negating the expected benefits of being to the west. Lewis was frustrated but determined to fight his way back to the front. "This cat has nine lives, and that was just a half day off one of them," he warned. "We are by no means out of the rat race to the middle of the earth." Flying every scrap of sail she could stand in the fresh northerly breeze, the big cat arrowed south in pursuit, hitting a top speed of 37½ knots, with the crew on deck whooping and hollering with excitement. No matter how grim the tactical outlook, aboard a sailboat there is no better tonic than going very, very fast.

While the Ollier catamarans sweated over their route to the Canary Islands, *PlayStation* completed her forty-eight-hour penalty in Gibraltar and sailed into the Atlantic to rejoin The Race. The weather had been merciful, to a point. By Fossett's calculation, *PlayStation* had lost fifty-six hours to the rest of the fleet. Yet when she finally departed Gibraltar, she was about 350 miles behind. "This is a huge deficit. At the anticipated pace of the race, we will have to average a half knot faster than the lead boat in order to win," Fossett calculated as *PlayStation* got under way. "But the entire crew is game and so much can happen during an around-the-world passage. SO WE ARE ON."

Fossett and Honey were grateful the deficit wasn't eight hundred or a thousand miles. Still, they were playing catch-up with heavier sails that already had endured thousands of miles of wear and tear. Fossett had also ordered some old Spectra jibs back aboard — he didn't intend to run out of sails again. All told, *PlayStation* was carrying around half a ton of additional weight in her chase across the oceans. All in all, Fossett and Honey figured they would be lucky if *PlayStation* could close most of the gap by the time the fleet passed through Cook Strait, between the North and South Islands of New Zealand, a little more than halfway around the globe.

Any mistakes up front would of course be welcomed, and Dalton was still enjoying the benefits of *Team Adventure*'s misstep off Madeira. "They went front-chasing and found it pretty rough at thirty-five knots, which is too hard on these boats, going upwind," he observed. But with the Canary Islands approaching fast, Dalton was about to make his own mistake. The Canaries are an archipelago of seven inhabited islands surrounded by numerous barren islets. They lie just below 30° north latitude and mark the start of the trade winds region. The islands were named by the Roman scholar Pliny the Elder, not for a prevalence of yellow birds but for the packs of roaming dogs (*canes* in Latin) he had seen while visiting there. Situated almost directly on the preferred sailing track from Europe to the Southern Ocean, the Canaries had become a familiar waypoint for the trading ships of the nineteenth century as well as for modern sailboat racers. Joshua Slocum had sailed close by Fuerteventura, the island closest to Africa, leaving all the islands to leeward.

Dalton and Quilter had originally intended to sail clear of the Canaries as well. After looking at the weather and routing models from his office in Australia, Badham urged them to change course to the west and stay with that plan. Dalton was wary, however. Badham's computer couldn't account for the greater abuse *Club Med* would suffer if she sailed closer to the wind on the new heading. "We can't point where you want me to point," he told Badham. "It would be too hard on the boat."

Dalton wasn't only worried about wind angle. He was also concerned that seas off the Canaries had been churned up by the front that had just passed through. He decided to cut inside the westernmost island, La Palma, expecting fast sailing and smooth water. Sometimes winds accelerated as they were compressed in the passages between islands, a phenomenon known as the Venturi effect. Unfortunately, *Club Med* instead ran into a painful blanket effect. The wind abruptly shut off between the islands, slowing the cat from more than 20 knots to less than 8. For five hours, in the dark of night, the crew remained locked in a tortuous effort to break loose from the lee of La Palma. By the time *Club Med* resumed the parade south, Dalton estimated that she had dropped fifty miles, handing the lead to *Explorer,* which maddeningly slipped without incident through the passage between Fuerteventura and Gran Canaria.

The pain was only partially mitigated by the arrival of the trade winds south of the islands. *Club Med* piled on the sail, and over the next twenty-four hours she clocked 450 miles. She was averaging more than 18 knots, three times the speed achieved by a typical nineteenth-century vessel in these same winds. Even Dalton, finally recovering from his flu, was up on deck enjoying the sun and beautiful sailing as he directed the crew on a stem-to-stern check of the boat and its hardware.

Explorer was also reveling in the trade wind sailing and the steady climb up the leader board. "We like our lead. I think we deserve it," coskipper Novak commented. But the advance took *Explorer* toward the African coast — "a beach strategy," as Peyron quipped, that was suitable for a tanning contest but not necessarily a race around the world. *Explorer* was well east of the preferred westerly crossing point for the equator. Shore-based router Pierre Lasnier and navigator Roger Nilson waited patiently for a good wind angle to move west to *Club Med*'s line near the Canary Islands, but the wind refused to cooperate. The Cape Verde Islands, seven hundred miles to the south, were fast approaching when Peyron decided to bite the bullet and steer west. When he did, both *Club Med* and *Team Adventure* would come screaming down from the north, devouring *Explorer*'s lead. "I know we are going to lose ground within the next twenty-four hours, but we need to get in some westing, there's no way to escape it," Peyron lamented.

Explorer had barely showed Africa her sterns when there was a loud, unnerving bang. Skip Novak rushed onto the deck, certain the fitting that anchored the large headsail had exploded. Peyron suspected a problem lower down. He ordered the boat to a halt and sent watch leader Loïc Le Mignon over the side with mask and snorkel to inspect the daggerboard. Le Mignon found no damage but did see a few shreds of flesh hanging off the leading edge. Apparently, the boat had hit a small fish, probably a shark. She was lucky. Anything larger, a small whale even, might have shattered the board or the trunk that held it in place.

The daggerboards and rudders on any catamaran were vulnerable to collision. Accordingly, Ollier had designed the board so that it could be removed from the trunk and reversed if the lower end was damaged — accepted design practice, since splintered boards were not uncommon. That wasn't necessary this time, but the danger posed by flotsam had been magnified by the higher speed of the maxi-cats. It was an x factor that technology had yet to eliminate. Small sonar systems that could be installed in the bows to warn of impending collisions with whales, ice, or containers were hitting the market just before The Race. The technology was unproven, however. And at $25,000 a unit, the cost and weight were hard to justify.

Aside from the occasional run-ins with marine life, the trade wind sailing was truly showcasing the unprecedented speed potential of the maxi-catamarans. All three Ollier boats reeled off a steady succession of 400-plus–mile days, frequently exceeding the best twenty-four-hour runs ever posted by clipper ships in the Southern Ocean (a single-day record of 465 miles was claimed by the *Champion of the Seas* in 1854).* *Club Med* and *Explorer* sailed from the Canaries to the Cape Verde Islands in under two days, a transit that took the Golden Globe racers more than a week to complete. *Team Adventure* was going faster than anyone as she pressed to catch up to the leaders, knocking off one twenty-four-hour run of 586.5 miles at an average speed of 24.4 knots. That was barely 39 miles shy of *Club Med*'s 2000 world-record mark of 625 miles (also set in the trade winds), and eclipsed by 6 miles *PlayStation*'s 1999 world record of 580 miles. By the time she reached Cape Verde, she had passed *Explorer* and closed to within 75 miles of *Club Med*.

Dalton watched this blazing display of speed sailing and grew even more certain that *Club Med* would have trouble matching *Team Adventure* boat for boat if they ever started sailing in the same water. He was also nervous about the flat-out pace being forced by the newer Ollier boats, because it was undermining his Juan Fangio strategy. "I'm really impressed," he admitted. "I didn't think they would be pushing so hard." Dalton had the crew conduct yet another full boat check, with a man up the mast to inspect all the rigging and Franck Proffit worming his way through the hulls in search of cracks or any other signs of impending failure.

Predictably, the breakneck pace victimized the boat that could least afford trouble. Almost one week into The Race, in the early hours of the day, *PlayStation*'s mainsheet parted. On *PlayStation* the pull of the mainsheet on the mainsail helped keep the mast in position while the boat was sailing. If the sheet parted under a load, the sudden release would cause the mast to whip forward. The force could easily send the mast crashing to the deck, which had happened on another Fossett catamaran a few years

---

*Chichester, ever skeptical, had scrutinized this claim closely and concluded it was probably bogus, an attempt at hype to win more freight and passengers. His vote for the greatest twenty-four-hour run by a clipper went to a 430-mile sprint recorded by the *Lightning* in 1857.

earlier. The on-deck crew waited in suspense to see if *PlayStation*'s beefy mast would survive the shock. To the surprise of many, it did. A substitute sheet was quickly put in place to stabilize the mast and allow *PlayStation* to keep sailing at half speed. But it took five hours to splice a replacement for the multistrand line and get the boat running at full speed again. "We were really lucky," Fossett admitted. *PlayStation* had thrown another fifty miles to the leaders. If Lewis was right and a big cat had nine lives, *PlayStation* had already used up two of hers.

The fleet might have been tempted to conclude that Fossett's hard-pressed cat was unlucky. But no one expected to complete The Race without some serious drama. A few hours later it was *Club Med*'s turn. As she sailed past the Cape Verde Islands, flying a full 1,200 square meters of sail in 30 knots of wind, the cable that connected the helm in the port hull to the steering quadrant jumped clear of its track. Neal McDonald felt the wheel go mushy in his hands, and at more than 20 knots *Club Med* turned up toward the wind and lifted a hull out of the water — the prelude to a catastrophic broach and capsize. Dalton was down in the nav station conferring with Quilter, and both stared helplessly through the large porthole that doubled as an escape hatch as more and more sky appeared under the opposite hull. "We're broaching, you know," Quilter observed with calm detachment. "The boat went right up, like right up," Dalton recalled. "We didn't know what had happened, but it didn't take long to work it out." Within seconds their race might be over and crew might be swimming for their lives to get out from under the nets. McDonald didn't say a word, but the crew in the cockpit with him responded with lightning reflexes. Steffano Rizzi, an Italian Whitbread and America's Cup veteran, and Fred Le Peutrec immediately eased the big mainsail, to release the pressure of the wind that was trying to turn the big catamaran over. *Club Med* settled back down on both hulls and rounded up into the wind. Ten crew raced to the deck and rolled up the huge foresail that was now flogging in the wind.

McDonald thought the rudder had broken, then suspected the culprit might in fact be the steering cable. When he had first inspected *Club Med* he had noticed the quadrant connecting the cable to the rudder didn't have enough lip and knew that if the cable lost tension it would slip off. But it was one of those pre-race problems that received only halfhearted attention. Now he was faced with the question of how to get *Club Med* going again. Maybe the wheel in the starboard cockpit was still working. "Fuck it," he told Le Peutrec. "I'm going down to look. There isn't much point in me holding on to the wheel on this side." He set off across the trampoline only to see a spectral half-naked figure, bathed in the light of a tropical moon, already manning the other steering station. It was Franck Proffit, helping *Club Med* out of the jam wearing only his boxers and a pair of socks. Proffit had raced to the deck from his bunk as soon as he sensed trouble, and he was slowly turning the big cat back onto its course. "So this wheel's working, then?" McDonald asked, suppressing a laugh.

The crisis was over. Ten minutes after the wheel went slack *Club Med* was racing again. The faulty steering cable was re-led and tightened so both wheels were back in service. McDonald reached for a cigarette and appeared to finish it in one long drag. "It was the only time I saw Neal with scared eyes," Rizzi said later. *Club Med*'s near-death experience was a reminder that even in pleasant sailing conditions the margin of error on the big cats was razor thin. Complacency could bring an end to The Race and even kill. It was one of the reasons that Cam Lewis had imposed a two-hour limit behind the wheel.

Endless maintenance — boat checks, winch servicing, sail repair, engine work — was another way to reduce the margin of error, particularly in anticipation of the Southern Ocean leg, when routine upkeep and repairs might be difficult to carry out. "I can think of twenty things which would have stopped us from finishing that we managed to get sorted before we started," McDonald said. "And probably another ten things during the race that would have stopped us if we had not got on top of them right away." One new maintenance item was especially onerous if not terribly threatening: flying fish patrol. Flying fish are silver and blue fish, usually six to ten inches long, that leap from the water and glide through the air to escape predators. They have been known to jump as high as thirty-six feet above the surface of the sea and can "fly" up to two hundred yards, sometimes whole schools of them.

For sailors past and present easing through the trade winds, flying fish were a tasty addition to the limited shipboard menu. Found each morning lying lifeless on the decks after inadvertently flying into the sails or hull, they could be scooped up and thrown into a pan. Many sailors believed that shining a light on the mainsail at night would dramatically increase the haul. Most of the seasoned single-handers ate them regularly, although lately sensibilities had changed somewhat. Ellen MacArthur, a young British single-hander sailing in the Vendée Globe, passed the same region a few months earlier and tired herself out running around her boat trying to return the gasping fish to the sea before they expired. The Race might have killed her, because the maxi-catamarans initiated a far more deadly relationship between boat and flying fish. "This kitty is a fish eater," Cam Lewis observed. "One hull scares them up; then as a genetic self-preservation they fly, not realizing that sixty feet away is another hull and above them is a tennis-court-sized cheese grater — our trampoline. Splat, splat, splat is the sound down here in the nav station."

The unique interaction of flying fish and maxi-cat might have been dismissed as an ecological curiosity save for two factors. A flying fish at 20 knots, closing with a boat or crewman moving at speeds up to 30 knots, can reach a collision speed as high as 50 knots. The fish, in short, were dangerous missiles that could bruise flesh or take out an eye. Goggles and helmets were the preferred protection, and even they didn't prevent the occasional body strike. Almost as bad was the stench from hundreds of fish carcasses rotting in the tropical sun. Each morning the decks were covered with fish guts and eyeballs. Sometimes they were hitting the hulls so frequently they sounded like popcorn.

Somehow the fish managed to find their way into the most obscure parts of the boat. In the southeast trades, one flew straight down an open hatch aboard *Club Med* and flopped around on the computer keyboards in the media station in the port hull. It was subdued by a surprised Jacques Caraës, *Club Med*'s cameraman, but not before sliming the sensitive equipment and infecting the cramped space with a lingering fishy odor. During his Whitbread years Dalton had had a reputation for slipping flying fish into his crew's gear, but this was too much even for him, especially since he liked a clean boat. "There is flying fish blood and entrails everywhere," he complained. "It is like a scene from *The Godfather*!"

The Southern Cross now blazed above the horizon. On clear nights it was the most recognizable constellation in the southern sky, and over the centuries it had become a sentimental beacon for Southern Hemisphere seamen. In the nineteenth century, when square-riggers in the nitrate trade on South America's west coast were ready for sea, a wooden representation of the Southern Cross, with fixed white and red lights, was hoisted to the top of the mast while the sailors sang, "Hurrah, my boys, we're homeward bound."

For navigators in The Race, the Southern Cross had a less benign import. It was a sign that the boats were descending toward the most devilish weather zone of the Atlantic, a twisted funhouse of torpid calms punctuated by violent squalls that lay across the equator. This was the Doldrums — technically known as the Intertropical Convergence Zone, or ITCZ — where the northeast and southeast trade winds meet, and air rising off the middle of the earth sucks all the wind up into the atmosphere. Sailors need air to move horizontally across the earth's surface. In the Doldrums it goes vertical, leaving large swaths of ocean with no appreciable breeze. The French refer to the region as the "Pot of Tar." The English name, Doldrums, probably derives from the Old English words "dol" (meaning dull) and "tantrum" and captures the painful contradictions of the zone.

It was a place in which races could be won and lost. The Doldrums are highly capricious, moving north and south around the equator according to the season, and breaking up or clamping down according to the passage of weather systems. Sometimes they're rife with squalls, sometimes quiet. Heavy, square-rigged ships could get lucky and cross in a matter of days, or they might drift for weeks. It was in the Doldrums and the Horse Latitudes that sailors desperate for wind turned to superstition. One ritual was to stick a knife into the mast and whistle — but softly, lest a storm be summoned. A more brutal solution, perhaps reflecting the madness brought on by blazing heat and no wind, was to flog the cabin boy with his back facing in the direction from which wind was desired.

Over the centuries, it became apparent that the Doldrums were roughly wedge-shaped, wider off the coast of Africa and narrower to the west. Many clipper and square-rigger captains learned to get out toward the middle of the Atlantic before daring a passage across "the Line." That took them past the St. Peter and St. Paul Rocks, northeast of Brazil, a strategy that Maury generally endorsed in his *Sailing Directions*. Sometimes, however, decent passages farther east could be made, which resulted in a faster sailing angle relative to the wind once the southeast trades were found. "The calm belts at sea, like mountains on the land, stand mightily in the way of the voyager," Maury advised. "But, like mountains, they have their passes and their gaps."

For the clipper captains and even for sailors like Moitessier and Knox-Johnston, finding those gaps was more a matter of luck than skill. The advent of satellite weather forecasting since their time had made picking a route through the Doldrums more scientific, but the technology wasn't accurate enough to entirely eliminate the mysteries of the fickle zone. Modern racing boats might be becalmed for days only to see another competitor sailing by just miles away on a fair wind. For any navigator or skipper, whether racing down the Atlantic with cargo or racing around the world, the Doldrums were a meteorological torment that could mean losing hours and days.

The navigators aboard *Team Adventure, Club Med,* and *Explorer,* after weeks of studying the North Atlantic weather picture before setting sail, had an idea of where they wanted to cross the Doldrums and the equator. Historically, most racing navigators followed nineteenth-century precedent and considered the longitudes around 30° west the most favorable zone in which to cut the line, balancing the desire to find a narrow band of calms against the tactical advantage of being to the east when the southeast trades finally kicked in. *Club Med*'s Mike Quilter had, over four Whitbread races, demonstrated a consistent affinity for 28° west. Quilter and Badham had been studying the Doldrums crossing off and on for almost a year, and they agreed before the start that that was about where *Club Med* should go. But the exigencies of racing and weather have no respect for advance planning. Tactics and winds kept the boats to the east, and it was proving hard to find a favorable wind angle for going the other way. South of the Cape Verde Islands *Club Med* was only at 23° west, trying to protect an eighty-mile lead over *Team Adventure,* just to her north and west. Sailing west to hit the preferred line would cost *Club Med* about five hours, more than enough to hand *Team Adventure* the lead again if she held her course.

Magellan's sixteenth-century fleet, the first to circumnavigate, spent three painful weeks in the fluky winds of the Doldrums. But Magellan had been navigating blind. Back in Australia, Badham was poring over high-resolution satellite images, showing visible light, infrared, and water vapor, to map out the contours and breaks in the Doldrums. Real-time data also provided wind strengths and directions. After twenty-four nearly sleepless hours, he came to a critical conclusion: the way the Doldrums were set up, crossing on the longitude *Club Med* was already sailing would probably be as good as crossing between 25° and 28° west. So why waste five hours sailing west? After a lot of satellite phone time, Dalton and Quilter rolled the dice and pointed their big blue catamaran's bows directly south. "We are basically applying as much technology as possible to solve a very random and complex natural phenomenon," Dalton said.

Team Adventure had detected the same eastern gap in the Doldrums and followed suit, drag racing *Club Med* to the equator. Pierre Lasnier, *Explorer*'s shoreside router, strongly argued for a traditional westerly crossing. Roger Nilson and Skip Novak, who had been schooled in fleet racing tactics in multiple Whitbread campaigns, disagreed. *Explorer* was already to the west of the other two boats and would make some gains if Lasnier proved right. If she sailed farther west, she might make even bigger gains. If Lasnier was wrong, however, she would also incur bigger losses. Sailboat racing tactics are all about evaluating risk and reward, and Novak and Nilson, huddled in the nav station with Peyron, were not inclined to separate themselves from the other two boats and risk a big loss so early in The Race. "If you want to go west, go fifty miles, not two hundred," Novak argued. "That's something you do at the end of a race and you need to gamble to catch up. Let's just see if we can stay in touch with these guys."

It was a crucial decision and laid bare the difficulty that Lasnier and Nilson were having working together. Nilson, an intense, careful navigator, was used to making decisions on the seas, because the Whitbread did not allow outside assistance when the boats were racing. Lasnier, on the other hand, liked to analyze weather and possible routes and then tell the boats he was working with where to go. He had teamed up with Peyron a number of times before on transatlantic races that allowed outside routing, and in such races the busy sailors were generally content to let the routers dictate the course. In Nilson Lasnier had a navigator who wanted to discuss the reasoning behind his advice, and he was not used to giving explanations. "You must go to the west," Lasnier insisted. "This is not my advice," Nilson told Peyron flatly. Peyron was caught between the strong views of his navigator and coskipper and those of his long-time router. Going farther west would be an early gamble, but maybe

Explorer needed to adopt a gambling style. If *Explorer* followed in the tracks of *Club Med* and *Team Adventure,* she was unlikely to gain many miles.

In the end, Peyron did not have time to both run the boat and debate navigation. He fell back on his relationship with and faith in Lasnier. His recommendations sometimes seemed a little nutty, but in Peyron's experience they delivered two out of three times. "We are probably not the fastest boat," Peyron told himself. "We have to do something different." He gave the order. *Explorer* turned west, sailing parallel to the equator instead of directly for it. Ironically, Peyron was adopting exactly the Doldrums strategy that Quilter and Badham had agreed on before the start and then abandoned. It was a costly repositioning, and Nilson had to suppress his frustration. At the Cape Verde Islands *Explorer* had been just seventy-five miles behind *Club Med,* in second place. By the time she made her turn south for the equator at 27° west longitude, she was more than three hundred miles behind.

Club Med hit the Doldrums wall first, at about 4° north latitude. Her speed quickly dropped from more than 15 knots to around 5 knots, allowing *Team Adventure,* on a line just to the west, to close to within forty miles. "We are in it here," Dalton announced. "Black clouds behind us, in front of us, all around." Unlike heavier, more conventional boats, *Club Med* did not grind to a halt but continued whispering along at a steady 5 to 7 knots. Still, it felt almost like a dead stop in a boat that had recently been cruising at more than 20 knots, day in and day out.

Picking through the Doldrums is a black art that requires constant attention to obscure signs. Satellite and weather forecasting technology can help the routers position the boats in zones of high cloud cover, which indicate some atmospheric activity, or in clear areas where winds have blown low-lying clouds away. Once the boats have chosen their line going in, however, they are sailing too slowly to reposition much if they get stuck. At its core, Doldrums sailing is good old-fashioned seat-of-the-pants sailing, with constant trimming and men up the mast looking for any sign of breeze. Sailors also scan the horizon for rain squalls, because they have plenty of wind on their peripheries. Crews that are both lucky and good can use the squalls to hopscotch across an otherwise windless zone.

The Doldrums do have one redeeming quality, though. A high-performance racing designer wouldn't give a second's thought to including the weight of a shower aboard. *Team Adventure*'s first severe rain squall saw a pack of naked crewmen on deck madly soaping themselves in hopes of having enough time to rinse off before the downpour let up. Other crews put the Doldrums to use too. During a lull, *Explorer* sent a diver over the side to take another look at the fish-eating daggerboard. *Club Med* did the same. In the really dull moments, sailors reached for their books, if they had been allowed to stow one or two aboard. On multi-lingual *Club Med*, Franck Proffit noted a clear-cut cultural distinction: "Anglos sleep, Frenchies read."

Most of all, everyone stresses. "My heart and brain are in my mouth at the moment as we cross this soft stuff," Badham admitted. "At this stage, I can't see *Team Adventure* or *Explorer* getting through without us . . . but it would be really nice if the opposite occurred." Dalton had been through enough Doldrums-related reversals to remain phlegmatic. In the 1997–98 Whitbread he had gained a few miles, but in the 1993–94 edition he had watched 140 miles evaporate. "I'm pretty philosophical about this. If they get ahead, we'll just have to pass them again," he said. "We won't really be able to assess who has done best with this until the first boat crosses the equator."

This time around Dalton bled a few miles. As *Club Med* entered the Doldrums they started to drift south with her. *Team Adventure*, following behind, stayed in the trade winds longer before she hit the calms. The two boats ended up just twenty-eight miles apart in the light and shifty breeze. In lockstep, they fought for every degree of southing they could manage, hoping to pop first into the southeast trade winds. Aboard *Team Adventure* the crew took perverse pleasure in dogging Dalton relentlessly. Mikael Lundh, a good-natured Swede, captured the mood in an e-mail to his wife, Inga. "There has been a rumor circulating *Club Med* has been surprised there is competition on The Race course," he wrote. "Funny, we think, but of course it's only a rumor."

Keeping in touch with Dalton and his crew was hard work, though. In Jean-Yves Bernot *Team Adventure* had a navigator who had spent much of his life studying the Doldrums. He had even lived on the equator for two months aboard a French research ship, making observations. Yet even with a certified expert, there was no way to escape the pain of sailing through the zone. One minute the sails would be slatting back and forth in a windless hole, threatening to snap more battens. Next, *Team Adventure* would be rocketing through a 30-knot black squall on the edge of control. Boat speeds ping-ponged between 1 knot and 30. "This is my first experience in the Doldrums," *Team Adventure*'s Larry Rosenfeld said. "And it's pretty amazing to see the hurricane factory."

Each mile of progress was so important and so hard-won that Dalton kept most of his crew on permanent standby to take advantage of every squall blast or cat's-paw of wind. As philosophical as he tried to be, it was hard for him to suppress his frustration as *Team Adventure* seemed to gain mile after mile in the black clouds and squalls. Adding to Dalton's somber mood was his expectation that, based on performance so far, *Team Adventure* would be slightly faster in the trade winds ahead. *Club Med* would have to keep pressing, putting more wear and tear on the boat and on the crew before she even got to the Southern Ocean. Lundh had been right: Dalton had not envisioned such a tough match race with a new, barely sailed boat. "We are all pushing harder than we would have expected to be doing when we started ten days ago. That may take weeks yet to come to the surface," Dalton admitted. "Close race. Probably not what we were all expecting."

Loïck Peyron, Skip Novak, and Roger Nilson also found the march of position reports excruciating. Their strategy to track west to near 28° west depended on finding a narrower band of the Doldrums and getting through it quickly to converge again on the lead boats. Now they were going slowly while *Team Adventure* and *Club Med*, approaching the equator, were picking up speed again. "They were fucking lucky," Peyron grumbled, which was exactly the outcome Nilson and Novak had feared. Lasnier's gamble had not paid off. At least the slow speeds allowed the bathing bucket to be tossed over the side, and almost everyone aboard the big cat indulged in a bucket wash. Peyron and crewman Xavier Dagault dealt with the swelter and stress in a different way. They each suddenly "found" a pack of cigarettes. To the disgust of the clean livers, a full-blown smoke-out erupted in the cockpit. The only thing that snuffed it out was the need to make yet another sail change.

Club Med crossed the equator with *Team Adventure* just 16 miles behind. *Explorer* followed about eight hours later and more than 150 miles in arrears. It had been nerve-racking, but the experience had been mercifully brief. It took *Club Med* and *Team Adventure* barely twenty-four hours to sail through the Doldrums and across the equator, averaging more than 11 knots. Double-digit speeds in the region were the stuff of fantasy. The maxi-cats' ability to sail as fast as the wind, and sometimes faster, had reduced the Doldrums from a speed trap to a speed bump. The first big gate had been transited, and the three Ollier catamarans were still in a group.

Dalton and his crew were so consumed by the competition that they neglected a hallowed ritual of the sea: the visit of King Neptune, to test all crew making the equator crossing for the first time. The tradition is believed to stem from ceremonies held when Viking ships crossed the thirtieth parallel of latitude during their voyages. The rituals were picked up by the Anglo-Saxons and Normans in Britain and eventually applied to the equator crossing. Then, and during the Age of Sail, the rite had a practical purpose: to see whether novices in the crew had the intelligence and fortitude to survive the rigors of a long voyage.

The modern racing version, popularized by dozens of Whitbread crossings, is mainly an excuse to have a bit of fun. King

Neptune and his designated veteran assistants, known as "shell-backs," appear on deck to pass judgment on all the "pollywogs" crossing the equator for the first time. Neptune, sometimes accompanied by Queen Amphitrite, tests the pollywogs' knowledge of trivia and charges them with a variety of mistakes and infractions. This phase is merely a humorous prelude to an orgy of hazing limited only by the imagination and mercy of the shell-backs. Regardless of their answers, the pollywogs always end up slathered in food slops, garbage, and fish guts before being welcomed into the Kingdom of Neptune. *Club Med* in any case had little excuse for such antics; her crew contained only one polly-wog, Fred Le Peutrec. Dalton had been known for his severe hazing in years past, so Le Peutrec was fortunate he was preoccupied with *Team Adventure*. As the big cat sped south, Le Peutrec was left to snooze in his bunk.

On *Explorer* Peyron threatened a more traditional passage. He warned that King Neptune — in the form of Roger Nilson — would be given free run of the boat when she crossed the line. When the moment arrived, a number of pollywogs abandoned a safety briefing on the Southern Ocean and disappeared below. Nilson, however, seemed more interested in reminiscing about his own equatorial initiation, years back in the Swedish Navy, when real tar was used to douse the unlucky, so the pollywogs escaped unscathed.

Aboard *Team Adventure,* the equatorial virgins — seven of them — would not get off as lightly as Le Peutrec and the *Explorer* crew. King Neptune, also known as crewman "Big Fred" Carrere, appeared with a trident fashioned from a scrub brush and three forks affixed with duct tape. Jacques Vincent as enforcer, Jean-Yves Bernot as accuser, and Micke Lundh, who meted out the punishments, followed, sporting mustaches made from leftover scraps of line. The seven novices had to kneel on the net as their crimes and sentences were read aloud. Randy Smyth was accused of excessive speeding and forced to paint his nails red. Navigator Larry Rosenfeld was charged with illegal trade in electronic equipment and ordered to do dishes and, worse, turn off all his instruments for thirty seconds. On it went, and everyone ended up with a thick coating of slops, along with permission from King Neptune to enter his realm. Rigger Rob Myles was charged with a particularly egregious offense — not putting enough water in the freeze-dried food. Myles explained the situation in detail on the Quokka sports Web site: "The gas this stuff produces is incredible . . . It's sort of funny at first, but then the fart game gets old, especially in the leeward hull where you can't always open the aft hatch and thus zero circulation. It's like living on a small farm, where the animal stalls are stacked up like bunks rather than side by side. Some guys have taken to sleeping on deck for fresh air. Me? Hey, what the hell. I can power blast with the best of them, so I sleep great in the bunk."

10

To the Southern Ocean

> "O for a soft and gentle wind!"
> I heard a fair one cry:
> But give to me the roaring breeze
> And white waves heaving high.
>
> — A. Cunningham

JUST TEN DAYS of racing had taken the Ollier catamarans from the Mediterranean to the equator. The brief span had also punctured any pretensions that *Warta Polpharma* and *Team Legato* might have had about staying anywhere near the new-generation boats. When *Club Med* and *Team Adventure* first put their bows into the Southern Hemisphere, *Warta* was already more than eight hundred miles behind. *Team Legato,* after a stop in Gibraltar to fix a fitting on the mainsail, was almost eighteen hundred miles astern. Barring a multiple and simultaneous collapse at the front of the fleet, this contest had decisively established the quantum boost in performance and design that fifteen years of advancing technology had brought to ocean racing.

Stuck between the two generations, at least in geographic terms, was *PlayStation*. As navigator Stan Honey analyzed the satellite pictures and weather forecasts for the Doldrums, *PlayStation*'s race was slipping away as well. Leaving Gibraltar, Honey and Fossett had hoped that a little Doldrums voodoo would slow the lead boats enough for *PlayStation* to make up a big chunk of lost ground. As it happened, the Ollier boats had slipped across the equator with ease. Worse, it looked as if the Doldrums trap was more likely to snap shut on *PlayStation*.

The more eastern passage that *Club Med* and *Team Adventure* had sailed was no longer favorable. After talking the situation over with router Bob Rice, Fossett and Honey headed west to approximate *Explorer*'s path. As they did, more bad luck struck when sailmaker Nick Moloney became the latest casualty of big-cat sailing. After sprinting across the trampoline, Moloney jumped into the cockpit as *PlayStation* gave a little hitch. He landed on a raised piece of flooring and turned his ankle badly. Fossett immediately contacted Dan Carlin, who had been signed on as *PlayStation*'s virtual doctor. Moloney's was the fourth ankle injury on *PlayStation* in a year, and it was by far the most severe. Carlin suspected a bad sprain and advised cold compresses and a half cast. In reality, Moloney had broken two little bones and torn all the ligaments around his ankle. Without knowing the extent of the damage, and after only a brief rest, he continued to hobble around, helping with crew work. Unable to walk easily on the springy trampoline, he took to dragging himself across while sitting down. That earned him the nickname "Lieutenant Dan," for the manic, legless character in *Forrest Gump*.

PlayStation hit the soft Doldrums wall just after 4° north latitude, about the same distance from the equator in which the other boats first encountered the humid, windless zone. A bubble of heated, unstable air from the West African desert arrived at the same time. Instead of frequent wind-generating squalls to assist the passage south, the Doldrums cloaked the largest, heaviest boat in the fleet in a frustrating miasma. "We are in the midst of the ITCZ now, at lat three north," Stan Honey reported. "We have had only one squall over thirty knots; the rest of our trials have been with light and shifty air and the calms associated with the rain cells." One especially bountiful rain cell allowed the crew enough time to lather up and rinse — twice. But racing sailors would much rather be unwashed and in the lead than squeaky clean and playing catch-up. In one deadly wind hole *PlayStation* managed a top speed of just 3 knots over the course of an hour. All the while the competition was streaking away at more than 20. The random airs forced *PlayStation* to steer east, then west, but rarely directly south. The demoralized crew gathered often in the cockpit, cursing the beautiful blue skies above them and talking about other races and other days.

In an ironic joke, Neptune sent the beleaguered cat across the equator at 26 knots, courtesy of a rare 30-knot squall. The disgusted crew was in no mood to show much appreciation. A fistful of granola bars — a type that almost everyone aboard had come to dislike — was tossed into the black waves as a token gesture of obeisance. Perhaps Neptune took note. The Doldrums clamped down again, expanding ahead of *PlayStation* and forcing her to endure additional hours of suffering. At 2° south latitude, a tentative breath of southeast trade wind finally whispered across the sails, and *PlayStation* started to accelerate.

Compared to any normal Doldrums passage in history, *PlayStation* had made good time across the equator. She had sailed from 5° north latitude to 5° south, a distance of six hundred miles, in just over sixty hours. But in the context of The Race, the experience had been brutal. All three Ollier catamarans had made the same passage in about forty-eight hours. "Cam and Dalton went from twenty knots to four knots for eight hours, and then back up to twenty," Gino Morrelli explained. "We went from twenty knots down to eight knots for two days."

The result was gutting. Approaching the Doldrums, *PlayStation* had cut the gap to the leaders to under four hundred miles, barely one day's sailing in favorable conditions. By the time she had resumed the chase in the southeast trades, the gap had ballooned to more than seven hundred miles. Morale sank even lower. The only remaining hope for Fossett and his crew lay in the St. Helena, or South Atlantic, High, which looked as if it might snare the boats ahead. Fossett and Honey spent hours in the nav station, in regular communication with Rice, trying to figure out a way to take full advantage of the developing weather picture. The strategizing was so intense, David Scully wondered whether he might have to squirt WD-40 into their ears to prevent the wheels in their heads from overheating. But, as so often in ocean racing, there was little to do except sail as fast as possible and wait to see what happened ahead.

Pure speed was also the priority for the front-runners. After clearing the equator, *Club Med* and *Team Adventure* began a tightly contested 2,400-mile drag race to the Southern Ocean. They had passed through the gates of Gibraltar and the Doldrums without either boat making a decisive break. The next opportunity lay with the west winds of the South, and Dalton and Lewis both knew that this was the first real prize of The Race. That meant continuing to drive the boats to the limit, at average speeds that quickly climbed past 20 knots in the fresh southeast winds. The two cats ran almost directly south — with *Explorer* just twelve hours behind — east of the Brazilian archipelago of Fernando de Noronha and close to the island of Trinidade. These rocky outcroppings, covered in guano, were familiar waypoints to the nineteenth-century ships that had traversed the South Atlantic on the way to Cape Horn or Australia. Then, as now, the key to sailing south was to keep to the west of the South Atlantic High, to stay in the favorable easterly and northerly winds near the coast of South America. The trick was deciding how far west to go in order to avoid the light winds and calms near the center of the high, and how far south to go to catch solid Southern Ocean westerlies before turning east.

The clipper ships and the first round-the-world racers had only their Pilot Charts, their barometers (which would rise as they approached the center of the South Atlantic High), and their sailing instincts to help them make these critical decisions. Robin Knox-Johnston, eager to start sailing toward Australia during the Golden Globe, turned east too soon in an attempt to cut the corner of the high; another week or so of heading south would have taken him to strong westerly winds. As a result, he spent three more weeks in variable and light winds before he reached the westerlies. By contrast, Bernot, Quilter, and their routers had satellite imagery and a wealth of weather data to show them where the South Atlantic High lay. The data also indicated the possibility of a split in the high, which might open up a beautiful highway to the Southern Ocean for the lead boats before closing back up.

Like many weather fantasies, it was fleeting. The high soon stretched over the entire South Atlantic, from Uruguay to Namibia, and far enough south that the boats would have to get almost to 40° latitude before the Southern Ocean winds kicked in. This was the forecast that was giving Stan Honey and Steve Fossett a flicker of hope as they sweltered through the Doldrums. If the leaders parked up, *PlayStation* might have a chance to roar down through the trades and rejoin the fleet. To "Clouds" Badham, back in Australia, it looked like a miserable light-air crapshoot for *Club Med*. He could see two or three routes straight south through the edges of the high pressure, which could either free her or imprison her. The traditional route west around the bloated high was not an option. To take it a boat would have to sail so far toward the coast of South America — away from the direct route to Australia — it was scary.

The developing weather scenario frayed nerves down in the nav stations. On deck, however, it was hard not to give in to the simple thrill of racing. *Club Med* and *Team Adventure* were flying in the southeasterly trades, easily covering more than four hundred miles a day and sometimes more than five hundred. No two boats had ever sailed south so fast from the equator, and it was hard for a monohull veteran like Dalton not to appreciate the experience of carving across the waves at powerboat speeds. It was also time to fly a hull.

Flying a hull was a multihuller's art. (Once the right sails were up, they were sheeted in until the pressure of the wind lifted the windward hull just clear of the water.) It was a spectacular sight, but it was all about speed. A hull that just kissed the surface of the ocean as the catamaran flew along its course reduced wetted surface and drag. Larry Rosenfeld on *Team Adventure* tried his hand at the wheel in southeast trades of 14 to 17 knots and discovered the benefits. "Get the hull flying and we are doing twenty-seven and a half to twenty-eight and a half knots. Drop it down and we are doing twenty-three knots. It's like trying to pull a wheelie on your bicycle for a city block," he remarked.

Once the hull was up, care had to be taken to keep it from flying so high there was a risk of capsizing. If the cat was sailing on a beam reach at a 90° angle to the wind, keeping the boat upright was the job of the trimmers. Catamaran drivers call this sailing angle "the line of death" because any change in course only increases the pressure on the sails and can flip the boat. The driver is helpless if the boat is hit by a sudden gust; only a quick ease of the mainsheet can keep the boat from tipping toward catastrophe.

Sailing upwind or downwind, however, it is all on the drivers. Small adjustments to the course can be used to increase or decrease the pressure of the wind in the sails. Maintaining the sublime balance between wind and water without thinking too much, reacting instantly to the feel of the helm and the rapidly changing readouts on the instruments relaying wind angle and boat speed — these are marks of a superior helmsman. The result is a hissing, sinuous trail across the blue seas. The best drivers — like Yves Loday, a French Olympic sailor, and Loïck Peyron aboard *Explorer,* Fred Le Peutrec and Guillermo Altadill on *Club Med,* and Cam Lewis and Randy Smyth on *Team Adventure* — could fly a hull with a concentrated skill that impressed even their all-professional crews. For a natural like Lewis, it was like driving "a Caddy Eldorado soft-top on the Texas big road."

It was an exhilarating ride. The boats raced along under the hot tropical sun at speeds that touched 30 knots and doused the decks in diamonds of spray. Any trips across the trampoline — to use the head, to ferry meals, to get to a bunk — meant a thorough drenching. The only question was whether it was better to make the trip practically naked or with full foul-weather gear. It was a time to relax and enjoy The Race before the cold, windy work of the Southern Ocean. *Team Adventure* passed Isla Trinidade, six hundred miles off the Brazilian coast and the last speck of land the crew might see until New Zealand, early one evening. To mark the event, Lewis called for a happy hour, featuring three bottles of wine, followed by a roast lamb dinner. "This is really neat racing," Dalton confessed on behalf of the fleet. "We are all loving it."

Nothing, however, could obscure the intensity of the duel for the lead under way between *Club Med* and *Team Adventure,* between Grant Dalton and Cam Lewis. In lighter winds, *Club Med* finally seemed to find a slight speed edge, which Dalton attributed to a special light-air sail called a Code 0 which had been developed during the most recent Whitbread race. In heavier winds, *Team Adventure* had a clear advantage. South of the equator, Lewis and company nibbled steadily at *Club Med*'s lead. When *Club Med* posted a 537-mile twenty-four-hour run, *Team Adventure* turned in a 570-mile run. "Christ, if *Team Adventure* holds together they are unbeatable," Skip Novak thought. "But are they going to hold together? There's a long way to go." At 20° south latitude, after a 1,200-mile speed trial from the equator, *Team Adventure* regained the lead, a moment Dalton had expected. This in itself didn't trouble him much — there were many miles to sail and plenty of opportunities for mistakes. *Team Adventure* and *Club Med* would ultimately exchange the lead four times in the race to the Southern Ocean. What worried Dalton was the accumulating stress on the boat from pounding the waves at top speed day after day.

There were twenty thousand miles still to sail, and even flying a hull in perfect trade wind conditions came at a price. When the windward hull popped free of the water, the entire righting moment of the boat — the force with which gravity tried to pull the hull back toward the water — was carried by the windward rigging. If the hull slammed down during a brief lull in the wind or when the boat slowed on a wave, the sudden addition of wetted surface acted like a brake, sending a shock through the rig and its hardware as inertia whipped the mast and sails forward. The steady trickle of broken pad eyes, which anchored the rigging, was a good measure of the unpredictable forces at work. The pad eyes were hefty, U-shaped stainless-steel fittings that were bolted through the deck. They were rated to loads of up to twenty-one thousand pounds but seemed to be pulling out at about one fifth that strain. One blew up at the aft end of a hull on *Club Med* as crewman Jan Dekker was taking a saltwater shower ten feet away. The pad eye, carrying the load of the large gennaker headsail, went whistling by his head. It could have killed him. The crew sent digital pictures of one failed fitting to the manufacturer. "No way that should happen" was the response. "Check the structure of the deck."

Gear failures, as long as they weren't drastic or deadly, were mostly a problem of lost time. In one instance, as *Club Med* plowed along at 20 knots, a welded titanium fitting securing the main sheet broke apart. The crew, which conducted daily patrols in search of maintenance problems, had been eyeing the piece for a few days so they were ready. The repair took just one hour. Even so, Dalton estimated that the downtime cost *Club Med* ten or fifteen crucial miles in her bow-to-bow race with *Team Adventure*. More severe breakages could mean dozens of lost miles or even the loss of The Race — and the boats had not even reached the Southern Ocean yet. Dalton could only imagine what sort of shape *Club Med* would be in for the difficult return leg up the Atlantic following Cape Horn, where the boats would have to beat back into the wind for days on end. "This continues to be a show of strength between *Team Adventure* and ourselves," Dalton said in an e-mail. "Neither boat can back off whilst the other is running this hard."

The only blessing in sight was mixed — the South Atlantic High. "The question for us [and for everyone else] over the next two days is how to get past the high-pressure zone. The bricklayers in the sky are building a nice little wall right across the Atlantic," noted Jean-Yves Bernot from the confines of his nav station on *Team Adventure*. He was feverishly scouring the data for the least painful solutions to breaching the wall, complaining to Lewis (only partly tongue-in-cheek) that *Team Adventure* was closing too fast for him to sort out all the scenarios.

Dalton and Quilter were going through the same exercise aboard their boat. As Badham expected, it looked as if they would have no alternative but to plunge straight into the zone of light winds and pick their way through with fingers crossed. There would be no black squalls, as there had been in the Doldrums, to provide intermittent blasts of wind. "Our lives are about to change. We are going to hit a wall soon," Dalton noted with resignation. "We are in exactly the same weather as *Team Adventure,* so we will pretty much stop together, but *Explorer* and *PlayStation* will come roaring in from behind to meet us both. The situation will last a day and a half." It was all part of racing around the world, but that didn't make it any easier to stomach.

PlayStation had found the trade winds south of the equator and was back in hot pursuit. Dalton could relax, though. As the cat powered along with a single reef in the main, the crew noticed a problem on the back edge of the old sail. Fossett climbed up onto the boom — which was three feet wide and built to catch the sail as it was lowered or reefed — and walked to the back end to take a look. The stitching securing the first reef patch to the sail was starting to pull out, and another six feet of stitching going up the sail also looked suspect. Nick Moloney hobbled out to the end of the boom to make a diagnosis. It seemed to him that the sailcloth was essentially sound and the damage mostly cosmetic. The crew lowered the sail to the second reef, letting the first reef patch drop onto the boom, so Moloney and David Scully could go to work with a needle and thread. The repair took nine and a half hours. Moloney had to support himself on the bucking boom with his damaged foot. The pain was hard to bear; it was finally clear he had more than an ankle sprain. Still, when he clambered back down to the cockpit, he thought the fix would hold.

That didn't resolve all the sail problems. While up on the boom Moloney had seen other areas of worn stitching. One possibility was to stop for as long as necessary and have a sewing party. Losing another day to the leaders was out of the question, however. Instead, Moloney figured he could keep sewing as needed, whenever the sail was reefed enough to let him get to the damaged areas. It was a possible solution, but far from ideal. *PlayStation* had lost another forty miles or so sailing with two reefs in the main to make the first repair. And mending stiff cloth with needle and thread in the trade winds would be a lot easier than sewing in the freezing gales of the Southern Ocean. "You just work with what you've got," Damian Foxall said. "But what we saw was another mainsail with problems and we weren't a quarter of the way around yet. It started to ring alarm bells in everyone's head, and maybe Steve's more than anyone's."

Moloney was concerned about his foot, too. He now suspected that there had to be some sort of ligament damage because when he picked up his leg, he could feel a brief hesitation before his foot came with it. A full cast was applied to stabilize the foot. Moloney's crewmates teased him about gangrene. An atmosphere of uncertainty and doubt pervaded the boat as she sailed into the tropical night.

Late in the evening Foxall was on standby with Gino Morrelli and Stu Wilson, *PlayStation*'s second sailmaker, when they heard a loud crunch followed by a horrific ripping sound. *PlayStation* didn't give much of a lurch to show it, but the port daggerboard had collided with something underwater. Crewmen Tom Weaver and Mark Callaghan were sleeping in bunks next to the daggerboard trunk, which ran down from the deck through the hull. The ugly mystery noise sent them flying from their bunks and up to the deck, half convinced that flooding was imminent. From the port side, under the shine of flashlights, the five-hundred-pound foil could be seen sticking out from under the boat. It had snapped almost completely free; only a few splinters of carbon fiber kept it with the boat.

When a daggerboard strikes an underwater object at speed,

there is a danger that the force of the blow will fracture the daggerboard trunk and open the hull to the sea. *PlayStation*'s board had not damaged the trunk in the collision, but the rush of water under the hulls continued to pound the broken board against the housing. To prevent serious damage to the hull the crew dropped a loop of line underneath the board and wrenched the broken section free. Twenty minutes after the impact there was a fourteen-foot piece of fluorescent orange board bobbing in *PlayStation*'s wake. No one knew for sure what had caused the breakage.

Before the start, the *PlayStation* team had discussed the possibility of losing a daggerboard. The boat had one in each hull to help prevent her from slipping sideways when the wind was blowing from ahead or the side. Two daggerboards were definitely better than one, but the team had decided that one would be enough to keep racing. The choice didn't seem so easy at sea, though. *PlayStation* was more than eight hundred miles behind the leader, relying on luck with the weather to help her get back in the race. The mainsail would require constant repair over the next twenty thousand miles. The remaining daggerboard, under a greater load now, was already vibrating in its trunk.

PlayStation sailed on for an hour while Fossett marshaled his thoughts. Then he gathered Morrelli, the designer; his senior crew, Brian Thompson and Ben Wright; and Stan Honey. He asked Stu Wilson and Nick Moloney to join the group and give an assessment of the sails. The two sailmakers were blunt: they could keep sewing, but they couldn't guarantee the mainsail would survive the Southern Ocean. *PlayStation* could put into Cape Town, South Africa, and incur another time penalty — sixty hours this time because the rules tacked twelve hours onto each successive stop — but there was no way that the damaged Cuben Fiber mainsail would be ready for pickup. Fossett thought that if the second daggerboard failed in the Southern Ocean, safety could become an issue, especially if they had to retrieve a man overboard, since *PlayStation* would have trouble sailing in any direction other than downwind.

All told, it was hard for Fossett to see a payoff in going the distance. Honey believed that *PlayStation* would make up a lot of miles as the three leaders bogged down in the South Atlantic High, but he also expected *PlayStation* to get trapped for a while too. Her only chance was a total meltdown at the front of the fleet. *PlayStation* was no better off than the slower, older boats. Morrelli agreed. *PlayStation* wouldn't be racing, she'd be on a cruise, a cruise that might leave her stuck on the other side of the world if she needed more repairs. That would jeopardize the possibility of moving on to other record-breaking attempts, such as the Atlantic crossing, later in the year.

Brian Thompson and Stan Honey were inclined to run with their emotions and press on just to finish the damn race. But Fossett was too rational to see any glory or romance in a quixotic circumnavigation with no chance at victory laurels or records. "That logic doesn't work for me," he said later. "To continue on, jeopardize the future, and not even have the opportunity to do anything other than make it around the world." Still, he didn't want to make a peremptory decision without giving the rest of the crew a chance to voice their opinions. So he gathered them together and told them he was inclined to withdraw from The Race and head for Miami, thirty-three hundred miles to the northwest. It would be an ignominious, heartbreaking end to a long project, but it would also allow *PlayStation* to go gunning for records the following summer and fall. Fossett encouraged the crew to discuss it among themselves and let him know if they could make a persuasive argument for continuing to race.

Many in the crew were in favor of pressing ahead despite the problems. They simply wanted to finish, even if they couldn't win. "There was a lot of 'Yes, let's get this bitch around the course whatever way we can,'" Foxall said. A few thought it was pointless to drag all their handicaps around the globe. All agreed, however, that Fossett had pretty much made up his mind, and since he was the skipper they should support his decision. Sailboats never work well as a democracy, and the crew instinctively deferred to the long nautical tradition of a clear chain of command.

Fossett rejoined the discussion and was told that it was his call; the crew would back any decision he made. He was touched and pleased by the support. *PlayStation*'s big bows were turned in a broad arc until they pointed north again. A little after midnight Fossett phoned Race headquarters and informed the directors that *PlayStation* was withdrawing. "We are destined to be struggling with sail repairs for the rest of the way. We just aren't prepared to tackle the Southern Ocean," he told them. Fossett was disappointed, as he was with any project that ended in failure, but he didn't dwell on *PlayStation*'s poor showing. Already he was thinking ahead, to the summer and the transatlantic mark.

The running was now left to three near-identical boats, fighting for every mile of advantage far to the south. *Warta Polpharma* and *Team Legato* were still sailing, but *Warta* was now almost fifteen hundred miles behind the leaders while *Team Legato* was more than two thousand miles adrift. Word of *PlayStation*'s withdrawal quickly spread through the fleet. Skip Novak could not suppress a shiver of relief. The lagging *Explorer* crew had been demoralized by the seemingly superior speed and preparation of their Ollier sister ships. *PlayStation* had also shown long legs in the Mediterranean, and since rejoining The Race seemed to be a threat to *Explorer*'s third position. "Christ, here they are coming down and catching up already," Novak had been thinking. "We were facing a last place, not counting the little boats," he said. Dalton, safely out front, could afford a whiff of regret. "Losing a boat so early in The Race in this way is a big disappointment for all of us," he commented. "However, this sort of thing could happen to any of us. Wear and tear will always be an issue in this race . . . There is no point in making predictions because you might be next. That's why the crew are constantly working on the boat to avoid breakages."

Dalton, in fact, was starting to feel nostalgia for the Whitbread format and the multiple stops that allowed broken gear to be replaced and new spares to be taken aboard. *PlayStation*'s withdrawal was in part a reflection of the fact that the new boats simply had not been sailed enough for the crews to discover and replace all the little parts that might fail. Instead, they just had to keep making repairs as best they could. The boats all carried stores of spares so they could try to remedy their problems at sea. Bruno Peyron had warned them that in 1993 *Commodore Explorer* had suffered breakages every day or two. But spares add weight, and it was hard to know how many spares, and which ones, to take. Sailing crews tend to be endlessly inventive when it comes to solving mechanical problems. *Club Med*'s crew had already become adept at replacing broken metal pad eyes with fiber strops. Even so, Dalton fully expected that by the time the big catamarans were heading back up the Atlantic for home, the crew's ingenuity would be sorely tested.

In the meantime, it was the navigators' wits that were required. As they approached 30° south latitude, all three Ollier catamarans sailed directly into the South Atlantic High. *Club Med* led the pack, after slipping past *Team Adventure* one more time, to open up a 40-mile lead. *Explorer,* still to the west, had closed to within 130 miles. Boat speeds dropped to single digits for the first time since the Doldrums. A five-hundred-mile ocean desert of variable, weak breezes stretched ahead, blocking the route to the Southern Ocean winds.

The crews took advantage of the slow speeds to check and double-check every piece of rigging and hardware. Not even Grant Dalton, Skip Novak, and Roger Nilson, who had spent months and months of their lives sailing the Southern Ocean, knew for sure what to expect in the month ahead on these big catamarans. None of the cats had really had a chance to sail hard in conditions that came close to approximating the high winds and steep seas of the South. *Team Philips* had been the only new multihull to get a realistic taste of Southern Ocean conditions, and the result had been catastrophic. "I guess we should enjoy this sailing as much as possible, 'cause it won't be long and we are all about to find out just what it is like on a runaway train in the Southern Ocean," Dalton warned.

Some incredible sailing, and probably a few world records, lay ahead. But the Southern Ocean was also going to be a severe test of the leadership on each boat, and Rick Deppe, for one, fretted that Cam Lewis wasn't quite ready for it. Deppe was a blond bantam who throughout his sailing career was always the guy willing to go up the rig or do the dirty work in a tight engine space. He had a bow man's toughness and wasn't afraid to speak his mind. In Deppe's view, The Race was an opportunity for Lewis to become more than a hot sailor. It was a chance to establish himself as a world-class skipper. Unfortunately, in the race down the Atlantic *Team Adventure* kept making mistakes. They were small ones, to be sure, like allowing a loose line to rip the blades off the wind generator, breaking battens, or inadvertently dropping the boom onto the satellite dome, but every mistake cost time and gave miles to the other boats.

Part of the problem was the crew had spent so little time sailing together. Deppe also felt that Lewis's leadership was a little inconsistent. Lewis seemed to encourage pouring on the speed, then got angry when something broke. As Deppe saw it, the call to shorten sail always seemed to come a little late. And sometimes sail handling led to mistakes because both English and French were being spoken, or there wasn't enough crew on deck.

Deppe and Lewis had talked about the situation up on the bow one sunny day. "Everyone knows you as Goofy Cam, Chemical Cam, laughing, joking Cam," Deppe said. "This is your opportunity to step up a bit. You're never going to be Grant Dalton, because you don't have his personality traits, and he doesn't have your innate speed-sailing ability. You're different guys, but you need to start thinking of yourself as the same class of leader."

Lewis listened. He knew what the stakes were. He also knew that molding fourteen guys of different nationalities into a tight-knit sailing team aboard a prototype catamaran was an enormous challenge. Just getting to the starting line with a full crew had been a feat. "It's really difficult," he replied. "I'm the captain, and you have to understand I've got my way of doing things."

The Southern Ocean would be the ultimate arbiter of how well *Team Adventure* was sailing, and getting there was fast becoming another high-stakes guessing game. The weather system that had enveloped the boats was highly volatile. Little bubbles of calm would expand and recede across the boats' paths. Sometimes a nasty chop would sweep in from a far-off storm, tossing the boats around and making life uncomfortable again. "None of the weather models correspond. I think if we had ten different models and ten experts, they'd each have come up with ten different opinions," Grant Dalton groused. For the first time in The Race, instincts and experience became more important than the forecasts.

In the very light winds, with their big Code 0 headsail, Dalton and Quilter focused all their efforts and racing know-how on positioning *Club Med* between *Team Adventure* and the westerly winds to the south. Their concentration paid off. *Team Adventure,* seeking any wind, turned slightly to the east and crossed behind *Club Med.* Dalton held his course until he had opened up some distance to the south of his rival and then matched *Team Adventure*'s heading. It was a decisive move. *Club Med* would now shadow *Team Adventure* so that the two boats sailed in roughly the same weather conditions, but with *Club Med* always closer to the escape winds in the south. "We've shut the door on [Lewis] a bit for now, which is nice," Dalton announced. "There are still 19,070 miles to sail to the finish, so we couldn't say he's totally under control, but we do have him where we want him."

The only boat Dalton could not control was *Explorer,* still out to the west. More often than not, that position should have given Peyron and his crew a chance to skirt the high pressure in somewhat stronger winds and find the Southern Ocean first. The west had in fact allowed *Explorer* to sail within a hundred miles of the two leaders, the closest she had been since the Cape Verde Islands, above the equator. *Explorer*'s luck was not that good, though. As Badham had warned, the South Atlantic High was so expansive that a boat would have had to be almost on the South American coast to find its windier edges.

How to get through had been another source of disagreement between Nilson and Lasnier. Lasnier wanted to try the western end run — with its promise of more wind — despite the spread of the high. Nilson, analyzing the extra miles required to circumvent the huge area of light winds, agreed with the boats in front: the best option was to punch straight into it. By now Nilson had lost faith in Lasnier's advice and was in contact with other shore-based forecasters to get a wider range of views. He thought Lasnier was an excellent meteorologist but lacked sailboat racing experience. Lasnier was also juggling other projects, and Nilson sensed he was unable to allocate enough time to the cash-strapped *Explorer*. "We need to take the decision-making back onto the boat," he told Peyron. At this stage Peyron was inclined to agree.

It almost didn't matter. Lasnier's westerly option through the Doldrums had made it difficult, once in the South Atlantic, to work back east against the southeast trade winds. *Explorer* never converged with the two leaders yet was caught in the same frustrating winds that bogged them down. Worse, just as *Explorer* started to slow, the crew heard a sound like paper flapping in a breeze.

On a high-tech sailboat with laminate sails, that is a noise to be feared. It was coming from the smallest of the downwind headsails — a workhorse jib needed for both the run in the Southern Ocean and light-wind work because it held a soft breeze without collapsing under its own weight. The sail was lowered to the trampoline. After close inspection, the crew found that the Mylar film sandwiching the sailcloth together was peeling away in a number of places. Consultations via satellite phone with the sailmaker in France produced a depressing conclusion: the material was defective. "This was the best sail, the absolute weapon for everything," Loïck Peyron said. "And that's the fucking sail that delaminates."

It seemed unspeakably unfair. *Innovation Explorer*, the underdog of the Ollier boats, had managed to surprise everyone, fighting for miles and staying in touch with the leaders. Now her race was being undermined by a sail problem that had started back in a loft. Over the course of a day, the annoyed crew did their best to repair the sail, using swaths of spare fabric and glue from their limited supply. The repair might hold, but they might have to limit use of the sail.

Explorer wasn't in a good position to husband any of her sails. The boat was already short and having trouble covering every wind angle and speed; there hadn't been enough money for a full wardrobe. Skip Novak, in fact, had tried to talk Grant Dalton and the *Club Med* team into lending them a spare headsail to fill a gap in *Explorer*'s inventory. Dalton was sympathetic and put the question to a vote of his crew. The answer came back: No. The Race was a competition, not just an adventure, and the *Club Med* crew intended to win. Novak offered a gentlemen's agreement in which he promised *Explorer* would not use the sail if for some reason *Club Med* lost the use of her newer equivalent anywhere on the racecourse. That might have been enough in the early, more relaxed Whitbread era of the 1970s. But round-the-world racing was now a big-money, high-stakes professional sport. The answer was still no.

Explorer was handicapped, and there wasn't much to do about it. "Right now we are just trying to keep in touch with these guys and try to get into the Southern Ocean weather systems in roughly the same area, within a radius of a couple of hundred miles," Novak said. "And then we'll just see what happens from there." How to get there was a problem that was now stumping Roger Nilson, despite his five Whitbreads. His boat seemed mired in a South Atlantic twilight zone, made all the more inhospitable by the fact that none of the usual marine or bird life was anywhere to be seen. "Probably because of all those flying fish we killed," Nilson suggested darkly. What he couldn't know was that it was about to get worse.

Grant Dalton had been patiently working *Club Med* south for two days when Badham spotted the break he had been looking for. Clouds was juggling four different global weather models, and sometimes good weather routing is simply knowing which forecast to gamble on. For the moment, Badham favored the medium-range European forecast and the short-range U.S. model, using satellite wind reports for confirmation. On his computer screen the bubble of high pressure *Club Med* had been trapped in, along with *Team Adventure,* started to break up and re-form. If Dalton headed southwest, away from Australia, he might be able to escape. Badham phoned the boat. "I know this is ugly, but it will work out," he told Dalton. Dalton didn't normally like to sail away from the mark, but he had enormous respect for Badham's skills and didn't hesitate. "Okay, we've got to do it," he replied. *Club Med*'s bows swung to the southwest, and she slowly accelerated.

It took just a few hours. The wind strengthened and steadied. As it did, Dalton and Quilter brought *Club Med* back around to the southeast, toward Australia, toward the fortieth parallel, and toward a decisive breakaway. *Team Adventure* tried to follow, but as Lewis recalled later, "When you have boats capable of cranking up over thirty knots, it's only a matter of a few knots of wind to get that jump." The jump was the key, because the re-forming high-pressure bubble moved with *Team Adventure.* She managed to escape eventually, but not cleanly. For almost a day she sailed in lighter winds than *Club Med,* which was rocketing along at a steady 25 to 30 knots. By the time *Team Adventure* started to match or even exceed *Club Med*'s speed, *Club Med*'s lead had ballooned from sixty miles to two hundred miles.

Lewis shrugged it off as random luck and tried to stay focused on the chase. *Team Adventure* had at least stayed in the same weather system as *Club Med.* Still, the two boats had been

within hours of each other for most of the Atlantic leg. Now
there were a lot of miles, Southern Ocean miles, to be made up.
"This is the break I've wanted," Dalton said. "We've played it
well to get this chance. It all started a couple of days ago when
he turned to the east before we did. I wanted the south like nothing I've ever wanted before. We crossed over his path and took
up position to the south of him, and that is when our situation
became the dominant one." The length of the Atlantic had been
a punishing tactical test, and as far as Dalton was concerned,
luck was the least part of it. The Race was always going to be a
navigator's battle, and Quilter and Clouds, his long-time broth-
ers-in-arms, had taken apart the famous French Wizard.

Explorer, which had been caught too far west and too far
north at the critical moment, suffered the most. The malign bubble of high pressure re-formed directly over their position, doom-
ing them to another thirty-six hours of limpid winds. Loïck Peyron, Skip Novak, and the crew could only curse their luck as
their two sister ships fled into the Southern Ocean, leaving them
five hundred miles and a full weather system behind.

"This is it. We're on the southern expressway," Dalton's coskipper, Franck Proffit, gleefully reported to race headquarters,
shouting to be heard against the background roar of a 110-foot
catamaran sailing at 30 knots. Lewis tried to remain philosophical. "Grant Dalton did a good job of working his boat through
a complex area of light wind," he commented. "Now we have
to sail smart and catch him. We are seventeen days into The
Race and have covered one quarter of the distance. There's still
a long way to go."

Club Med made a rapid transition to Southern Ocean sailing.
Gone were the shorts and light clothing of the scorching Horse
Latitudes. Now, at around 40° south, fleece pullovers appeared.
Thick socks, boots, and one-piece Gore-Tex suits followed.
Quilter and Dalton had the big blue boat aimed at the back
side of a massive low-pressure system whose center was hun-
dreds of miles southeast. If *Club Med* could latch on to the
westerly winds in its northwest quadrant, she might be able

to ride the system for thousands of miles. If *Team Adventure* missed this "train," she would fall a weather system behind, and *Club Med* could at last fulfill Dalton's deep desire to sail more conservatively.

Positioning the boat just right in the Southern Ocean's weather systems would be tricky, though. With the dearth of commercial traffic in this ocean wasteland, the ship reports that give detail to most forecasts were rare. In the heavily traveled North Atlantic, three- or four-day forecasts were about 80 percent accurate. The same forecasts in the Southern Ocean were right only about 40 percent of the time.

Dalton didn't care. He was in his element. "A nip in the air this morning, started to see the odd Alby [albatross] today," he wrote in an e-mail from the boat. "The [Southern Ocean] beckons and we have the boat 100% ready after a feverish 3 days of maintenance. Bring it on."

11

Southern Ocean Derby

However man may brag of his science and skill, and however much, in a flattering future, that science and skill may augment; yet for ever and for ever, to the crack of doom, the sea will insult and murder him, and pulverize the stateliest, stiffest frigate he can make.

— Herman Melville

THERE IS NO clear boundary between the Southern Ocean and the Atlantic, Indian, and Pacific Oceans. Latitude 40° south is as good a geographic threshold as any. But the Southern Ocean is really defined by its distinctive characteristics: the winds, the seas, the isolation, even the birds. When Grant Dalton saw the first albatross gliding in to take up station over *Club Med,* he didn't have to ask Mike Quilter where he was.

Over the centuries, the great wandering birds had become synonymous with the South, where they spend five to ten years at a time cruising the skies on wingspans of twelve feet or more and rarely, if ever, touching down on land. "Albatross" derives from the Portuguese name for pelican, *alcatraz.* The enormous birds are ungainly on land — in the Pacific they are sometimes called gooney birds — but near-perfect flying machines, gliding almost motionless above ships as they navigate the air currents with the subtlest adjustments of their wingtips. Samuel Taylor Coleridge, in *The Rime of the Ancient Mariner,* imbued the albatross with a reputation for luck. The epic poem is supposedly

based on a true story, related to Coleridge by William Words-
worth, about the privateer George Shelvocke, who shot a black
albatross off Cape Horn in 1720. Coleridge's Mariner kills an albatross with a crossbow and his ship endures terrible suffering
as a result. ("Ah wretch! said they, the bird to slay, / That made
the breeze to blow!")

Not all sailors were superstitious enough to heed the Ancient
Mariner's lesson. During the long nineteenth-century sailing
voyages to Australia and around the Horn, albatrosses were
often caught on baited hooks to relieve palates weary of salt
pork and hardtack. Their webbed feet were made into tobacco
pouches and their hollow wing bones transformed into pipe
stems. Those practices disappeared with the square-riggers, but
modern fishermen are much deadlier. They inadvertently kill
tens of thousands of the slow-breeding birds every year. The albatrosses dive on thrashing squid and fish caught in nets and on
longline hooks. The birds get caught as well, and drown.

Modern racing sailors, however, have resurrected reverence
for the wandering albatross — as an omen of good luck and a
vanishing symbol of the surpassing wildness of the Southern
Ocean. From the Golden Globe to the Whitbread, they have
watched the birds follow their boats for days, making sweeping
passes or simply tagging along in tandem. The albatross, which
can fly at speeds of fifty to seventy-five miles an hour, was master of those slow-moving monohulls, the best of which were
lucky to average 15 knots.

In The Race, Southern Ocean albatrosses were confronted
with a more worthy design, maxi-catamarans whose enormous
wingspans drove them at top speeds of 30 to 40 knots. "We are
going so fast that they struggle to get out of the way," Dalton reported. One discombobulated bird flopped down on *Club Med*
and took shelter behind the main beam. In the pocket of still air
created by the beam the big bird couldn't take off again. Dalton
took pity — or maybe he didn't want to haul the added weight.
He picked up the albatross and held it high in the slipstream created by the slot between the jib and mainsail. The draft was

more than enough to relaunch the bird, which flew off to resume patrolling the skies.

Dalton was probably happy for any luck the bird could give back. The Race had entered an exhilarating but dangerous phase. At the speeds the boats were attacking the Southern Ocean, he knew that getting *Club Med* to Cape Horn safely was going to take more than good seamanship. "We have thirty knots, but unfortunately we can't use it all," he reported to race headquarters. "The weather is horrible, very, very wet and trying conditions. It is ugly sailing. This is a bad part of the world. Nighttime is weird. We were sailing sometimes at thirty knots in pitch black. Often can't see a damn thing. We have to be really careful." The crew on *Team Adventure* also appreciated the stakes. "Sailing in the Southern Ocean is a mixture of good and bad," Micke Lundh e-mailed Inga. "On one hand, you surf down these massive waves at incredible speeds. On the other, you are playing with your life."

Dalton wanted to be sensible, but he couldn't really afford to be. It had taken the length of the Atlantic to get a two-hundred-mile jump on *Team Adventure,* and he had no intention of letting it bleed away now. Unfortunately, the risks of sailing an easily driven, high-powered catamaran in big winds and following seas were, after months of speculation, becoming readily apparent. Southern Ocean depressions, whose centers tend to track along a corridor at about 60° south, are generally associated with a cold front that arcs off from the center toward the north. Ahead of the front, in the depression's northeastern quadrant, the wind blows from the north or the northeast. Seas here tend to be more uniform and easy to sail because the depression has just moved over them as it travels eastward, and the winds haven't had time to whip the seas up to more dangerous heights. This is the depression's sweet spot, the place where a boat can be pushed fast in windy yet relatively flat seas. On the back side of the cold front, however, in the northwestern quadrant, it is another story. As the cold front approaches, the wind shifts from the northeast to the north to the northwest. When the front passes, the wind shifts rapidly to the southwest.

This new wind consists of cold, dense air from Antarctica. The new wind direction also whips up a vicious cross-sea that hammers at boats and throws them around. Colliding waves send tons of white water tumbling into the troughs. The faster a boat tries to sail in this agitated sea state, the worse the abuse becomes. Sailing the maxi-cats aggressively in these chaotic conditions was like trying to drive a delicate Formula 1 racecar at top speed on a dirt track. Stuff was bound to break. As Fossett and Morrelli and Melvin liked to say, the boats were "sea-state limited." This was the problem that Goss tried to solve with his wave-piercing "suspension" system. It was the problem that Fossett had tried to address when he lengthened *PlayStation* and raised the bows until the forward crossbeam was about a meter higher than the forward beam on the Ollier catamarans. And it was the problem that Grant Dalton and *Club Med* were confronting as they tried to preserve both their lead and their boat.

Club Med arrived in the Southern Ocean just in time to latch on to the rough back side of the depression Quilter had been eyeing to the southeast. When you're desperate to break into the Southern Ocean, you hitch a ride on the first system that comes along, no matter where you end up in it. Dalton and his crew were always willing to tolerate physical discomfort as long as the boat was speeding along. And there was the chance that the maxi-cats, for the first time in sailing history, might be able to accelerate through a moving cold front, to land in the sweet spot out front. *Club Med*, in fact, began to catch up to the cold front ahead. But instead of breaking through she got stuck in the 30-knot winds and nasty seas Dalton had reported. Spray was everywhere and *Club Med* was leaping off waves and crashing into troughs.

Dalton was relying on instinct and experience to tell him how fast *Club Med* could be driven in these conditions. The Southern

Ocean chipped in with a blunt warning. One wave steeper than the rest picked *Club Med* up from behind and sent her surfing down its face to the trough below. The crew on deck could only watch with detached curiosity as the bows buried themselves in the wave ahead and brought the boat to an abrupt stop. Dalton was in his bunk at the time, and as the sterns started to lift he found himself standing on the normally vertical bulkhead at the foot of his bunk. Neal McDonald had been tending the mainsheet. The sharp deceleration threw him the length of the cockpit and down the main hatch. Powerful shock loads rippled through the rig. This was the scenario that had dismasted *Team Legato* (sailing as *Royal & Sun Alliance*) during a 1998 Jules Verne record attempt and almost pitchpoled *PlayStation* during her first transatlantic run. *Club Med* was luckier. McDonald was surprised but uninjured. The catamaran settled back onto her hulls, then took off again. "You have to watch it in this place. One bad wave and it's all over," a chastened Dalton commented. "It will bite you in the backside if you let it."

Pitchpoling had been a widely recognized danger before the maxi-catamarans ever reached these seas. *Club Med* now discovered an unanticipated Southern Ocean specialty: the geyser effect. When sails were not in use, they were often stowed in sail bags and tied down to the trampoline between the hulls. That way, they would be ready on deck if needed, and the crew would be spared the work of lugging the heavy sails in and out of the hulls. This stowage system had worked fine back in the Atlantic, but the Southern Ocean wasn't as agreeable. The heavy, wet sails tore at the netting as the boat pounded along. And in the rougher seas, waves frequently shot through the nets. In the middle of one night, unseen by the crew, a large swell surged up underneath the bagged staysail with enough force to rip ten feet of the trampoline away from the main beam. The gap was just at a point where crewmen often landed as they hopped over the beam to move forward during sail-handling maneuvers. In the morning light, the rip was spotted before it could do any harm.

But if a sail change had been called for in the black night, anyone headed to the bow could have plunged into the sea between the hulls. Eventually the crew would store the biggest headsails below, on the floor amid the bunks, to keep their weight aft (which helped keep the bows out of the water) and off the vulnerable nets.

Aside from capsizing, having a man go overboard was the most feared and potentially deadly event on the big catamarans. Sailors rarely fall over the side in calm weather. They drop off the deck in bad weather, in big waves, or at night. In any kind of seaway, a person in the water soon becomes hard to see, much less rescue (Eric Tabarly died in 1998 when he was knocked into the sea in rough conditions). A Race-class catamaran was so large and noisy the loss of a man overboard might not be detected right away. At night the *Club Med* crew took to signaling with their flashlights when they left the cockpit and crossed the net, to let their mates know they had arrived safely on the other hull. But even if the alarm was raised immediately, the math was not encouraging. A catamaran traveling at 30 knots covers a mile every two minutes. By the time the crew could lower the enormous sails and stop the boat, a man in the water might be miles away. If the cat happened to be running downwind in the Southern Ocean, the problem was worse. In a monohull, the boat can be brought to a quick stop by turning into the wind. Sails may be damaged, but the boat stays close to the victim. In a maxi-catamaran, to turn head to wind with full sails up was to risk flipping over. That would put the lives of all the crew in danger, something that *PlayStation*'s Steve Fossett had bluntly warned his crew he would not do if they faced a man-overboard emergency in the Southern Ocean.

All the sailors in The Race had small packs with location beacons and flares that could help the boats track them down if they were swept into the sea. The GPS systems included a Man Overboard button that when pressed would record the exact position of the boat. Buoys with strobe lights and waterproof radios, which could be thrown over the side, were placed within easy reach of the on-deck crew. But there were a lot of ifs. What if the man overboard hadn't been wearing his survival pack? What if, on boats that were more than one hundred feet long and usually enveloped in a cocoon of noise, no one noticed a man over the side right away? What if the beacon's tracking technology, which relied on a clear line of sight between the beacon and the receiver on the boat, suffered interference from waves or bad weather? A man in the near-freezing sea might have twenty minutes before severe hypothermia set in. In the 1989–90 Whitbread, one sailor was recovered after just forty-five minutes in the Southern Ocean. Yet it was too late to revive him, and he became the fourth man-overboard death in five Whitbread races. Fossett, the inveterate number cruncher, estimated that any man that fell into the ocean during The Race would have only a 50 percent chance of survival.

Team Philips had attempted to improve those odds. One of the innovations Pete Goss and his project devised with the help of Philips's engineers was waterproof radio headsets for the crew to communicate over the length and noise of the supersize catamaran. The headsets were also a valuable man-overboard tool. It would be much easier for a man in the water to see *Team Philips,* with her thirteen-story masts, than it would be for the crew on board to see him. The radio headset would allow the swimmer to direct *Team Philips* back to his position once she had been slowed and turned around. The Goss team tested the concept by dumping one intrepid crewman into the English Channel during a force 7 gale (next to a marked buoy). The system worked. The Race inspired other novel strategies. More than one sailor half jokingly suggested that the big cats should carry Jet Skis to make the pick-up. No matter what technologies were in play, however, the sailors knew — as most sailors instinctively do — that there would be only one decent man-overboard strategy in The Race: stay on the boat. Attitudes and boat speeds had come a long way since Robin Knox-Johnston casually streamed a line from the stern of *Suhaili* during the Golden

Globe, jumped overboard to bathe, and staked his life on being able to catch the line as it went slipping by.

For the moment, Grant Dalton was thinking more about the survival of the boat. He was still trying to get a feel for how much speed *Club Med* could handle, throwing up a big downwind headsail for the first time in Southern Ocean conditions to see how the boat would respond. The crew were bundled up in their cold-weather gear — gloves, boots, balaclavas, and thermals — and settling in for the long, wet chase around the bottom of the globe. Average speeds hovered between 27 and 32 knots. During one trick at the wheel, Dalton had the speed readout dancing around 30 knots, with occasional bursts up to 35. At that speed one bad wave or mistake at the helm could be disastrous.

If *Club Med* was sailing fast, *Team Adventure* was sailing faster. Maybe *Team Adventure* had found slightly smoother seas on her parallel track just to the north, or maybe she hadn't yet hit the churning water just behind the cold front. Perhaps Lewis and his crew were simply pushing their boat harder, taking greater risks in an effort to close the gap. Whatever the explanation, all Dalton and his team could see as Quilter tracked the competition's progress was that *Team Adventure* was sailing at record speeds and rapidly cutting into *Club Med*'s tenuous lead. "Cam has been attacking like a madman since last night," marveled *Club Med* coskipper Franck Proffit.

Dalton was in a bind. If he pushed *Club Med* even harder, he risked a serious wipeout or major breakdown. But if he played it safe, if he flinched and backed off to preserve his boat, he would be giving up the lead with no guarantee that he would get it back. Dalton's unease surfaced in a not-so-veiled warning to Lewis. "It was always our wish to get to the S[outhern] O[cean] first if possible, not be chasing, and then be given an option to slow down if necessary," he wrote in an e-mail to race headquarters. "This is a very unforgiving place to those who think they are out on a short offshore race. It will bite back unless treated with a lot of respect."

The experience of hundreds of thousands of miles at sea was telling the Southern Ocean veteran that the two boats would never be able to survive this pace all the way to New Zealand. Even so, Dalton wasn't inclined to take his own advice and throttle back. He had always had a bit of the gunslinger in him, a bit of swagger. Handing over a lead without fighting to the last mile was not in his nature. "Don't give a fucking inch, and if we break at least let's not be behind" was the way he later described his mindset. Winning in the Southern Ocean meant taking risks and never giving up. Dalton had learned that lesson in his first Whitbread race, in 1981, when Cornelius Van Rietschoten, his skipper aboard *Flyer,* suffered a heart attack south of Australia. Rietschoten appeared to die and was revived, but he refused to drop out and *Flyer* went on to win. "*Team Adventure* was bloody fast. They also showed they weren't afraid to push the boat beyond what we figured was safe," Roger Badham recalled. "Grant had his foot down. But there is a difference between foot down and foot through the floor."

Dalton, in fact, was gambling on this distinction. He felt *Club Med* was close to the red zone but not in it. Even so, he knew it was dangerous to flirt too much with the red zone in the Southern Ocean and fervently hoped he didn't have to do it all the way to Cape Horn. He also knew that after his confrontation with Ollier *Club Med* had been beefed up more than *Team Adventure.* He wasn't sure how much more, but if a boat was going to break, Dalton decided the odds favored *Team Adventure* being victimized first. He chose to play those odds. *Club Med* kept flying headlong across the cold, gray seascape in a cloud of spray. All movable gear and sails were shifted to the back of the boat — some sails were folded around the rudders down inside the hulls — to keep the bows up. Water ballast was added when insurance seemed a good idea. The crew went about their duties with professional deliberation. Still, stress was building with every blast of wind, every surge of acceleration, and every hour that passed.

About one hundred miles away, Lewis lay in his bunk, every

sense keenly attuned to the boat around him. Winds were building to 35 knots and a watch change was approaching. Randy
Smyth and Jacques Vincent were on deck, pouring on the speed.
Team Adventure always seemed to fly a little faster when those
two were on watch; even the officials tracking the boats from
race headquarters in Paris believed they could tell when Smyth
was behind the wheel. This was the first time Smyth had sailed
in the South. He had been dreading the cold, but his layers of
fleece and Gore-Tex, with a hat and gloves, were keeping him
comfortably warm. The thing that impressed him most was the
sheer energy all around him, in the hard blast of the wind and in
breaking waves so large he lost any sense of whether they were
twenty-five or forty-five feet high.

In the brief hours *Team Adventure* had been in the Southern
Ocean, Smyth had discovered that racing a maxi-catamaran
across these waves was a wholly unique exercise. At normal
speeds of around 30 knots the boat traveled faster than the
waves. Instead of being caught from behind like most boats,
Team Adventure would race up the back of the wave ahead of
her. At the top she would pause until the bows and about forty
feet of the hulls were suspended over the wave trough in front.
The weight of the bows would then tilt her forward in an accelerating rush down the steep wave face.

Every wave presented an obstacle and a delicate choice. If
Smyth steered too directly down the wave face, he risked bury-
ing the bows and the front beam in the wave ahead. He needed
only to experience once the violent stop that resulted — he compared it to a train hitting a wall — to know the boat and the
crew wouldn't survive that kind of driving long. But if he cut too
hard across the wave face, the breaking top would slap at the
sterns and knock the catamaran broadside to the wind and seas,
where she would be in danger of being rolled. The trick was to
find just the right angle down the wave face, find the fast, narrow groove that somehow got the catamaran safely across the
trough to the smooth back of the next wave ahead. Then the
process would start all over again.

Smyth had gotten the hang of it, but now he found himself fighting big waves that did not line up evenly. Trying to steer through and around them was like trying to ski in the moguls. Each one had its own personality and forced him to make a snap judgment on how to keep the boat under control. Rick Deppe had already voiced his concern that the motion of the boat didn't feel right. Smyth and Vincent were having a hard time deciding — they had never sailed *Team Adventure* in these conditions during training — whether it was safe or not. One possibility was to add water to the aft ballast tanks to help keep the bows and front beam out of the waves. As the sail designer, Smyth had worked closely with the Ollier design team and knew that the ballast tanks had been configured to tame the boat's motion in just these sorts of seas. With ballast in, the boat would descend horizontally into the wave troughs instead of tilting bow down, so that the ride was more like an elevator than a roller coaster.

But water ballast was not an option. Throughout The Race, Lewis had adamantly resisted filling the tanks, either for safety or to help hold the windward hull down in fast reaching conditions. Each aft tank could hold about a ton of water, and there just hadn't been time to play with the tanks before The Race, to learn how they affected the boat's motion and performance. Lewis was reluctant to experiment in the heat of battle. More important, he worried that the added weight of water in the tanks would give the cat more inertia when it slammed into waves, increasing the impact. He preferred to reduce sail area instead. Smyth had given up even asking.

While Smyth and Vincent discussed taking more sail area down — evening was approaching, and when you couldn't see the waves you had to slow down anyway — Deppe, Micke Lundh, and Rob Myles started to shift sails to the back beam. That would at least get some more weight aft. Down below, Lewis was thinking about a reef too. He had been stung by *Club Med*'s escape into the Southern Ocean and was eager to recoup his losses. There was no deadline to catch up; the idea was simply to sail as hard as seemed safe and drive every puff and every wave just that much better than *Club Med.* He knew he was pushing *Team Adventure* more than he and Peyron had pushed *Commodore Explorer* in these same conditions. But *Team Adventure* had nearly three times the crew and was in a tightly contested race against another boat. And the sprint was paying dividends. He had Dalton looking over his shoulder, and the gap between the boats had been halved, to just over one hundred miles.

Nevertheless, Lewis knew he had to be patient. Plenty of Southern Ocean lay ahead, and the crew had never sailed *Team Adventure* downwind in high winds and monster seas. It was hard to know where the edge really was. Even from his bunk he could feel the conditions deteriorating. Maybe it was time to throw another reef in the main or switch to a smaller headsail. A watch change was a good time for sail handling because two watches would be on deck at the same time. An old rule of thumb in sailing says that as soon as you start to wonder about a reef, you probably need to reef. Nervous, Lewis got up and looked at the speed readout near his berth. It told him the catamaran was flying along above 30 knots most of the time. Too fast. He headed for the companionway to tell Smyth and Vincent to slow down. He didn't get there in time.

It was quick. Rick Deppe, Micke Lundh, and Rob Myles were at the aft beam, securing one of the sails to the trampoline. Jeffrey Wargo, a twenty-eight-year-old sailor who worked the front of the cat, was down in the starboard hull struggling into his wet gear in preparation for his watch. A gust of wind, maybe 40 knots, hit the cat. She leapt forward in the rough seas and set up like a surfer on a wave face. Myles felt the boat accelerate sharply. *Team Adventure* always felt like a powerful train at high speed, but this burst felt a little different. Smyth knew it was different too. His instincts told him he had no choice but to drive straight down into the trough. If he cut across the wave face this time, he sensed he might lose control and risk flipping the cat. He could see an impact coming with the wave ahead; he

just couldn't tell how bad it was going to be. He waited. The entire front beam smacked solidly into the hard water. It was bad.
Team Adventure slammed to a near stop.

To Larry Rosenfeld it felt like a bus crash. Any bodies that
weren't snugly encased in a bunk went flying. Lionel Lemonchois, Lewis's watch mate, had just come up through the hatch
and was tossed against the radar screen. The wind was knocked
out of him and he grunted in pain, desperate to fill his lungs.
"Say anything! Are you okay?" Smyth shouted, adding, "Hey,
we've got a problem here." Deppe, Myles, and Lundh, facing aft
as they worked, were hurled backward onto the trampoline.
Deppe was pulled up short by the tether of his safety harness.
Lundh and Myles, who weren't clipped in, slid away. "Whoa,
we've got two more down!" Smyth yelled as he saw them
writhing on the net. Myles popped up unscathed, but Lundh's
hood had caught in the trampoline, wrenching his head around.
Infused with adrenaline, Lundh struggled to his feet. A minute
or two later he felt a shooting pain in his neck and knew that he
was hurt, maybe seriously. Seven months earlier he had injured
his neck in a car accident. The pain was in the same spot. A neck
brace was brought up to immobilize his head, and he was carried to a bunk.

Lewis was on the ladder when he felt the boat accelerate and
then lurch to a sudden stop. Somehow he managed to hang on
and raced topside, yelling that the boat had been carrying too
much sail. Down below, Wargo was also in agony. He had been
catapulted from the companionway steps like a circus performer.
He came up hard against a bulkhead in the galley, slamming into
it with his head and pelvis. The impact knocked him unconscious. "The last thing I remember was adjusting my harness,"
he recalled later. Lewis asked someone to check the starboard
hull for injuries, and Jacques Vincent found Wargo lying on the
floor. When he came to, his legs were numb and he had trouble
focusing. He vomited. Two minutes later he passed out again.
He was showing all the signs of major concussion. He was taken
to a bunk too.

Fred Carrere and Vincent, the designated medics, got on the satellite phone with the race doctors back in France. Lewis didn't need a professional opinion to know that Wargo and Lundh needed to be taken to a hospital. Wargo was in shock, and Lundh might have spinal damage. To continue chasing *Club Med* was out of the question. An hour after the accident, *Team Adventure* was headed for Cape Town, eleven hundred miles to the northeast, sailing at a reduced speed of 15 knots. Lundh lay motionless, feeling an ominous tingle along his left side. He tried to stay cool, but the uncertainty and distance to medical assistance made it difficult. Whenever *Team Adventure* lifted a hull or started another sickening rush down a wave, Lundh would cry out a plea to slow down. He was scared, and asked Deppe to hold his hand.

Just before sunset Deppe went topside and toured the deck. It was a routine inspection, normally carried out every day by Lundh or Wargo. Moving forward, he happened to glance at the starboard side of the main beam. During *Team Adventure*'s construction — after the delamination experienced by *Club Med* while undergoing her trials — the beam had been reinforced to withstand fifteen tons of pressure per square meter. Apparently it wasn't enough. Deppe saw cracks in the outer skin and black carbon fiber peeking through. He called to Lemonchois, an experienced boat builder. Lemonchois took one look and sighed. "Take some more sail down," he called. "This is bad." A blanket-sized area of carbon-fiber skin had been torn open. Water was working its way into the Nomex honeycomb core, turning it into a soggy mass. Lemonchois disappeared below to look inside the beam. Reinforcing bulkheads had buckled too. The boat was broken.

The damage was puzzling because the main beam had not suffered any great impact in the recent incident; the front beam had borne the brunt of the collision. Perhaps it had occurred a few days earlier, when another wave — which came to be known as Philippe's Wave because sailmaker Philippe Peche had been at the helm — smacked into the main beam. As far as Lewis knew, the internal damage could even have occurred during the stormy delivery to Barcelona before The Race started. Either way, *Team Adventure,* like both *PlayStation* and *Team Legato* before her, was going to endure a pit stop that would last at least forty-eight hours and probably much longer, given the need for extensive repairs.

It was a gloomy, quiet boat that sailed for Cape Town. If the collision and injuries hadn't happened, *Team Adventure* might have found herself much deeper into the high latitudes before anyone discovered the structural damage. Still, it was a crushing blow to have failed so early in the Southern Ocean leg. "We only lasted one day and crashed," Randy Smyth recalled. "It was kind of intimidating." A full team meeting to analyze what had gone wrong would have to wait for Cape Town. But *Team Adventure,* which had surprised everyone with one of the most dramatic match races the Atlantic Ocean had ever seen, was in deep trouble.

Mike Quilter had been closely monitoring *Team Adventure*'s speed and progress since the arrival in the Southern Ocean. *Club Med* finally seemed to be holding her own and was even drawing away a bit when he knocked off to grab some much-needed sleep. Dalton was on standby for his watch and reviewing the weather and fleet positions in the nav station. *Team Adventure*'s heading and speed were starting to look a little funny when an e-mail came from race headquarters. He clicked it open. Lewis was headed to Cape Town, it said. Dalton's reaction was immediate and brutal in its simplicity. "Fantastic," he whispered to himself. "Thank Christ for that." The tensions brought on by the intense racing, and the worries over the breakneck pace in the Southern Ocean, were suddenly released. Dalton would never wish injury on another competitor, but for almost three weeks and more than six thousand miles, Lewis and *Team Adventure* had been ratcheting up the speed in a way Dalton had never anticipated and didn't believe safe. The *Club Med* crew had made hundreds of small refinements to their boat during the six months of training before The Race. It was hard to believe that *Team Adventure* was racing so well after sailing so little, and watching her relentlessly close the gap in the Southern Ocean had been excruciating. Some of the *Club Med* crew had coped with the stress by joking and bantering. Others had turned inward. Everyone had been jittery about the pad eyes and other fittings that had been breaking. "A lot of the time we were just sitting there looking at the rig and thinking it can't last," Ed Danby recalled. "But you can't be the first to slow down."

It was hard not to feel a certain vindication that in the end *Club Med* had played the high-stakes and unwelcome poker game just right and that it was Lewis and his team, and not *Club Med*, that "fucked their boat," as Dalton later put it with characteristic bluntness. But there were other emotions — sympathy for the wounded not least among them. "It's like watching your mother-in-law go over the cliff in your car. You don't know exactly how to feel," Dalton quipped.

Maybe. But the relief on *Club Med* was palpable. In a single afternoon the nature of The Race had changed entirely. One minute *Club Med* had been sailing at gut-twisting speeds to protect a lead that could be measured in hours. The next minute the gap to the nearest threat, *Explorer,* was more than seven hundred miles. Now it was *Club Med*'s race to lose, and the only way she could do that was by breaking the boat too. As darkness fell and the sea howled with greater malevolence Dalton ordered the headsail dropped to the deck. For almost twenty-four hours, *Club Med* stooged along at two-thirds throttle, two reefs in the main, refocusing, regrouping, and preparing for a different sort of run across the Southern Ocean. Then it was back to racing.

Cam Lewis was also stunned by the sudden reversal. He knew he had a reputation for recklessness and was going to be second-guessed about the speed at which *Team Adventure* had been sailing. In fact, when *Explorer* got word of the crack-up, Novak and some of the other crew also felt a measure of vindication. Five of *Explorer*'s sailors had been involved with *Team Adven-*

ture at one time or another before jumping ship to sail with Peyron. The decision had been costly — the underfunded *Explorer,* wags joked, had the only true amateur crew in the fleet. But each had questions about Lewis's management style and ability to exercise sound leadership in the Southern Ocean. Julien Cressant, an acrobatic twenty-seven-year-old who had been raised on a Mediterranean charter yacht and sailed for France in the America's Cup, had agonized over which boat to sail on. His gut told him *Explorer,* and he listened. "It can be dangerous. You are putting your life into someone's hands," Cressant said. "And with Loïck you knew that he was going to handle the boat safely and still go fast."

It wasn't entirely clear cut, though. Speed in rough water is a matter of judgment and seamanship, and judgment comes with time on the boat. Perhaps Lewis should have been more conservative and set firm speed limits for the drivers. Perhaps he should have been more open to the idea of experimenting with the water ballast. But Loïck Peyron on *Explorer,* though he used the ballast tanks, also viewed them with some trepidation. Yes, they raised the bows. However, he agreed with Lewis that a ton of water slowed the boat — tempting drivers to speed up by taking a more dangerous line across the wind and waves — and increased the impact when the bows did plow under. "Sometimes less sail area is better than ballast," Peyron concluded. Similarly, with or without speed limits a skipper has to be able to rely on his watch captains to make the right decisions while he sleeps. Grant Dalton would later express sympathy for Lewis on this point. Dalton knew the importance of setting standards, but in his view boat speed on *Club Med* was a self-regulating process that depended on having the right hands on the helm. He had gone to a lot of trouble to find crew he could trust to make the right seamanship decisions. Lewis, he believed, had fielded a team of strong personalities who would test the limits of prudence unless kept firmly reined in.

In hindsight, though, Lewis was reluctant to criticize the team on deck. It was hard for any of the sailing team to be sure just how much abuse the structure of their new cat could withstand in the extremes of the South, and the fever to catch *Club Med* had been running high. In any case, all the Ollier boats discovered it was impossible to avoid the occasional nosedive while racing fast. Even *Club Med,* with the most experienced, disciplined skipper in the fleet, had been driving her bows under. Dalton, in fact, later stuck *Club Med* in so hard the Plexiglas canopy protecting the ladder going from the cockpit into the hull was shattered. "Jesus, Dalts, what the hell are you overdoing it for?" his surprised watch mates chastised him.

Injuries during these sudden decelerations were mostly a matter of chance. "I think we had a lot of luck nosediving," *Club Med*'s Steffano Rizzi admitted. Rizzi, a gregarious young Italian sailor, was twice tossed through the air — once landing against a grinding pedestal and once crashing facedown on the bowsprit — but survived without serious damage. Neal McDonald could easily have ended up like Jeffrey Wargo when he was thrown down the hatch, but it was *Team Adventure* that happened to put two crew into the hospital. "Our incident is due to bad luck," Lewis told race headquarters in the immediate aftermath. "We have a lot of respect for the Southern Ocean and [were] not attacking like madmen. But we're also competitors and we knew our boat was faster than *Club Med.*"

Yann Penfornis, from the Ollier design team, wasn't quite ready to write the damage off to bad luck. "The boats are so wide, it is easy for the crest of a wave to come between the hulls and hit the main crossbeam full on. If you do this at thirty knots plus, there is great energy in the impact," he responded. "They are not bulletproof. They are not made of steel." Penfornis was preparing to fly from Multiplast to South Africa to help supervise the repair work. He was disappointed, of course, to see one of his boats heading to port with a breakdown. Gilles Ollier, however, was relieved. If Lewis hadn't broken the boat, he told his colleagues, he probably would have flipped it.

Team Adventure limped into Cape Town three days later. On the way, it had become clear that major repairs would be needed to get the boat safely to sea again. From the inside, even at reduced speeds, the crew could see the center beam twisting with each wave. Larry Rosenfeld pondered some unconventional modifications, such as the removal of sharp protrusions and the installation of additional handholds below. Any sailboat at sea can be tossed violently, and injuries below — bumps, bruises, cuts — are common. Extreme speed, however, had turned these catamarans into manned torpedoes. The forces at work, particularly in the cramped spaces down in the hulls, were obviously sufficient to cause brutal injuries, maybe even a fatality. Micke Lundh had been up on the expanse of the trampoline, where there were few hard, sharp objects to run into. He still ended up in a bunk, sustained by a diet of painkillers and anti-inflammatories, feeling lucky to be alive. Jeff Wargo was lucky too. Their injuries had occurred one thousand miles from land, in the ice and gales of the Southern Ocean, on a boat sailing at 30 knots. "This is no child play," Lundh wrote Inga. "This is for real."

Before *Team Adventure* even touched a dock, the Cape Town Sea Rescue Team approached in a boat and put a doctor aboard to examine Wargo and Lundh. As soon as the big catamaran was safely moored, the two were transported to a local hospital. The medical verdict arrived the following morning. Wargo had a compression fracture of the first lumbar vertebra. He would have to keep the area of the injury immobilized for three weeks; full recovery would take two to three months. Lundh had strained a tendon in his neck and bruised a nerve between his number four and number five vertebrae. He would have to wear a neck brace until he was healed. Neither man would be sailing from Cape Town.

Team Adventure's prognosis was only slightly better. While Wargo and Lundh were being checked out, the damaged section of the main beam was cut open. Penfornis, just off a flight from Paris, immediately went to work, snaking around inside the beam to examine the damage. Delamination on the main beam's underside appeared limited to the area observed while under way. Inside the beam, Penfornis's inspection confirmed that an

internal bulkhead had fractured and a number of half-frames —
all intended to help stiffen the beam — had popped loose. The
damage was consistent with a powerful impact and had to be
fixed if *Team Adventure* was going to continue racing in the
Southern Ocean. The delaminated section would have to be cut
out and a new carbon-fiber skin layered on. Inside, the bulkheads would have to be repaired and new stiffeners added to
make the beam even stronger.

Lewis hoped for a quick repair and wanted to get back to sea
after the forty-eight-hour penalty had expired. The crew, particularly the French contingent, led by Lionel Lemonchois, were
not so eager. Everyone's confidence in both the sailing style and
the structure of the boat had been shaken. No one wanted to return to the dangers of the South unless a complete and reliable
repair had been made. Penfornis pegged the time frame at closer
to four days.

Even with a sound boat, it wasn't clear how many crew would
be setting out again. *Club Med* and *Explorer* were sailing away
at a rate of five hundred miles a day, building an almost insur-
mountable lead as *Team Adventure* languished in port. When
she first arrived in Cape Town, a number of sailors, including
Rick Deppe, Rob Myles, and even Randy Smyth, were wondering about the wisdom of continuing. Smyth had a long history
with Lewis and was no stranger to grueling races. But to Smyth,
sailing the Southern Ocean seemed to be a sort of Russian roulette. It had taken the seas there just one day to smash the boat
and seriously injure two men. What would the remaining eight
thousand miles have in store?

The *Team Adventure* crew sat down to talk it all over. Despite
the odds, Lewis wanted to keep racing. "It's a long event. I don't
want to wish anyone bad luck, but if they break something and
stop, it increases our odds," he explained. He assured the crew
that the necessary time would be spent to make sure the boat
was sound. He also agreed that water ballast would be used
whenever conditions threatened to overwhelm the catamaran.

Lewis didn't get through to everyone. Rick Deppe didn't see

the point of simply following the other two Ollier boats around the world. More important, he had lost faith in Lewis as a skipper. Deppe believed the accident never would have happened on the other top boats. Fossett, he thought, would have set firm speed guidelines, and Dalton's crew would have known better than to push the boat past its limits. Deppe's frustrations with Lewis's leadership style had boiled over on the way to Cape Town. "If you are lying in your bunk thinking we should get some sails down, why didn't you get out of your bunk and come and tell us to take some sails down?" he had asked him. "Lying in your bunk saying you are thinking that doesn't justify it. Your job is not to lie in your bunk."

These were harsh words, but Deppe's disillusionment had been building for thousands of miles. Lots of little things had started to bother him, even Lewis's tendency in hot weather to wander about the hulls naked. More important, his feelings had been compounded by a disagreement with Lewis over how candid he could be in telling *Team Adventure*'s story with the film and photos beamed from the boat. Deppe was already regretting his decision to sail with *Team Adventure* by the time the boat hit the South. "Fuck, I'm in the Southern Ocean staring at icebergs going by," he was thinking at the time. "My canary window is shut, and two months of this is just going to be miserable." Now he had an unanticipated opportunity to do something about it. After he had a chance to sit in the sun in Cape Town and drink a few beers, Deppe made up his mind. He met with Lewis and Larry Rosenfeld in a hotel room. There was no beating around the bush. "I think you guys know what my thoughts are," he said. "I'm not going to keep going."

Rigger Rob Myles told Lewis he was getting off the boat too. Lewis knew Myles had been reluctant even before the start. The delivery to Barcelona had been a rude awakening to the unruly nature of big catamarans in bad weather, and Myles had also been laid low by suspected food poisoning. Lewis had talked him into sailing anyhow. Lewis didn't want to lose two able-bodied crew in addition to the injured Wargo and Lundh, but he knew that an America's Cup job was waiting for Myles and that in any case both he and Deppe had made up their minds. He didn't argue. "I was not going to call them scared or chicken," he explained later. "And I didn't want people on the boat who didn't want to be there."

Race rules banned bringing new crew aboard. Larry Rosenfeld queried the rest of the fleet via e-mail to see if the other skippers would support allowing *Team Adventure* to replace her injured sailors. *Innovation Explorer,* determined to hold to at least second place, quickly answered "No way," and in any case race headquarters made it clear that adding crew was unacceptable. *Team Adventure*'s future hung in the balance. If any more sailors defected, there might not be enough manpower to handle the big catamaran. Each man considered the decision carefully. A few days in Cape Town with hot showers, bars, and restaurants had taken the edge off the recent memory of the Southern Ocean. Ultimately, the rest of the crew stuck together, leaving a total of ten. Sailing the boats with that number was certainly feasible. In fact, it was a configuration Dalton had contemplated early in *Club Med*'s training. When *Commodore Explorer* had raced around the world in 1993, Lewis and Jacques Vincent had been part of a crew of just five. It was not ideal, however. The maxi-catamarans had proved to be demanding, unforgiving machines. A smaller crew would mean less sleep and more work for everyone, and two thirds of the globe was yet to be sailed.

Lewis tried to make light of the situation. "Our conavigators, Larry Rosenfeld and Jean-Yves Bernot, may have to spend more time grinding," he predicted. But he was smart enough to know that *Team Adventure* was fading from contention. She had too many miles to make up and too few people to sail her at her full potential. It would have been easy to retire, and Lewis liked nothing better than to be the first sailor across a finish line. But he had sweated, worried, and worked tirelessly to enter a boat in The Race. Despite the setbacks, he intended to finish it. He and his team would have to make do with whatever reward came with that.

Team Adventure set sail again after four and a half days of round-the-clock repairs. The main beam's interior and exterior had been rebuilt and strengthened. In the living spaces padding had been added to any sharp corners that had not been rounded off. Webbing with easy-to-open carabiners was strung across the entries to the nav station and galley, ready to snare any flying bodies. Lewis was also better prepared. "We will continue to learn the limits of speed . . . It's always a fine balance in the Southern Ocean. In hindsight, we should have had less sail up and been going slower," he finally admitted. "We will be a little more aware of the speeds the boats can maintain in The Race."

Rick Deppe watched quietly from the dock as *Team Adventure* headed back into the fray. He was sorry to leave the team shorthanded but did not regret his decision. "Anyone who says they're not scared is lying," he said before he headed for the airport to fly back to the United States. "When I saw the state Jeffrey was in and the state of the beam, I started to wonder whether all this was really sensible." In the end, *Team Adventure*'s exact departure time hardly mattered. Cape Town Harbor was nicely blanketed in an enormous lull, with only the mildest of zephyrs ghosting over the water. After that, the forecast called for strong headwinds.

Club Med was three thousand miles and an ocean ahead, already approaching Australia. Dalton was impressed Lewis had managed to rally his demoralized crew back onto the ocean. "I never thought for a second *Team Adventure* was going to come out of what happened," he said later. He watched Lewis and his short-handed crew continue to bleed miles as they struggled to work the cat back into the Southern Ocean westerlies. Once she was there, Vincent found himself at the helm, rushing through the black night at speeds of 40 knots and more. It was an exhilarating ride and a defiant show of *Team Adventure*'s still-intact performance potential. This time, though, he called for the smaller storm jib to slow the boat down. Water was also added to the aft ballast tanks as a precaution against submerging the bows. *Team Adventure* nevertheless cracked the 600-mile twenty-four-hour barrier one more time with a 607-mile run (a record for the Indian Ocean). She was a fast boat with a good crew, but The Race had left her behind. One bad wave and one moment of incaution had transformed her fate.

12

SOUTHERN OCEAN EXPRESS

The work was hard, the voyage was long . . .
The seas were high, the gales were strong.
— "Leave Her, Johnny" (sea chantey)

SKIP NOVAK had rarely been so happy to be cold and wet. Lanky, with shaggy brown hair and a mustache, he had devoted his life to high-latitude adventure and was practically a native of the Southern Ocean. Like Dalton, he had raced there in multiple Whitbreads, and for more than a decade had run an expedition sailboat called *Pelagic* back and forth between Tierra del Fuego and Antarctica. Novak loved the austere terrain of Cape Horn, South Georgia Island, and the Antarctic peninsula, and sailed paying clients throughout the region to explore and climb. Sitting in the South Atlantic High, watching his competition sail away into the Southern Ocean westerlies, was an exercise in patience and self-control. It was tough on the rest of the *Explorer* crew as well. Mounting losses and fickle breezes will eat away at any racer's equanimity. Little annoyances — not showing up for watch on time, not washing the dishes, leaving gear and clothing strewn around — began to fester and corrode cohesion.

The lack of discipline aboard *Explorer* only made the problem worse. Accommodations on the maxi-catamarans were relatively spacious. They were situated in the back half of each 110-foot hull, which meant that the twelve crew had almost double the space of the crew on a typical Whitbread boat. Still, they were far from luxurious. The twelve bunks were divided evenly between the two hulls and stacked closely together. Workspaces (such as the galley and the nav and media stations) bracketed the sleeping areas fore and aft. A narrow corridor connected them all. The sailors had to squeeze by each other as they went on or off watch or moved from one part of the hull to another. Managing such close quarters to minimize friction and clutter requires strict routines. And while Skip Novak admired Loïck Peyron's sailing skills, he and Roger Nilson had become frustrated with Peyron's reluctance to establish and enforce rules aboard the catamaran. "Loïck is not super-organized," Nilson said. "He's like an artist, an amazingly talented sailor."

It was also partly a matter of culture. Novak and Nilson had spent their racing years in the Anglicized naval environment of the Whitbread, where firm schedules and responsibilities were the rule. Grant Dalton was an exemplar of the Whitbread ethic. He brought an almost military style of organization to his boats, and *Club Med* was no exception. It was a new experience for many of his European crew, and some had trouble adapting. But Dalton's force of will, backed up by McDonald, Danby, and the others on *Club Med* who were used to his style, prevailed. Peyron and many of his crew, in contrast, had raced most of the time alone or with just one other sailor on board. Short-handed sailing requires improvisation and flexibility. Peyron was not used to managing a crew of twelve.

Early in The Race, Novak tried to put Whitbread-type schedules in place to keep *Explorer* running smoothly, lists that would dictate who would clean, who would cook, who would run maintenance surveys, who would check the leaky ballast tank and when. But most of the crew were steeped in the more casual French approach, and in any case went to Peyron for direction. "There was a Breton clique and I didn't realize it would be that strong," Novak said. "They didn't move without Loïck saying something. Call for a sail change and they'd look right through you, until it was checked out with Loïck, even if that meant waking him up." Novak appealed to Peyron to impose some order and a chain of command. "Yeah, yeah, I must do something," Peyron would tell him, but he had a hard time confronting his crew. It was a style Novak and Nilson found totally alien, but they were in the minority and had to adapt. The standby crew — needed on short notice for sail changes — was often sleeping and not even dressed to come on deck. "People just got sloppy and lazy. That evolved into not taking care of the boat and not taking care of sail changes," Novak recalled. "If we had had more time before the start, we probably would have made massive crew changes."

Tensions among a crew are always greatest when things are going badly. So when *Explorer* slipped free of her light-air purgatory and started to pick up the first chill gusts of the Southern Ocean, the crew could not have been more upbeat about layering on the fleece and wet gear for the ten-thousand-mile sleigh ride around Antarctica. It felt as if the boat were finally rejoining The Race. The weather-induced pause had only heightened anticipation for what lay ahead — five-hundred-mile days with steady winds and long surfing runs, the possibility of ice, whales, and birds, and the pleasures of riding an extreme sailing machine on the fastest racetrack on the planet.

It would be important to make the most of those pleasures. With *Club Med*'s breakaway and *Team Adventure*'s breakdown, the tight, three-way chess game of the Atlantic was over. Two boats remained in contention for the lead, but they were separated by hundreds of miles. Novak and Peyron understood that overtaking Grant Dalton's well-prepared catamaran, now in full Juan Fangio mode, was going to take some work. Windless highs sometimes drifted south from the Indian and Pacific Oceans to upset the steady parade of Southern Ocean weather systems, but with Clouds Badham on the lookout they were unlikely to catch *Club Med* unawares.

The most likely place for weather funky enough to allow *Explorer* to come racing up from behind was the required passage through the Cook Strait, between the North and South Islands of New Zealand. The strait was notoriously fickle; winds could blow — or not blow — from opposite directions on any given day. Then there was the return trip up the Atlantic. More probable, though, was a breakdown on *Club Med.* The boat had been driven to its limits in the match race with *Team Adventure.* It took only one bad break — collision with a wave, ice, or a whale, or just rig fatigue — to put a maxi-catamaran out of commission. "Gear failure on the other boats is a sad way to win an ocean race," Novak admitted. "But it has always been part of the formula in around-the-world racing."

If bad luck with gear or weather lay ahead for either *Explorer* or *Club Med,* neither crew could do much to prevent it. The boats were no longer close enough to affect each other with tactics. Instead, the new focus of each crew was sailing smart and fast. Before the start, Grant Dalton had predicted that the most difficult competition might well come from the sea itself. And he was right. The Race was about to become a test of technology and seamanship in a merciless environment. Bruno Peyron had always fantasized about the speed, excitement, and danger the world might witness if monster catamarans tackled the Southern Ocean. Now, after twenty days of hard running that had decimated and dispersed the fleet, two crews, on two boats, were about to redefine the Southern Ocean sailing experience.

The shortest distance between any two points on the globe can be found by stretching a piece of string between them. When the path or course of that string is transferred to the more practical flat charts that navigators use — known as Mercator projections — it retains the curve of the globe. Thus, on a chart the shortest distance between two points is known as the Great Circle course. The 5,800-mile Great Circle course from the island of Tristan da Cunha in the South Atlantic, a popular clipper entry point into the Southern Ocean, to New Zealand presents problems: it runs through the continent of Antarctica, close to the South Pole. In short, it's impossible. But sailing along a track closer to 60° south might save more than a thousand miles over a track closer to the northern boundary of the Southern Ocean at 40° south latitude. The Great Circle course from New Zealand to Cape Horn isn't as dry, but it runs 4,200 miles and would take any ship following it close to 67° south latitude.

The geography of Southern Ocean sailing, then, tempted any skipper to sail as far south as he dared in order to shorten the distance from point to point. That took ships deep into areas of sea ice and close to the worst weather of the Southern Ocean storm track. The clipper captains were notorious for driving their ships down to latitudes of 60° south and beyond. Clipper sailors spent so much time around Southern Ocean ice they claimed they could smell it before they saw it. The gale- and storm-force winds close to the centers of depressions would drive the ships at 15 to 20 knots day after day. But it was a calculated gamble. Ships collided with ice. Sometimes they got south of the depressions and found themselves battling headwinds, even calms. Other times they sailed into horrific storms that drove the decks under or rolled the great clippers on their sides to founder. Often, little evidence or wreckage remained to tell the story of a ship's fate. Shipping publications simply listed such vessels as missing.

Modern Southern Ocean sailors — the racers from the Golden Globe on — were also tempted to sail their boats far south to save distance, and frequently did. In the 1989 Whitbread, Dalton sailed *Fisher & Paykel* to within about one hundred miles of the Antarctic icepack and saw icebergs every day for a week. Eventually, race organizers specified waypoints along the route, which forced boats to stay far enough north to protect the sailors from their own competitive instincts.

There were no such safety waypoints in The Race. However, *Club Med* and *Explorer* had other reasons to avoid the higher latitudes. One of the greatest dangers to the lives aboard the catamarans was hurricane-force winds of 65 knots or more. At that velocity wind is like a giant fist, and Gilles Ollier questioned the ability of the boats, with their tall wing masts, to stay in control or even upright. Both *Explorer* and *Club Med* carried drogue systems that could be deployed from their sterns if excessive speed threatened disaster. The system had yet to be tested in realistic conditions, though, and no one was eager to find a storm to run trials. "We really don't want to see fifty knots on these boats if we can help it," Skip Novak acknowledged as he contemplated *Explorer*'s Southern Ocean strategy.

Aside from the risks of higher wind speeds closer to the storm centers down south, trying to shave miles at high latitudes also meant a greater probability of encountering ice. The heavy oak timbers of a clipper ship might withstand a collision; the brittle carbon fiber of the catamarans — traveling at 20 to 30 knots — almost certainly would not. It was hard to escape the risk of ice in the Southern Ocean entirely, but the closer to the Antarctic pack the boats sailed, the more likely they were to come upon apartment house–sized bergs and regions littered with deadly growlers.

History had proved that racing sailors were more than willing to brave such risks if they could steal a few miles on their competitors. On the big catamarans, however, there was a more prosaic reason to stay out of the high latitudes, one that even the most risk-happy sailor would listen to: performance. As everyone had learned, the maxis didn't like headwinds or rough seas, which forced the crews to slow down or risk gear failure. Both were more likely to be found at 60° south than at 40° south.

After weighing these factors against one another, Dalton and Peyron, along with their navigators, opted for the same strategy, which was to try to keep their boats in following winds of 25 to 40 knots. Generally, that meant staying in the corridor of the Roaring Forties and avoiding the violent centers of the Southern Ocean depressions sweeping by to the south. The occasional foray beyond 50° south would be justified if light winds threatened in the north or miles could be saved without routing the boat into a storm center. The one place where geography intervened was the barrier of Cape Horn, which would require a descent to 56° south. Cape Horn's high latitude was one of the reasons it was so dangerous. Sailboats trying to round it from the west were eventually forced south by the coast of Chile, and sailors had to hope that their arrival at the Horn didn't coincide with the arrival of a vicious storm, which is what made *Commodore Explorer*'s experience in 1993, with its 85-knot winds, so memorable.

Nigel Tetley, the first sailor to cross the whole of the Southern Ocean in a multihull, would have recognized the strategy. During the Golden Globe he stayed well to the north in an effort to keep *Victress* away from bad weather that might capsize her. He sailed most of the Indian Ocean, between Africa and Australia, north of the Roaring Forties, and didn't cross 50° south until he ran out of ocean off Chile and had to dive for Cape Horn. Tetley would have been amazed, though, at the technical resources Grant Dalton and Loïck Peyron had to refine their routes by placing their boats precisely in each weather system that came along. By the time *Victress* reached the Southern Ocean, instrument failures had reduced Tetley to estimating his boat speed by looking into his toilet — the boat's passage across the sea tended to siphon water from the bowl. If it was half empty, *Victress* was making 4 knots. If it was completely empty, 8 knots. Yet here were two crews that knew exactly where they were all the time, that talked to a shore-based weather forecaster several times a day, that could move at unheard-of speeds to pick and choose their weather.

They could even hunt for wind speeds that matched the nuances of their sail inventories. *Club Med* unveiled a small storm spinnaker, a balloonlike sail for downwind sailing in up to 50 knots of wind. This "chicken chute" was half the size of the gennaker, their large headsail, and allowed *Club Med* to keep just the right amount of fabric before the wind when it really started to blow. The chicken chute also allowed her to keep the Southern Ocean westerlies more directly behind her and sail a straighter course toward Australia and beyond. Dalton, who always preferred to head right for the mark whenever he could, fell in love with the sail. He hoped it was one of the advantages *Club Med* could use, without taking too many risks, to build a two-day cushion over *Explorer*. If *Club Med* could somehow stretch her lead to one thousand miles or so, the team would have the option of stopping in "windy" Wellington, right on the Cook Strait, if any major repairs were required to complete The Race.

Explorer had nothing in her limited sail inventory to match *Club Med*'s latest weapon. In fact, her choice of sails had gotten even smaller in the Southern Ocean. To save the damaged small gennaker for the final leg up the Atlantic, Peyron decided to take the much-patched sail out of the rotation, overruling arguments in favor of just flying the damned thing and risking disintegration. That left the crew to choose between the large gennaker, which they felt comfortable using in winds up to about 30 knots, and the much smaller Solent jib, which was about one third the size and needed closer to 40 knots to keep the boat moving fast downwind. Initially, the crew — racers, after all — were inclined to keep the gennaker up past its safe wind range, putting the boat on edge and convincing Peyron and Novak that it was only a matter of time before she found her one-in-a-million wave and smashed up her beam like *Team Adventure,* or, worse, capsized.

They held a crew meeting to emphasize the importance of prudence and seamanship, even if it meant a little hit in boat speed. Nilson and the routers would do their best to keep the boat out of the 30-to-35-knot wind range, which was where the gap in the sail inventory was most painful. Instead, they would look for gennaker weather, with winds between 25 and 32 knots, or Solent weather, with winds between 35 and 40 knots.

But even in the superfast catamarans it was hard to dictate the weather. There was no way to avoid entirely wind ranges that would catch *Explorer* without the right sail. When that happened, *Explorer* would have to steer some funny angles to change the apparent wind speed to suit the sails she did have. That meant sailing slightly closer to the wind, which increased apparent velocity, when the smaller Solent was flying, and more directly downwind, which reduced apparent velocity, when the larger gennaker was up. Which sail was flying would depend on which angle was the lesser of two evils. *Explorer* was going to have to sail a zigzag course and more miles to cover the Southern Ocean — there was no way around it. Meanwhile, *Club Med,* with sails to match most wind angles and speeds, would be sailing whatever heading took her to New Zealand fastest. It was a depressing tactical disadvantage that the *Explorer* crew tried not to dwell on. "We have to really forget about *Club Med* for a while and sail our own strategy, as if we were on a Jules Verne," Novak explained. "And try to make small gains on them as they try and loosely cover us . . . There is a long way to go."

If *Explorer* was going to sail a longer route, it was preferable to err to the south, where the Great Circle route would at least cut the distance to New Zealand and keep her in the strong breezes. That meant a greater risk of ice, so a radar watch was set up after reports of ice started arriving from race headquarters. This involved switching the radar from standby to transmit at regular intervals to take a peek ahead. Like most routines aboard *Explorer,* it grew a little lax. One night Roger Nilson decided he had better check himself. He switched the radar to transmit and was startled to see a large return just four miles ahead. That was about ten minutes of sailing. The chastened crew quickly changed course to pass the berg to windward. In the dark and fog, no one even saw the monster.

In the Atlantic the boats had fought to get south. Now they were in a race to see which boat could cover the 270° of longitude between the Cape of Good Hope and Cape Horn quickest. *Club Med* and *Explorer* were "running their easting down," like every clipper ship and round-the-world racer before them. The big difference this time was that no two boats had ever flown across the Southern Ocean so swiftly, knocking off twenty-four-hour runs of 450 to 550 miles day after day. The distance between the two catamarans would expand and contract, depending on whether one happened to be in fast, flat sailing conditions while the other was backing off a bit in heavy winds and waves.

Nevertheless, they moved over the seascape in tandem, as if attached by an elastic band.

The high-speed traverse took place in long hours of sunlight provided by the austral summer. Still, behind the passing cold fronts, air temperatures dropped to near freezing, and with wind chill factored in, well below. *Explorer* blasted the heaters in her hulls for hours on end. *Club Med,* which had no heaters other than one used in the clothing locker, to save weight, just suffered. The brief period of darkness each night was a time of nervous anticipation, with the boats hurtling along blind, the drivers often unable to see well enough to avoid smacking into the tumbling waves. "Sea and sky blend together into an impenetrable opacity. The helmsman is then on his own, cut off momentarily from his more concrete senses," *Club Med*'s Franck Proffit explained in an e-mail. "It's the moment of instincts and intuition. You come out of it an hour later, soaked, exhausted and groggy, as if you had just gone ten rounds with Mike Tyson."

Progress was measured on the glowing screens of the navigational computers on each boat. It was also measured by the appearance of remote island groups, familiar only to nineteenth-century sailors carrying cargo to Australia or to today's racers hurrying to complete the long passage to Cape Horn. Each archipelago they approached required a tactical decision: go north or south. Sailing close by usually meant rough seas, as the seabed rose to the surface, tripping up the open-ocean swells. One thousand miles south and east of Cape Town lay the Prince Edward Islands, at 46° south latitude. Near the islands, the seabed rises from 3,200 meters to just 315 meters. During the 1993–94 Whitbread, Grant Dalton lost the mizzenmast of his ketch-rigged *New Zealand Endeavor* shortly after passing by here. He completed the leg with the mainmast alone and went on to win the race. This time around he had only one mast and no margin for error. *Club Med* stayed safely to the north.

After the Prince Edward Islands came the Crozets, a chain of

volcanic summits that culminates in Est Island, which reaches
more than three thousand feet above the ocean's surface. The
Crozets were discovered on January 23, 1772, exactly 229 years
before *Club Med* arrived. They are a perfect illustration of the
damp, gray Southern Ocean climes. Rain falls, on average, three
hundred days a year, and the wind blows sixty miles an hour or
more on one day out of every three. Even in summer the temperature never exceeds 18°C. This dreary combination made the
islands unattractive to humans but very popular with seals.
Throughout the nineteenth century, Southern Ocean sealers
stopped regularly in the Crozets, decimating the population.
Dalton and Quilter guided *Club Med* within thirty miles of the
Crozet Islands and then east toward the Kerguelen Islands, a
psychological halfway point of the Indian Ocean route to Australia.

The Kerguelens were also discovered in 1772, by the French
explorer Yves-Joseph de Kerguélen-Trémarec as he was searching for the Antarctic continent. Captain Cook followed in 1776
and for his purposes named Kerguelen Island, the largest in
the group, Desolation Island. It is desolate indeed, with no native fauna. But explorers and sailors sometimes stopped by to
harvest "Kerguelen cabbage," famous as a preventive against
scurvy, a horrific disease brought on by vitamin C deficiency and
marked by bleeding gums, skin lesions, and occasionally death.
Dalton remembered the Kerguelens mainly for his decision to
stay north of them in the 1989–90 Whitbread, which cost him a
healthy lead in the Southern Ocean leg of that race. This time,
with no competitors nearby, he elected to stay north again and
continued on toward Australia.

Two days later, Loïck Peyron on *Explorer* contemplated a
more pleasant memory of the islands. In January 1990, as he
sailed past them in the first Vendée Globe single-handed race
around the world, his first daughter was born. Feeling lonely
and isolated, Peyron was so moved by the news that he named
the child Marie-Kerguélen. It took Kerguélen-Trémarec a month
to reach the islands across two thousand miles from Mauritius.

It took *Explorer* a little over three weeks to reach them from Spain. Now she ducked south of the island group, to avoid a large high-pressure system pressing down from the Indian Ocean, and gained almost two hundred miles on *Club Med*.

With each passing day, both crews grew more confident in their abilities to drive the big boats in gale-force winds and rough water. Watch in and watch out, the sail changes to adapt to shifting conditions became more efficient and automatic. The watch captains learned to favor the "middle gear" rather than wear out their crews with sails that pressed the boats to the edge of control and had to be changed more frequently. The routers on shore did their part as well, keeping the boats clear of storm centers. More conventional boats — the square-riggers and racing monohulls — often hunted for lashing winds deep inside storms because that's what it took to find top speed with a heavy lead keel under them. The Ollier catamarans were so light and powerful that it was easier and safer to crank them to top speed — or the top speed allowed by the sea state — in more moderate winds.

That didn't mean a moderate ride. Traveling at 20 to 30 knots in any kind of seaway was a bruising experience. In cross-seas the motion was even worse. Water frequently hammered at the beams — a relentless and corrosive reminder of the possibility of structural failure — or surged up through the netting to mug the crew and rip away at any gear stowed on deck. "For the first time in this race," Skip Novak reported, "I would categorically say it is getting dangerous to be working anywhere on the net, fore or aft." He was almost relieved that his boat was hundreds of miles behind *Club Med* and could sail her own race. If it was just fifty, he was certain, both crews would be pushing their cats to excessive velocities, their judgment impaired by the adrenaline rush of competition. *Club Med* and *Team Adventure* had already starred in that movie, and it had a bad ending. "We have to get our heads firmly screwed on here to get to the other end of the Southern Ocean in one piece," Novak warned.

During one 45-knot gale, a big wave exploded through *Club*

Med's netting and threw a sail stowed on deck straight over the back beam, ripping out lifelines as it went. Anyone working with the sail might have gone with it. A few sail ties held it dangling over the beam, preventing an expensive sail from disappearing into the deep. The crew rushed to heave it back aboard, watching carefully for any new trapdoors torn in the netting. "The boat looks like a battleground right now," Dalton commented. It wasn't getting any better, either. One of the consequences of sailing along at the speed of the depressions is that the weather — whatever weather you happened to be in — didn't change for days. "You can't really change your conditions," Mike Quilter discovered. "It makes everything go slow motion."

Neither *Club Med* nor *Explorer* could afford to have anything go badly wrong. In the Southern Ocean mishaps are magnified by the reality that the racing line — along the clipper track — takes boats into zones beyond the normal reach of rescue services. The Kerguelens, for example, are more than two thousand miles from either Africa or Australia. And that is the region where *Club Med* experienced the sort of glitch that can easily be transformed into a full-blown crisis.

Each hull contained a diesel engine that was used for a period each day while racing, to drive an alternator and charge the batteries. During routine charging, the exhaust fitting happened to blow off the engine in the port hull. Ed Danby, *Club Med*'s bosun, dropped down into the engine space to secure it. As he did, he noticed that a valve that passed through the hull and was used to open the aft ballast tank to the sea looked cracked — apparently it had been struck by the exhaust fitting when it flew off the engine. Even the hull around the fitting looked cracked. Danby tried to turn the valve. It came off in his hand.

Club Med now had a hole in her hull. The Southern Ocean shot through in a cold, high-pressure stream, rapidly flooding the compartment. Danby raced up to the deck to raise the alarm. With all her separate watertight compartments and inherent buoyancy, *Club Med* wasn't in danger of sinking, but if the leak could not be stopped, and stopped fast, she could be crippled. Electronic gear might short out; thousands of pounds of water would press the port hull down into the sea. Her ability to continue racing, to sail at more than a crawl, was at stake. "Get your ass over here, we're fucking going down," Danby shouted, to get Dalton's attention.

Dalton ordered the sails dropped, to slow the boat and allow the crew to devote their full attention to this emergency. To try to keep up with the influx of water while he planned a possible fix, Danby powered up an electric bilge pump in the compartment and threw some portable pumps into action. Some of the crew grabbed buckets and stood by in case they needed to start bailing. Plugging a hole at sea is never easy. One traditional approach was to make a mat that could be pressed along the outside of the hull. Water pressure would force the mat into the hole and plug it. Robin Knox-Johnston had fixed *Suhaili*'s leaky hull by plugging the open seams with canvas and tar from the outside. He had been in the Tropics, though. Dalton and Danby decided it was too cold and rough to put anyone in the water. In any case, a mat protruding from *Club Med*'s slick hull would slow her down. It was a last-ditch solution, not a racing solution. *Club Med* carried a supply of epoxy that would harden even when wet or underwater. Danby cut open tubes of the stuff, thickening it with chopped-up carbon-fiber cloth and jamming it into and around the broken fitting. Bandages from the medical kit were used to hold it in place while it hardened. As it did, Danby would tear his hand loose and slap another pile of epoxy on top. Within three hours the gush of water was stopped and *Club Med* returned to the race. A bypass to allow the aft ballast tank to be filled with seawater was rigged.

Club Med's crew slipped back into the regular watch routine, barely giving the leak a second thought. Perhaps it was easier for modern sailors to forget the close calls because they were so much less vulnerable than their predecessors, even in the reaches of the Southern Ocean. During the 1960s, a sailor needing rescue or assistance, in the busy shipping lanes of the North At-

lantic or anywhere else, was in real trouble. Using traditional
sextant navigation, most sailors — even the good navigators —
rarely had their positions pinpointed. When he abandoned his
Victress catamaran off the Azores in the Golden Globe race, Tetley knew only that he was "approximately 100 miles north-east
of San Miguel." He was rescued promptly because the race
sponsor, the *Sunday Times,* happened to include an emergency
radio transmitter in his survival kit, which he used to guide a rescue aircraft to his life raft.

More often than not, however, surviving shipwreck meant
floating for weeks and sometimes months in a raft. In 1952 a
young French doctor named Alain Bombard concluded that
thousands of people died at sea every year because they didn't
know how to stay alive in their life rafts. To give hope to future
castaways by proving that a person could survive indefinitely on
what the sea alone provided, Bombard crossed the Atlantic,
from the Canary Islands to Barbados, in a fifteen-foot rubber
dinghy that carried no food or water. He took sixty-five days to
complete the journey in his little boat *L'Hérétique,* eating the
raw flesh and drinking the blood of fish that he caught. He also
collected rainwater and drank small amounts of saltwater, which
he believed safe as long as he wasn't totally dehydrated. He arrived in Barbados fifty-five pounds lighter and wrote it all up in
a book called *History of a Voluntary Castaway.*

As communications and emergency position-finding technology steadily improved, the need to drink fish blood in life rafts
diminished. Today, emergency beacons give precise positions
over international distress frequencies monitored by aircraft and
satellites. Commercial vessel positions are constantly updated by
maritime search-and-rescue authorities so that nearby ships can
be diverted for a pickup, as the *Hoechst Express* was for *Team
Philips.* Of course, the efficiency of the modern search-and-rescue process is predicated on being able to get a ship or an airplane to the sailor or vessel in distress. And the one ocean that
stubbornly resists easy accessibility is the Southern Ocean. Vast
swathes of the Indian and Pacific Oceans beyond 40° south are

as remote as any place on earth. These areas — like the position where *Club Med* was bailing — are well beyond the range of rescue helicopters that can pluck sailors from the sea. And cargo vessels generally prefer to go from ocean to ocean via the safer, more convenient Suez and Panama Canals. In the 1994–95 BOC single-handed race, one sailor activated his emergency beacon halfway between New Zealand and Cape Horn. A ship was diverted to search for him but took days to reach his general position. By the time it did, his beacon had stopped transmitting. He was never found.

There have been successful rescues from the nether reaches of the Southern Ocean, but they usually entail considerable time and expense. Isabelle Autissier was rescued about one thousand miles south of Australia on New Year's Eve, 1994, by the Australian Navy. The navy also picked up Bullimore and another racer, Thierry Dubois, in the 1996–97 Vendée Globe. The Australians even plucked Steve Fossett from the Coral Sea after he ditched during a 1998 round-the-world balloon attempt. The cost of all these rescues, which ran to hundreds of thousands of dollars, provoked an angry backlash from Australian taxpayers, who naturally resented footing the bill for risk-taking adventurers (particularly since one of them was a multimillionaire). The Australian Navy didn't seem to mind, appreciating the real-life training and experience, but the Australian Marine Rescue Coordination Centre did post a cartoon illustrating its worst nightmare: Steve Fossett crash-landing a balloon on Tony Bullimore's sailboat.

The taxpayer backlash was one of the reasons that round-the-world race organizers introduced required waypoints to keep competitors out of the most remote zones of the Southern Ocean. Bruno Peyron, aside from the passage through Cook Strait, did not want to restrict the course of The Race in any way. He also did not want to be forced to turn to the rescue services if one of his boats got in trouble, so a four-tiered safety plan was devised for The Race. It relied first and foremost on the other race boats if assistance was needed. This made sense. If the fleet wasn't too reduced by mishaps or too spread out, the other multihulls would likely be in the best position to help a stricken boat, and in any case could sail faster than most ships.

As a backup to the race competitors themselves, a former Whitbread monohull, with a doctor and trained emergency personnel on board, had been chartered to shadow the fleet across the Southern Ocean. This boat, named *Watcher,* waited in Cape Town until *Club Med* and *Explorer* raced by, and took up a position in the middle of the fleet. Only if *Watcher* or one of the other competitors was unable to assist a catamaran that had capsized or suffered some other catastrophe would commercial shipping and, finally, conventional marine rescue authorities be called into action. It was a better safety net for the Southern Ocean than most races provided. Australian and South American rescue services, which were facing three separate races in the Southern Ocean at the same time — the 2000–01 Vendée Globe, The Race, and the BT Global Challenge, an amateur round-the-world race with paying crews — appreciated the gesture. Blondie Hasler might also have appreciated the slight reversal of a racing culture that increasingly took rescue for granted.

Robin Knox-Johnston and the first Southern Ocean racers had none of this reassurance. They were more isolated than any humans on the face of the planet, and knew that if they could not save themselves in an emergency, there would be no one coming to their rescue. They would die, and it would be months before anyone realized they had gone. It is almost impossible to approximate such extreme isolation in the wired world of today or the effect it has on the psyche. Still, the deep Southern Ocean latitudes, like the upper reaches of Everest, come closest. A safety net, regardless of its technological sophistication, cannot take that away. There, self-reliance, preparation, and experience count above all else.

On board *Club Med,* Grant Dalton was perhaps sensing this truth more than the others. Even throttled back to 95 percent since sending *Team Adventure* to the repair dock, *Club Med* was taking a beating. There was no way around it. Sailing the big catamaran at racing speeds in the Southern Ocean meant taking the boat "down the mine." Not every hour of every day, but often enough. And Dalton was learning to live with the unsettling reality that rig failure, beam structure problems, and perhaps capsize lurked in every weather depression, every storm gust, and every graybeard that picked *Club Med* up and sent her humming forward on a long surfing run.

Clouds Badham and Quilter were doing their best to hold *Club Med* north and protect her from the ocean they feared most in any round-the-world race. "The Indian Ocean is a cow," Badham said. "What you get at forty-five degrees south is usually equivalent to what you find at fifty-five degrees in the Pacific." Even so, the seas were as bad as any Dalton could remember in his five previous races through the region. "Surfing off these waves is like starting at the top of a hill on a skateboard. Once you are off there is no way to stop without falling, you just have to ride it flat out all the way to the bottom," he explained. "When you hit the bottom of the valley, it is like standing on the back of a flatbed truck that suddenly slammed the brakes on. If you are not holding on you will go flying forward. It is just like constantly running aground." Dalton elaborated further in another communiqué: "We have found that the boat accelerates down the face of the wave and over 35 knots of wind you may ride out the bottom of the trough but then again you may not. Every now and again you bury the bows and come to an abrupt and sudden stop. Not so much a full-on nose dive, more a sudden deceleration caused by the tons of water that [are] being pushed. Not particularly safe." The dangers were real, but sometimes the effect was comical. Once, crewman Alexis de Cenival was caught unprepared as *Club Med* decelerated sharply from 29 knots to 3 knots. He was launched from the back of the trampoline, ending up in a heap twenty feet away near the main beam. Only his dignity was wounded.

This was a novel sort of interaction between boat and sea, one that didn't necessarily appeal to all sailors. Asked whether he would have liked to have been racing one of the maxi-cats through the Southern Ocean, Chay Blyth, the Golden Globe and Whitbread veteran, was clear. "Not me . . . I'd rather watch them on video and via the Internet," he said. "To be on board at those sorts of speeds you'd need the steering wheel in one hand and a prayer book in the other." The *Club Med* crew shrugged off the tendency to submarine and instead honored it with a new description, "pile-driving," as in, "We did some pile-driving this morning because the sea was really bad." The only reassuring aspect of the experience was that while it was violent — especially for anyone who got tumbled — the boat never felt as if she were about to pitchpole. Instead, damage to the rig and beams was the main worry.

To adapt, Dalton and his crew, unlike Cam Lewis, spent a lot of time playing with water ballast. When the bows started to show signs of driving under, seawater would be added to the aft tanks to raise them up. Ballast helped, but the additional weight perceptibly slowed the boat. Even the aft beam, connecting the back ends of the hulls, was becoming a source of concern, particularly the leeward end, which was repeatedly slammed by waves as the wind in the sails pressed the leeward hull down into the water. In the Atlantic, Dalton had fretted that the weight of the extra structure he had added to *Club Med* slowed her a touch. Now he wished she had about fifty more kilograms of carbon fiber reinforcing a few strategic spots. "The beams take such a hammering from the waves, it is unbelievable," he observed. "The force of the water hitting them at high speed is just brutal."

With so little experience on the boat, Dalton was forced to make instinctive decisions about how much abuse *Club Med* could take. In flat water, winds as high as 35 knots seemed easy to handle, and the boat could be raced hard. In winds above 35 knots and in big seas, however, Dalton shifted from racing to what he called a "total seamanship strategy," which made preserving the boat the dominant priority. Sometimes that meant water ballast (during one storm he called Multiplast to ask whether it was safe to fill both aft tanks at the same time). Sometimes it meant sailing under mainsail alone. Always it meant being careful, doubling tie-downs on any sails left on the netting and dragging any unused sails down into the hulls. The banging and bucketing were so severe that Dalton found himself looking forward to the lighter winds expected in the Tasman Sea on the approach to New Zealand. They might allow *Explorer* to make up some miles, but they would soothe his jangling nerves and give the crew the conditions needed to thoroughly inspect their battered craft.

Seven hundred miles behind *Club Med,* the Indian Ocean was giving *Explorer* a much smoother ride. Julien Cressant got all the way to Australia without ever wearing a safety harness. Skip Novak, more a stickler for safety, put one on just once. Cressant was at the helm one night with the big gennaker hauling *Explorer* through the blackness at more than 30 knots. The wind and waves kicked up a notch and Cressant felt the boat set up on top of a steep roller. He instinctively knew what was coming, but all he could do was try to keep the cat's bows pointed downwind with the set of the seas. "Let's go for a ride," he whispered, and *Explorer* took off on a wild surf, vibrating like a well-struck tuning fork. Cressant watched transfixed as the speed readout climbed to 40 knots. This was the sort of exhilaration he had signed on for. Peyron was less impressed and popped up to the deck. "Hey, you're not supposed to go that fast," he chided, unnerved by the sensation of his 110-foot catamaran hurtling along on the edge of control. "Well, I'm trying to do my best to slow down" was all the sheepish Cressant could say. It was like asking a teenager in a Ferrari to keep to the speed limit. Loïc Le Mignon pushed even further into the red zone during one trick at the wheel, hitting 42 knots. Sometimes it's the machine that does the driving.

Even with the relatively manageable depressions *Explorer* was riding to Australia, the boat received its share of nicks. As *Club Med* had discovered, sailing fast meant battering the beams. The core structure of *Explorer*'s main beam — which was identical to *Team Adventure*'s — survived intact. But the Ollier catamarans had been designed with two life-raft bays built along the aft side of the beam, on either side of the mast. The "bomb bays," as they were known, had two doors, one above and one below, so the life rafts could be retrieved whether the catamaran was upright or upside down. It did not take many Southern Ocean miles before a single wave ripped the bottom door off one bay and left it spinning in the wake. Sail trouble also continued to plague the crew. The big gennaker, which had become a workhorse sail in winds around 30 knots or less, started to show some tears. The crew had it down on the net for sewing whenever possible. During one repair session a knife lying on the netting was kicked into Elena Caputo-Novak's thigh; only her heavy waterproof clothing prevented a serious wound.

Explorer finally ran into a real Southern Ocean storm south of Australia. Winds blew steadily at 35 to 40 knots, with gusts to 45. In a run of twenty-four hours, Novak, Peyron, and the crew discovered all the pluses and minuses of the Southern Ocean experience in a big catamaran. On the plus side, *Explorer* cracked off her first 600-mile day, hitting 605. On the minus side, the screeching winds and confused seas exacted a series of tolls on the speeding French boat.

In the dead of night, with boat speeds hovering around 30 knots and a new watch preparing to come on deck, there was a familiar submarine crunch. A few meters of the port daggerboard had sheared off below the hull, leaving the remnant vibrating noisily in the trunk. The crew turned *Explorer* dead downwind so they could slow down and investigate. Attempts to raise the broken daggerboard through the hull were unsuccessful. Whatever was left at the bottom of the board was jamming as the crew pulled it up through the casing. They eased it back down, whereupon another large piece broke off and gave the rudder a solid whack as it went by. The thing was disintegrating, but at least the remaining board could now be raised into the hull. Steering and tracking would be a little harder, slowing the boat a fraction, but the board could be reversed to regain some performance, and *Explorer* thundered on. No one could be sure whether the board had hit an underwater object or simply had exploded under the force of the water pressure.

The Southern Ocean had consumed two big chunks of carbon fiber and was hungry for more. Shortly after the daggerboard went to pieces, the second life-raft bomb-bay door was smashed in two by a wave — despite the line placed around it after the first door went swimming. Half an hour later, a large wave crashed down onto the Plexiglas canopy protecting the starboard companionway and shattered it. *Club Med* would also lose a bomb-bay door in addition to her cracked canopy.

The canopies were not vital racing components and were eventually glued back together. The fractures provided a good illustration of the guesswork involved when the boats were being designed, though. Multiplast's engineering models had calculated that the canopies should be ten millimeters thick. Jean Maurel, a sailor with vast experience on the sixty-foot trimaran circuit who was acting as a design consultant, suggested that four millimeters would be lighter and had proved sufficient on his sixty-footer, which could sail almost as fast. The Multiplast designers didn't argue the point, and in any case couldn't know for sure what was required because a boat like theirs had never been built before. So they split the difference and made the canopies six millimeters thick — not strong enough.

For a malicious finale to the orgy of destruction aboard *Explorer*, water somehow found its way into the much-beloved heater in the starboard hull. The unit was rendered inert, forcing Roger Nilson to shiver in a navigation station that began to drip with condensation. "Now we know what Grant was making all the fuss about," Novak wryly commented in an e-mail. "One thing we can say is that the boat is getting lighter with every piece that falls off it."

Novak could afford to joke because the big catamarans were inflicting some damage of their own. Bruno Peyron's old *Commodore Explorer* would hit the wall at around 27 knots. The new *Explorer* cruised comfortably above 30 and had to be taken past 35 before things got hairy. "There's just a huge jump in speed," Novak said. Almost one month into The Race, *Club Med* crossed the longitude of Cape Leeuwin and sailed south of Australia into the Great Australian Bight. A storm with gusts over 50 knots and squalls of sleet and snow hastened the big blue catamaran past the headland, one of the milestones of a Southern Ocean passage. Just seven days and eighteen hours earlier, *Club Med* had been at the longitude of the Cape of Good Hope, at the southern tip of Africa. The meridians between Africa and Australia had never been covered so quickly. *Sport Elec* had set the previous record for the Indian Ocean during its 1997 Jules Verne circumnavigation, with a time just shy of nine days. *Club Med* was thirty-three hours faster.

Not to be outdone, *Explorer* passed Cape Leeuwin a day and a half later. In the early evening, race headquarters received an e-mail from navigator Roger Nilson: "Just to inform you that we crossed the longitude of Cape Leeuwin . . . at 1810 GMT today the 29th. That makes for us a total time of 7 days, 14 hours and 10 minutes from the longitude of Cape of Good Hope." Nilson didn't mention it, but he didn't have to: *Explorer*'s time was four hours less than *Club Med*'s. The resilient crew hadn't taken many miles off *Club Med*'s lead, but they had snatched her newly minted record.

Explorer now seemed blessed, sailing out from under roiling storm clouds into warm sunshine. The wind eased into the 20-knot range for some fast, easy running, and crewman Thierry Douillard made Roger Nilson a happy man by fixing the heater in the starboard hull so the Swede could restore his preferred sauna conditions. Even better, *Explorer* sailed into the Tasman Sea, between Australia and New Zealand, and found herself perfectly positioned between a high-pressure system to the north and a low-pressure system to the south, with a northwesterly wind whistling between them over flat water.

By now the crew had learned that with the big catamarans it was impossible to force the pace. The sea either opened the way for a full sprint or it didn't. You had to take what was offered or risk damaging the boat. What was offered here was a beautiful runway. Boat speed rapidly climbed toward 30 knots, faster in the gusts. After a few hours of watching the speed readout, Skip Novak went down to the nav station to review with Nilson the boat's speed over the past eight or nine hours. "Christ, if this keeps up we could be up for a twenty-four-hour run," he exclaimed. Nilson projected their course ahead on the chart. "Yeah," he said. "Except New Zealand is in the way." Novak looked to see what Nilson was talking about. He was right. In a couple of hundred miles *Explorer* was going to have to start curving north toward the Cook Strait. The twenty-four-hour record was measured point to point rather than by actual miles sailed, so that arc might kill her chances. There was no reason to give up, though. Regular watch schedules were almost entirely abandoned so the full crew could squeeze every increment of speed from the boat. Loïck Peyron shook Yves Loday from a deep sleep so the best drivers could be available on deck. *Explorer* began to spit out the miles at a blistering pace, the windward hull just skimming over the waves. Novak spent an hour on the helm and never saw the readout drop below 31 knots. Race headquarters was asked to closely monitor the boat's position and speed.

All night the sweet northwest wind blew true, and the 110-foot catamaran flew along under mainsail and the hardworking big gennaker. In the hours before dawn, with *Explorer* touching 36 knots, the on-deck crew considered a reef in the main. How to balance the thrill of gunning for a cherished sailing record against the risks of pushing too hard in a race that still had half a world to cover? Down in the nav station Loïck Peyron was on the satellite phone, giving an interview and fidgeting as boat speeds kept climbing on the readout in front of him. Knowing that a world record was possible, the crew didn't want to tuck in the reef without Peyron's assent. Finally, Peyron called for the reef. When morning broke, *Explorer* was still cruising at 30 knots. The reef in the main was let out again. Twelve more hours and the record would fall.

Throughout the day, the perfect conditions held up. The corridor of wind between the weather systems stretched all the way to New Zealand's South Island, which *Explorer* was rapidly approaching. Late in the afternoon, though, when she started carving northeast toward the Cook Strait, the lighter winds of a high-pressure system sitting over New Zealand wafted in. No one in the crew could bear the idea of slowing down just when the record was within reach. Peyron considered the situation. The only sail that might preserve the record chances was the jib that had been damaged and retired in the South Atlantic. He had been saving it for the chase up the Atlantic following Cape Horn. Now he decided to risk it.

The much-patched sail still needed a little mending before it could be flown safely. Jean-Philippe Saliou and Thierry Douillard went back to work trying to strengthen it. An hour later, as darkness descended, the sail was ready. Nervously, the crew hauled it up the halyard and sheeted it home. "We did this at night so we can't see how awful it is," Peyron joked later. The sail may have been ugly, but it was right for the conditions.

Explorer pressed forward, racing the dying breeze. Peyron took the wheel. A tense Roger Nilson kept up a steady stream of advice on angle and heading, shuttling between the nav station and the helm. The crew continued trimming with every little flaw in the wind. Someone thought to check the faulty ballast tank in the starboard hull. It was full. Plenty of cursing helped pump it dry. The wind kept dropping along with the boat speed. At last the breeze gave out. Gloom settled over the boat. Surely they had just missed. Nilson retired to his nav station. As he sat, a satellite message came through from race headquarters. *Explorer* had just sailed 629.59 miles, it said. Nilson raced to the deck one last time. "We have broken the record!" he shouted.

Explorer had sailed farther in twenty-four hours than any vessel in history, and *Club Med*'s record was beaten by just under four miles (not even ten minutes of sailing time). No one cared that they had cut it so close. A record was a record. In the dark the entire crew gathered on deck to drink another bottle from Xavier Dagault's celebratory stock of grand cru. "*C'est super*," someone said with satisfaction. It was a sublime moment.

13

Cape Horn and Home

> A great cape, for us, can't be expressed in longitude and
> latitude alone. A great cape has a soul, with very soft, very
> violent shadows and colors. A soul as smooth as a child's,
> as hard as a criminal's. And that is why we go.
>
> — Bernard Moitessier

W HILE *Explorer* was slowly winding up for her record run,
Grant Dalton and Mike Quilter were entering familiar waters
after a month at sea. Both men had sailed into Auckland at
the head of the Whitbread fleet, Dalton twice and Quilter three
times, and it was an experience to be savored. Few nations are
as devoted to sailing as New Zealand is, and when local boys
arrive in port at the front of a big-time race the reception is tu-
multuous.

Yet approaching New Zealand the Kiwi pair had been uneasy.
The high-pressure system over the Tasman Sea threatened to expand into a trap that might snare *Club Med* and let *Explorer*
come screaming up from behind. It is the skipper's job to worry
about such possibilities, and Dalton found himself wishing that
his native land didn't figure quite so prominently in the course.
Club Med was making great time riding a Southern Ocean depression that he believed could carry her all the way to Cape
Horn, four thousand miles away. Now they would have to hop
off the system to head north toward the Cook Strait and the uncertain winds along the coast of New Zealand.

In the end, the weather was kind. *Club Med* found a nice band of wind that carried her toward Cape Farewell, at the western edge of the Cook Strait, at speeds that touched 40 knots. In sunshine and flat seas Dalton had the crew scouring the boat for any signs of equipment or hull damage that might prevent them from completing the circumnavigation nonstop. If *Club Med* needed repairs, Wellington was the most painless place to take the forty-eight-hour hit.

Skip Novak and Loïck Peyron clearly were hoping the lead boat would have to stop. It seemed to be their only hope of catching and passing *Club Med*. To make a stop more tempting, Novak, along with Peyron and Nilson, cooked up a ruse. If they could convince Dalton that *Explorer* had to pause for spares, maybe he would put into Wellington ahead of them and allow *Explorer* to come sailing up. In communications from the boat, Peyron and Novak hinted broadly that *Explorer* needed a new sail and daggerboard, and that replacements were being readied. They talked of a cargo plane preparing to depart France. The devious *Explorer* team had Multiplast pack up a spare daggerboard in case Dalton called from the boat and had *Club Med* allies verify that preparations were indeed under way. The sailmaker played along too, even though no spare sail was available. Bruno Peyron knew what was going on but was sworn to secrecy. Although it seemed a little unsporting, there was a long tradition of head games and double dealing in grand prix sailing events like the America's Cup and the Whitbread. To Novak it was just the usual shenanigans — "Spy vs. Spy" he liked to call it. He didn't give the scam a second thought and devoutly hoped it would work. As far as Novak was concerned, Dalton was due for a little payback. The more Novak thought about the effort to secure a spare medium gennaker from *Club Med* before The Race, the more convinced he was that Dalton had strung him along until it was too late for *Explorer* to order a new sail, and then delivered the "no."

Most pundits ashore were convinced *Explorer* would pull in. Dalton had been steeped in the same sailing traditions as Novak and was cagey. What if *Club Med* stopped, only to watch *Explorer* sail past Wellington and continue? It would be a sucker play unmatched in racing history, and as long as his cat was afloat, Dalton wasn't going to fall for it. *Club Med* had her share of broken pad eyes, busted sail battens, and damaged hardware, but the checkup on the way to Cook Strait hadn't turned up anything more serious. The Race was nonstop, so Dalton intended to sail nonstop. *Club Med* arrived at Cook Strait just as *Explorer* was shooting down her twenty-four-hour record, making it obvious that the pursuing cat was still capable of top speeds. The grizzled Kiwi was almost insulted that Peyron and Novak believed they could toy with him. "If they thought they were playing a game that would affect a bunch of professional yachtsmen ahead of them, fuck it, they were really on the wrong planet," he said. Dalton thought the whole thing was stupid. "Why don't they spend more time pulling headsails up and down instead," he groused. "They might go faster."

Club Med came upon Wellington in the late afternoon, just in time for a joyous welcome in the waning light. All the crew turned out on deck to gaze at beaches and crowds for the first time in a month. Helicopters buzzed overhead, taking pictures for the newspapers. Enthusiastic boaters, braving the chop in Cook Strait, pulled alongside in powerboats and dinghies, struggling to keep up with the fast catamaran. A group of tipsy fishermen followed for more than an hour, impressing everyone with their shambolic, shirtless version of the *haka,* the Maori challenge dance popularized by New Zealand's All Blacks rugby team. Traditionally, visitors had to either answer the *haka* or leave. *Club Med*'s crew was spared the need to perform; they were leaving. Directly off Wellington, *Club Med* dropped her staysail to allow all the waiting boats the chance to draw even. A bag of videos was passed over the side. Grant Dalton's wife, Nicky, with their two sons, Eli and Mac, pulled up to wave hello to her itinerant husband.

Everyone was happy to see friendly faces and soak up the ambience of the world ashore. But with *Explorer* checking off the miles at a record pace, *Club Med* had little time to break from racing. Dalton gave the word, and the staysail was raised again. The quick fly-by was over, and it was time to get back to the Southern Ocean. The weather did nothing to ease the crew's anxiety about the miles to the boat behind. Light winds clamped down on *Club Med* just clear of Wellington. All through the night the deck watch could see the steady blink of the lighthouse on Cape Palliser, a ceaseless, annoying reminder that the catamaran was going nowhere. Ten hours later she had sailed only twenty-five miles. The crew stoically endured *Explorer's* record sprint. "I see Lolo is enjoying himself!" noted Franck Proffit, who had raced often with Loïck Peyron. "I'll send him a little message to tell him he should stop for a while to clean the boat."

Proffit would not have been in the mood to joke if *Club Med* hadn't enjoyed such a big cushion on the trailing boat. In a mere twenty-four hours "Lolo" and his crew took more than 320 miles out of *Club Med's* lead. That lead had been cut to fewer than five hundred miles — a one-day run in the Southern Ocean — for the first time since the South Atlantic High. As Peyron and company closed on Cape Farewell, at the western entrance to Cook Strait, an increasingly nervous *Club Med* finally broke free of the calm patch and sped south again. There she hopped onto the westerly winds of the depression that *Explorer* had just abandoned and set her bows for Cape Horn and home. One more item had been added to Dalton's race agenda: recouping his twenty-four-hour record. "Good on them, records are made to be broken," he commented. "But it really annoys me. We'll have to do something about that on the way to the finish."

On the sweep north to Cape Farewell, the *Explorer* crew also combed over the boat, looking for major problems and making any necessary repairs. In the flatter water of the passage through New Zealand the broken daggerboard would be removed from its trunk so the splintered end could be sawn off and smoothed. The board was then reversed and returned to the casing, shorter but still serviceable. When the work was finished, Peyron and Novak were both confident that their catamaran, though still handicapped by lack of sail choice, was ready to take on the second half of the globe without any danger of losing her place in the fleet. The Race was more than ever a two-boat duel at the front. *Team Adventure, Warta Polpharma,* and Tony Bullimore's *Team Legato* were strung out over six thousand miles. Even *Team Adventure* lagged by more than four thousand miles. There was no reason to pause in Wellington and throw away a chance, however slim, to catch *Club Med.* A surprise 50-knot squall off Cape Farewell and three more broken battens did not change the calculation, although when the main was down so the battens could be replaced a much more serious problem was discovered. The headboard at the top of the mainsail, which held up the main and carried its full load, was close to failure. Frantic work overnight yielded a workable repair, and the need for an ignominious and ironic stop was barely averted.

Off Wellington, *Explorer* was surrounded by the same buzz of helicopters and spectator boats that had greeted *Club Med.* It was the height of the lunch hour, but Peyron and Novak barely slowed. On they sailed to take up the long chase in the Pacific, giving back some miles in the light winds of Cook Strait. Ultimately, the diversion to New Zealand had cost *Club Med* about 150 miles of her lead, leaving the cushion at around six hundred miles. Dalton was in the mood to keep the pressure on. Earlier in the day, a newspaper article written by Novak appeared in Britain's *Sunday Telegraph.* It flat-out admitted what Dalton had suspected all along: all the noise from *Explorer* about damage and stopping had been a con from the start. "What a crack it would have been to pass him by as he sat in dock and continue on our merry way," Novak wrote wistfully. "Give us your best shot, Skip, we're more than ready," Dalton replied from *Club Med* as the race to the last great cape began in earnest. "We have played this game before. But be careful. Cam learnt the hard way."

Every mile *Club Med* and *Explorer* now sailed took them closer to the Mediterranean instead of farther away — a huge emotional lift. They were so far ahead of the trailing fleet that

Grant Dalton was closer to catching Tony Bullimore, still south of Africa, than Tony Bullimore was to catching Grant Dalton. *Club Med* could take an extra lap around Antarctica, à la Moitessier, and still have a good chance of beating *Team Legato* to the finish in Marseilles. *Club Med* and *Explorer* had sailed from Europe to New Zealand in just thirty-two days, less than half the time it took the fastest clippers to make the same trip (most clipper ships were happy if they reached the Roaring Forties in the South Atlantic in forty days). Both had sailed half the world at speeds that averaged well over 18 knots (*Club Med* was averaging an amazing 19 knots).

First, though, Dalton and his crew would have to negotiate Cape Horn, which lay just over four thousand miles ahead. To get there, both *Club Med* and *Explorer* would have to sail past a point in the Pacific Ocean calculated to be farther from dry land than any other place on earth. Magellan had named the Pacific for its seeming lack of storms, which was a reasonable view of a circumnavigation that tracked much closer to the equator than the voyages of sailors bound for Cape Horn. Yet in the previous decade it was in the Pacific that single-handed racers Harry Mitchell and Gerry Roufs disappeared and where Isabelle Autissier almost died after capsizing her boat. Titouan Lamazou, the winner of the first Vendée Globe, dubbed this part of the Southern Ocean "the Dark Country."

Grant Dalton and Mike Quilter had no such superstitions. They expected the Pacific to be a smoother ride than the Indian Ocean, and that allowed a different navigational approach. *Club Med* had so far sailed a fairly northerly track across the Southern Ocean — to keep the boat away from high winds, confused seas, and ice — even though it meant sailing more miles. She had crossed into the Furious Fifties only once, to duck under the high pressure lying across the Tasman Sea. Dalton, Quilter, and Badham had dealt with the approach to Cape Horn many times among them, and all their experience argued for a new strategic priority. "In the Indian Ocean you avoid the south, but in the Pacific you need the south," Dalton explained. "Yes, it is colder.

Yes, it is windier. But the miles are just so much shorter you have to bite the bullet and head on down."

The traditional clipper and Whitbread route was to bite the bullet early and then run east across the Pacific along the latitude of Cape Horn. This was brutal on the crews, particularly in clipper days when sailors had only wool, cotton, and leather to insulate them from rain, sleet, wind, and flying seawater. The southern approach to the Horn was more dangerous, reintroducing the risk of ice. Nevertheless, it was the most direct path to the exit, and faster sailing too.

Quilter and Dalton also wanted to shave as much distance as they could to Cape Horn. But they favored a more gradual descent, once again to minimize the possibility and duration of winds above 40 knots and breaking seas. If there was a chance to push south safely in moderate conditions, they would; there was no profit in risking a breakdown or a collision with ice at this stage of The Race. Peyron, Novak, and Nilson were inclined to agree. For the first time in the Southern Ocean they had managed to latch on to the same depression that *Club Med* was riding. It was a mixed blessing, however. *Club Med* was enjoying better conditions on the leading edge, while *Explorer* was bucketing though the rougher seas and stronger winds tucked farther back.

That's not to say *Club Med* had a luxury ride. Working south, she ran into 40-to-50-knot winds. Hervé Jan, who had come to be considered the autopilot on his watch for his willingness to stay at the helm hour after hour in the worst conditions, got mugged by a wave while crossing the trampoline and sprained his ankle again. He continued to limp about his duties until medic Alexis de Cenival finally tracked him down. De Cenival ordered Jan into his bunk and threw some plaster around the joint, just in case.

As the long Southern Ocean days trickled by and the finish moved ever closer, it was getting easier to think — even to fantasize — about life ashore and its comforts. If both *Club Med* and *Explorer* made it to Marseilles in one piece and without stopping, they seemed destined to be at sea for about the same amount of time as a clipper crew heading to Australia or returning to Europe via the Horn. Whitbread crews would spend only about half the time at sea on any given leg, which meant that Grant Dalton exceeded his longest continuous stint at sea when *Club Med* was halfway between New Zealand and Cape Horn.

Dalton and his team had it easy, though. The clipper crews suffered terribly in comparison, with the dangerous, exhausting work of driving a big square-rigged ship, the rancid food and dubious water, and clothing that was no match for polar conditions. Even worse off were Robin Knox-Johnston and the trail-blazing nonstop single-handers. No one can be sure where Donald Crowhurst's demons originated. But Knox-Johnston was at sea alone for five times the expected duration of The Race, and solitude for that length of time was a severe mental trial, even for a man who considered himself "distressingly normal." Knox-Johnston succumbed to bouts of listlessness and depression, and suffered recurring bad dreams in which the grueling voyage turned out to be only a preliminary heat in the Golden Globe. Only Bertrand Moitessier seemed to transcend — and even embrace — the loneliness and physical stress of being at sea for a prolonged period of time.

Since eating was one of the few diversions available during these sojourns, a preoccupation with food became a natural theme in global racing. Provisioning in earlier years meant thousands of cans and a tremendous addition of weight to the boats. It is hard to believe that Knox-Johnston's list of stores, read in the abstract, didn't sink the thirty-two-foot *Suhaili* below the waves. It included well over 1,500 cans of everything from corned beef (216 cans) to stewing steak (144 cans) to Stafford pork sausages (48 cans). Knox-Johnston also piled 350 pounds of potatoes and 250 pounds of onions into the hold. Even so, he became thoroughly disgusted with the choices. Some of the only excitement after months at sea came from guessing what was inside cans that had long ago lost their labels as they slopped around in the bilge water. When he finished in Falmouth, he still had a three-month supply of food because he couldn't force himself to eat more of it.

The early Whitbread years were undoubtedly the high point of Southern Ocean cuisine. During the first races in the 1970s most boats carried full galleys and often a designated cook. With multiple stops along the way, crews could load up on fresh provisions, and if the boat had a freezer (many were designed for both cruising and racing) they could enjoy a good roast well into the Roaring Forties. With each successive race, the competition became more intense, the crews more professional, and the rations more geared toward weight-saving. Through the 1980s, in both the Whitbread and the single-handed races that took up the legacy of the Golden Globe, provisioning became a game of maximizing nourishment — which ranged from three thousand to five thousand calories a day, depending on temperatures and the physical demands of the sailing conditions — while minimizing stores. That meant freeze-dried food, which made its Whitbread debut in 1981. Water makers, which eliminated the need to carry heavy tanks of drinking water, completed the weight payoff.

The range and quality of freeze-dried food steadily improved. Curries, pastas, porridges, stews, all manner of entrées and desserts could be had. The *PlayStation* crew tried out five hundred different meals in the three years preceding The Race. A seven-day rotation was created in which every lunch and dinner was different. Altogether, food stores weighed about two pounds per person per day. *PlayStation* and the Ollier catamarans set out with enough food for about seventy days of sailing, which meant that the total weight of stores for crews of twelve to fourteen people weighed less than the stores that Robin Knox-Johnston carried just for himself.

That was a huge performance boost. Yet even with the variety available, freeze-dried meals quickly grew tiresome. Ernesto Uriburu, a passionate cruising sailor, detailed a novel solution to the standard food woes in his book *Seagoing Gaucho:* "I tolerate no grousing; whenever mutiny seems imminent, I read to the crew the menu of a banquet offered by King Leopold of Belgium to England's Edward VII. They cannot stand it. Before I have finished detailing the third or fourth course, they feel full."

The Race skippers apparently didn't know about Uriburu, or what King Leopold served for dinner. For all their research, the *PlayStation* crew kept referring to meals of "salty brown slurry." *Explorer* was not far into the Southern Ocean before Elena Caputo-Novak noted several new vegetarians in the crew, who ate mostly rice or mashed potatoes and ignored the bland sauces that came packaged with the meals. Spurning food was a dangerous practice, though. Roger Nilson, a trained doctor, consulted with a sports nutritionist before sailing in the 1993 Whitbread. They concluded it was hard enough to replace all the calories a body burns sailing in the Southern Ocean eating only freeze-dried food. The amount required is too great to force down, particularly when the sailors are sick of the taste. To increase carbohydrate intake and enhance flavor, Nilson recommended that for The Race at least 40 percent of the food should be dried pasta. *Explorer* also carried a protein powder and diet supplements because the water maker stripped water of almost all minerals. Unfortunately, the protein powder tasted so bad it was eventually thrown overboard. Perhaps Nilson and Xavier Dagault, in charge of the provisioning, should have followed the example of Francis Chichester. He enjoyed fresh greens throughout his long voyage by growing mustard and watercress sprouts on a damp facecloth.

The bland diet aboard *Explorer* did prevent significant weight loss among the crew, with the exception of one picky eater who lost 15 percent of his starting body weight. A couple of the crew even added a few pounds. But aside from special treats, such as pâté and foie gras and caviar, brought out to mark milestones in the voyage, eating enough food to stay healthy was a constant chore. The *Club Med* crew struggled to choke down their freeze-dried calories too. Alexis de Cenival rated "Mr. Heinz" the best chef aboard. Thankfully, some of the gustatory tedium was relieved by the mutinous work of a few gourmands. Before leaving Barcelona for the South, a large Serrano ham was smuggled aboard and hidden in a bag of life jackets. Dalton, a well-known "weight Nazi" (as they are respectfully known in the sailing world), discovered the large hock and ordered it off his boat. It was extraneous poundage that, if it had to be carried at all, could be better devoted to spares. Dalton also couldn't stand the idea of *Club Med* being turned into a greasy butcher shop. The gourmands were equally devoted to their principles, however. Co-skipper Franck Proffit smuggled the offending ham back on board and hid it in the boat's hollow wing mast. When Dalton was off watch it would be retrieved so that pieces could be cut from it and put into individual bags for each crew member. Eventually Dalton discovered the stowaway. He managed to keep his sense of humor, but on principle he refused to touch a morsel of the contraband.

To add injury to insult, freeze-dried rations had another objectionable quality beyond blandness, already noted by *Team Adventure:* they produced flatulence. This sometimes made sleeping, even for exhausted sailors, as much of a chore as eating the stuff. The port hull of *Explorer* gained a reputation as a particularly malodorous address. The starboard hull wasn't much better, but there the culprit was smelly feet.

That wasn't surprising. Personal hygiene in the Southern Ocean, with water temperatures barely above freezing, was a rare and fleeting affair. To save weight, crew were limited to just two or three changes of clothing for the entire trip. Just before reaching New Zealand, Elena Caputo-Novak surveyed the crew. Since the warm weather of the South Atlantic High, no one had braved a wash; baby wipes were a popular substitute. Loïck Peyron confessed that he hadn't changed any clothes since beginning The Race. Yves Loday's strategy was to change only his socks. Loïc Le Mignon had a different approach: he never changed, but slept in the nude, reasoning that as long as everyone else smelled like him, everything was fine.

The food gripes and smells accumulating on the way to Cape Horn might have been easier to bear with regular rounds of grog (until 1970 the Royal Navy antidote to crew discontent). Unfortunately, while *Club Med* and *Explorer* carried small amounts of wine or liquor to celebrate special moments, the professionalism of the modern era mandated virtually dry ships. (*Explorer* made do with one case of wine — a bottle per sailor for the entire voyage.) In contrast, Chichester, Robin Knox-Johnston, and the Corinthian adventurers who pioneered round-the-world racing were practically fueled by alcohol. They sailed slowly, but they really knew how to enjoy themselves. In addition to plenty of hard liquor, Chichester carried a keg of beer on each of his two legs around the world in *Gipsy Moth V*. The keg was rigged with a hose and nozzle that ran straight to the nav station. In the foulest of weather Chichester could fill a glass with beer without leaving his seat. He also celebrated the milestones, but in a way entirely alien to the hardened masochists of The Race. For his sixty-fifth birthday, England's first yachting hero donned his green velvet smoking jacket, a tie, new trousers, and black shoes. Closing on the equator as he sailed south, Chichester opened a present from his wife (silk pajamas) and sat in his cockpit drinking a bottle of champagne.

Knox-Johnston, although less elegant, was equally attached to the rites and rhythms of life ashore. Whenever possible, he had a whiskey or a beer at 5 P.M. and got into bed by 10, waking up only once in the night to have a look around. That civilized schedule fell apart in the Southern Ocean, where he resorted to removing the lee board of his bunk so he would be pitched onto the floor whenever the weather got rough enough to require a sail change. Yet large quantities of medicinal brandy or whiskey continued to sustain him through the extreme cold and endless abuse the seas heaped upon his little craft. The liquor stores on *Suhaili* ran to a case of Scotch, a case of brandy (by Cape Horn, he had averaged a bottle of one or the other every sixteen days), and five cases of beer. (Knox-Johnston also carried three thousand cigarettes, and still ran out.)

Of course the best narcotic for the crews of the big cats was sailing at speeds Chichester and Knox-Johnston couldn't imagine at the time of their voyages. And the conditions across the Pacific had the sailors on a permanent IV. The big depression they were riding moved east at the same velocity as the boats, pushing *Club Med* along in front in good sailing conditions and dragging *Explorer* along behind in rougher, colder seas. Following Dalton and Quilter's desire to push south, *Club Med* worked her way past 57° latitude, as far south as any boat had yet been in The Race. Water temperatures cooled with each mile, edging down toward an iceberg-friendly 3°C.

Dalton ordered a radar watch. Almost as soon as the set was switched on, a large echo showed on the screen, about eight miles ahead and directly in *Club Med*'s path. At seven miles, the crew could see it, and it was huge — about three hundred feet high and perhaps half a mile long, the largest berg Dalton had ever seen. "Big Mother iceberg at 58 degrees S, 135 degrees 31 W, please advise others," Quilter warned race headquarters. Dalton and Proffit sent crew forward for a better look anytime anything appeared on the radar screen or flashed on the visible horizon. Icebergs meant growlers. And with *Club Med* moving at more than 25 knots no one wanted The Race to end early. "Mercifully, visibility is good, a nice moon, flat sea," Proffit commented. "It's very beautiful but very cold." Aside from the ice, it was also excellent for sprinting. The Southern Ocean was opening a smooth, windy path to Cape Horn.

Badham, Dalton, and Quilter had carefully worked *Club Med* into the sweet spot of their depression, where the winds blew at 30 knots and the seas were flat. It was a unique position. The boat was right at the leading edge of the system, and ahead a ridge of high pressure with light winds was calming the waves. Throughout The Race the possibility of a twenty-four-hour record had hovered in the background. But the ideal track — which had to be close to seven hundred miles long, heading in the right direction, and offering consistently favorable winds and seas — never materialized. Until now. *Club Med* was almost two thirds of the way around the world and had shed much of her excess weight in food and fuel. She was in record-breaking trim and Dalton didn't hesitate. The maxi-cat accelerated until she was humming along at an average of more than 27 knots.

The only real suspense was whether she would run into the high-pressure ridge ahead, with its light winds, before she could reclaim the record. Dalton and the crew were feeling the adrenaline. He got on the satellite phone with Clouds Badham. "I think we can break the record," he told him. "How long do you think we can stay in this pressure before we hit the ridge?" Badham was pessimistic. He expected the high pressure to peter out and broaden, slowing *Club Med* as she bumped into the light winds. "I expect you'll have about twenty hours of good pressure," he predicted.

It was hard to be pessimistic on the water. *Club Med* felt as if she were on rails. With a reef in the main and a staysail, she frequently surged past 30 knots, and the ridge of light winds seemed to be moving toward the Horn in tandem with the flying cat and the depression that was driving her forward. The crew kept a close eye on the barometer. If it went up, *Club Med* was overrunning the high pressure ahead. If it went down, they were falling safely back into the depression behind. "The extra speed these boats sail at means that we can just move around at the same speed as the weather systems," Dalton discovered. "It is quite incredible compared to monohull sailing. It really changes everything."

Twenty-four hours after starting the run, *Club Med* had reeled off more than 630 miles and reclaimed her title as the fastest ocean racer in the world. And Badham, for once, was off the mark. Instead of twenty hours of prime conditions, *Club Med* got forty. The crew kept her cracking along and raising the record with every hour that passed. The steady winds eased only slightly, to about 25 knots, late in the run. Dalton wanted to take the reef out of the mainsail and change to the bigger Solent headsail. Normally, that might take the crew forty minutes, which would mean sacrificing a handful of miles. With the chance to lay down a really big number, he roused all the crew up to the deck to help speed the sail change. No one minded losing sleep for a shot at glory. *Club Med* slowed to 20 knots for the first time in a day, but the full mainsail and new jib were up and drawing in just eighteen minutes. The catamaran resumed her sprint, cold spray flying. By early evening the record had been raised to 642.4 nautical miles. And still the crew drove her forward.

Dalton knew he was taking a risk, but the thrill was impossible to resist. A big iceberg popped up out of the drizzle, directly ahead. There wasn't time for Ed Danby, at the helm, to alter course to pass it on the windward side. Dalton sprang forward of the mast to guide Danby — arms waving like a traffic cop's — through twenty minutes of ice chunks and "bergy bits" that littered the sea. Dalton shrugged off the drama later, a devilish grin creasing his weatherbeaten face, but ace helmsman Fred Le Peutrec, a Southern Ocean virgin, found the experience a little unnerving. "You're playing Russian roulette when you are steaming along at thirty-five knots in the middle of all that," he commented. "It's a bit like driving the wrong way up a motorway." Quilter felt the same way, but to him it was all part of taking on the nether regions of the globe. "It's terrible seamanship, it's ridiculous sailing in the ice area, doing thirty knots at night," he admitted. "But there's nothing you can do about it. Your seamanship says 'Stop, get out of there,' but then you would lose the race. So you just close your eyes and full speed ahead."

When it was all over and *Club Med* slowed as she finally brushed the light winds ahead, she had sailed just over 655 miles in twenty-four hours, at an average speed of 27.3 knots. "It was a lovely bit of sailing. The ridge kept moving and extending the runway," Badham recalled. "If that weather system were stronger, we could have had a much better record." It was impressive enough as it was. *Club Med* had been the first boat in history to sail 600 miles in a day. Now she had become the first boat to break the 650-mile barrier. Dalton had been annoyed to lose the twenty-four-hour record to *Explorer* and was thrilled to have been dealt the weather needed to get it back. "It happened quite naturally. You can't force that pace," he said. "It's either there or it's not." The happy crew celebrated with a round of toasts drunk with well-aged calvados. Cape Horn and the last leg to the Atlantic finish were less than two days away.

The approach of Cape Horn was much more than the approach of just another landmark. Any circumnavigation via the Southern Ocean takes sailors south of three great capes: the Cape of Good Hope, Cape Leeuwin, and Cape Horn. Of the three, the Horn is by far the most meaningful. It is the exit from the privations of the South, the most dangerous and captivating headland in the mind of any sailor. Rounding Cape Horn was like summiting the Southern Ocean. Its challenge was one of the reasons that racing sailors kept coming back.

Cape Horn is actually located on an island, to the south of Tierra del Fuego. It has a sheer rock face that rises from the sea toward the heavens with a grandeur that befits the geographic boundary between two great oceans. Sir Francis Drake was the first to report seeing the great cape, in 1578. He did not pass by and go on into the Pacific Ocean, preferring to return north to the safer confines of the Strait of Magellan, which winds from the Atlantic to the Pacific through Tierra del Fuego. A Dutchman, Willem Schouten, rounded it first, in 1616, while searching for a new trading route to the Pacific — the East India Company alone had rights to use the Strait of Magellan. He named the stark promontory after his birthplace of Hoorn, in Holland.

Over the centuries, Cape Horn became the gateway to the Pacific for traders, whalers, and fast merchant vessels like the clippers, which had trouble in the fickle winds and narrow confines

of the Strait of Magellan. But it is a gateway attended by fear
some winds and seas that extracted a heavy toll in ships and
lives. Southern Ocean depressions barreling down on Cape
Horn from the west, and the mountainous seas they bring with
them, are compressed into the relatively narrow Drake Passage
between Cape Horn and the Antarctic peninsula, about five hun
dred miles to the south. The long ridge of the Andes, running
north up the spine of Chile, also channels weather down into the
gap. Beneath the surface, the Pacific seabed rises sharply from
more than thirteen thousand feet to less than one thousand feet
around the Horn, catching the deep, even ocean swells from
below and knocking them into steep, sometimes breaking seas
In every dimension, geography conspires to push wind and wave
energy through a funnel, and the result is unusual violence.
Winds at Cape Horn blow at gale force five days out of every
seven. The seas are often closely spaced and dangerous. Sailors
who feigned illness to avoid ships going there were said to be
suffering from "Cape Horn fever." Veterans of the Horn wore
their earrings and formed societies to talk about their exploits
and the hundreds of wrecks that litter the region's waters. Sur-
vivors of all three great capes — most of all Cape Horn — were
considered so lucky it was said they could piss into the wind
without getting wet.

Doubling Cape Horn from east to west, against the westerly
winds and currents, could at times be the most harrowing passage in the world. On average, it took square-rigged ships almost three weeks to bash their way into the cold winds and seas,
often losing men over the side as green water swept the decks
and suffering sail and mast damage as storms ripped away at
gear and rigging. At its worst, rounding the Horn could take
months or seem so futile that ships simply turned back and
sailed all the way around Antarctica, to enter the Pacific via Australia and New Zealand. This added ten thousand miles to the
voyage, but at least it was downwind. Rounding from west to
east, with the prevailing winds, was a lot easier, although storms

:ould sweep in to drive ships onto the lee shore of Tierra del Fuego. To avoid getting pinned by the westerly winds, clipper ship captains tried to arrive at Cape Horn's latitude as much as three hundred miles to the west.

Club Med's crew did not fear Cape Horn. They looked forward to it, not least because it meant that they would be heading north again. Even with the most sophisticated clothing money could buy — a high-tech amalgam of thermals topped by fleece wrapped in Gore-Tex — the sailors were weary of the bone-chilling cold and frequent bouts of rain. Staying warm had become an obsession, and there were always volunteers to brew the next round of tea or coffee. Getting dry was almost impossible. It was so cold that even the ham bone languished in the mast; no one had the stomach to cut greasy strips from it.

Dalton and Quilter had seen Cape Horn in all its moods. This time they anticipated a relatively easy passage. Their favorite depression looked as if it would grant them one last favor and sweep *Club Med* around the Horn in manageable winds and then give her a good nudge north past the Falkland Islands. *Club Med* might get as far as Uruguay before facing the tricky zone of the South Atlantic High again. Quilter, who had rounded Cape Horn four times, was in fact more worried about the run up the South American coast than the cape itself. "It is this part of the round-the-world course I have had the most unpleasant time with, just after Cape Horn and on the way to the South Atlantic High," he commented. "It is often really rough, with cold headwinds and dangerous, confused seas."

At least the veteran navigator could see some good in the transition. "You can put your bow north," he emphasized. "Every mile you make, the weather improves. Every mile north, the sea conditions improve, the weather, the temperature, the condensation stops. You can take some of your layers of clothing off. It's a doorway back into the real world." Grant Dalton, in contrast, expected only trouble from the South American coast. In the 1993–94 Whitbread nasty seas in this region had almost cost him his victory, pounding so hard on *New Zealand Endeavour*'s bow that it started to peel apart. Bunks had to be ripped from the interior and used to shore up the hull. Dalton didn't know exactly what meteorological forces and currents were at work there; he only knew it was a place where many round-the-world racing boats had come to grief, either through dismasting or structural failure. "Stop being a prophet of doom," one friend e-mailed him. "You're not even there yet." Still, Dalton couldn't shake a sense of foreboding.

Club Med closed on Cape Horn at more than 20 knots, surfing on a nice, easy swell. In the middle of the night she passed about ten miles south of the rocky promontory. It was bathed in moonlight, and Dalton was reminded of how impressive a landmark it was. Quilter notified race headquarters — adding that he now authorized everyone to piss into the wind. Even with the detour through New Zealand, it had taken *Club Med* just over forty-one days to arrive at the Horn. That was almost a week faster than Olivier de Kersauson's time to the same point during his Jules Verne record run. *Club Med* had also demolished the Southern Ocean, sailing from the Cape of Good Hope to Cape Horn — across both the Indian and Pacific Oceans — in just twenty-two days.

A three-week passage across this part of the world had been inconceivable until Bruno Peyron started sketching in the nav station of *Commodore Explorer* and dreaming about an unusual race. Appropriately, Peyron was there to witness this high point. He hadn't been able to race the enormous boats born of those rudimentary drawings, but he flew to Chile and sailed out to Cape Horn in a seventy-foot ketch to watch *Club Med* become the first maxi-cat to conquer the famous headland. He caught only a brief glimpse of her as she flew by in the gloom at 25 knots. It was enough, though. His fantasy was reality. A new generation of sailing machine had made its mark at Cape Horn. *Club Med*'s crew didn't pause to celebrate. They had an outside chance at another milestone — a sixty-day circumnavigation — and in any case were eager to clear the region before a major storm rolled in. "There is a hell of a blow on the way," Dalton warned. "*Explorer* are going to get their heads kicked in with a real 'belter.'"

Eight hundred miles astern, Loïck Peyron and Skip Novak were contemplating the same grim forecast. Their catamaran had suffered a grueling trip across the Pacific, enduring one storm, seven hundred miles southeast of the Chatham Islands off New Zealand, in which the wind increased to almost 60 knots. The crew had learned the boat could be made safe in those conditions, with water ballast in the aft tanks, three reefs in the mainsail, and just a storm jib up front. Roger Nilson found the experience reassuring. The Race was the most uncertain enterprise he had ever jumped into, with all the talk of death and destruction in the Southern Ocean. Yet *Explorer* was in exactly the conditions he had feared, still making more than 20 knots. "The boat was like a duck, taking the sea very well," he said.

Nevertheless, the power of the wind-churned ocean had brutalized her, ruffling her feathers and setting her hull and rig squealing and groaning in protest. One abrupt stop in a wave slammed Elena Caputo-Novak's head into the computer as she typed. The only safe place, she concluded, was in her bunk with her knees bent to absorb the blows. Waves crashed into the cockpit, inundating the crew on deck with cold water that relentlessly worked its way through every gap and seam in the foul-weather gear. Water spilled below as well, leaving the floors sloppy despite desultory efforts to mop it up. The crew kept at it, dragging wet, heavy sails across the trampoline to make whatever sail changes were required. Caputo-Novak, exhausted and unsettled, neglected to drink enough liquids and ended up dehydrated and vomiting. Whether the wind howled or eased to a more amenable range, the seas remained riotous. It was a gut-wrenching, tiresome ride. And now the Chilean weather bureau was forecasting more 60-knot winds, with gusts to 80 knots, for *Explorer*'s arrival on the shallow continental shelf at Cape Horn.

Peyron hoped that was an exaggeration as he pushed the boat

as fast as prudence allowed in a bid to beat the storm to Cape
Horn. *Explorer* started to pitch and bury her bows. Water was
again added to the ballast tanks, but before they were full the
catamaran stuck both bows in hard. Skip Novak was thrown the
length of the cockpit, landing headfirst near the companionway
hatch that led below. In a sailing career that had covered hundreds of thousands of miles of ocean and negotiated millions of
waves, he had never been launched like that. Somehow, his tra-
jectory took him past winch-grinding pedestals and sharp corners without maiming him. "That scared the shit out of me. All
of a sudden you are lying facedown wondering what happened,"
he said. "You are building a case for wearing a hard hat the
whole bloody time on these boats."

Explorer approached the South American coast in a freezing
drizzle. Little pieces of gear — a block guiding the steering cable
and a snap shackle at the top of the Solent — failed and were
fixed. The black weather was ominous, but the crew mostly
worried it would force *Explorer* away from the coast and de-
prive them of the long-anticipated sighting of Cape Horn. Water
depths gradually decreased off the Chilean coast, throwing up
short seas that caused the usual drumbeat on the hulls and
beams. Drogues were prepared and laid out. Peyron ordered all
sails stowed on deck moved to the aft beam, both to help keep
the bows up and to protect against seas washing under them
and ripping the forward netting to pieces. The winds built to 40
knots and kept rising. Gusts topped out at 60 knots. The crew
progressively shortened sail until there were three reefs in the
main again. Boat speeds slowed to 20 knots, yet the hulls and
bows continued to slam, setting everyone on edge. Hail joined
the rain that steadily fell. The wind angle prevented *Explorer*
from sailing a straight course toward the Horn. Instead, she was
forced to jibe back and forth repeatedly to work close.

Skip Novak was at the helm when relief arrived. The frontal
system they were sailing in, which had been spitting out a succession of squalls, finally pushed ahead of the boat. Novak
called everyone on deck. The off-watch crew rushed up from

below, expecting some sort of crisis. They were greeted by a world transformed. The low gray clouds of the front had cleared away, leaving a deep blue sky. Sunlight poured onto the rocky crags of Tierra del Fuego. The wind howled, but when *Explorer* jibed one last time toward Cape Horn — clawing past a fearsome cluster of rocks — the big seas came more directly astern and sent her rampaging forward on long surfing runs that touched 39 knots. Bruno Peyron was also waiting for his brother, just as he had when Loïck first rounded Cape Horn in the Vendée Globe eleven years ago. Two hours earlier, Novak had sent him an e-mail: "Fasten your seat belts and take your seats, big bird is coming."

The big bird ended up sailing within two miles of the cape. Yves Loday, who as a young boy lived in the apartment just above the Peyron brothers, was at the helm as *Explorer* returned to the Atlantic. The rest of the crew gathered along the rail, taking it all in. Olivier Lozachmeur, affectionately known on board as Mouette ("Seagull"), gazed at this lifelong dream and his eyes glistened with tears. "I feel like a child discovering water for the first time," he said.

Loïck Peyron stood silently as *Explorer* rushed down on Bruno. Attempts to contact him on the radio yielded only static, so the two brothers had to settle for a quick wave at the bottom of a continent. It seemed enough. *Explorer* slipped quickly past Bruno and the great cape and turned northeast, toward Staten Island and the Falklands beyond. Roger Nilson was pleased to note that *Explorer* retained her distinction as the fastest boat in history across the Southern Ocean. She had beaten *Club Med*'s time from the Cape of Good Hope by an hour and a half. "An interesting record," Nilson observed. "It shows that with quality sails we could have really worried *Club Med*." Almost six thousand miles astern, *Team Adventure* was slowly approaching New Zealand, where she would have to stop for additional repairs. *Warta Polpharma* and *Team Legato* were stretched out over another fifteen hundred miles of ocean behind her.

*　　　*　　　*

Cape Horn was seven thousand miles from the finish in Marseilles. One thousand miles of sailing remained to get north of 40° south again. Still, after Cape Horn and the Southern Ocean, the length of the Atlantic seemed a small impediment to completing The Race. Almost as soon as *Explorer* cleared the Horn, temperatures warmed. Sailing speeds dropped as unusually light and fluky winds clamped down over the region.

Frustration set in, and the exhausted crew turned to sleep and housekeeping. Yves Loday, who had refused to cook during the entire voyage — claiming he was a vegetarian, and in any case had not been raised at a stove — shocked everyone by giving the galley a thorough scrub. Skip Novak used the lull to take his first bath since New Zealand, a brave act in 50° water. Like all cold-water bucket baths, it stimulated further virtuous action — manicure, pedicure, fresh clothes, the works — and a certain air of righteousness. "The others are still brewing away in their gear from the last ten days, and some, dare I say it, well before then," Novak observed.

He was also inspired to write his wife a Valentine's Day note. She was more touched by the fact that he aired out her sleeping bag. The rest of the crew settled for the ocean-racing equivalent of a gourmet meal. Cooked by Xavier Dagault, it featured foie de canard on toast, tinned ham, and a mushroom omelet accompanied by rehydrated, reconstituted crabmeat. A couple of bottles of wine washed it all down. *Club Med* had lengthened the lead to more than nine hundred miles while *Explorer* languished near the Falklands. It would be hard to catch her, barring a disaster, which tugged at the crew's cohesion and motivation. For the moment, though, they tried to enjoy their brief respite.

Grant Dalton and Mike Quilter were not so relaxed. Psychologically, it is easy for crews to feel that once they have rounded Cape Horn they are almost home. But Dalton and Quilter were now preparing to face the leg of the racecourse they feared most. To get to the equator *Club Med* would have to pound her way north into the prevailing northerly winds on the western side of the South Atlantic High. This would be a final trial for the race-weary catamaran, a trial that would decide the outcome of two months of all-out sailing. If only *Club Med* could get to the southeast trades intact, she could run directly north to the equator and head home. "The next few days will be tough on the boat and tough on me mentally," Dalton admitted. "I've been worried about this beat for three years. I'll be glad when it's over."

Roger Badham, working overtime with his computer models and on the satellite phone with Quilter, had a plan. It was complicated, but the gist of it was to keep *Club Med* in favorable winds by snaking the boat up the east side of a small high-pressure system off Uruguay and then racing her around the western side of a developing low-pressure system farther to the north. It was an ambitious strategy, made possible only by the sophistication of the weather and routing models on Badham's computers and a sailboat capable of covering close to one thousand miles over forty hours to catch the systems in the right place. As usual, *Club Med* would have to push hard, and Dalton would have to worry some more. But if they pulled it off, they would prove that smart, fast routing can finesse the most complex weather. "We could get lucky," Dalton noted. "If we slip through before the gate closes, we may well be through with this part of the world and on course for a finish in Marseilles pretty early."

That was a reward worth one final gamble. Dalton moved to improve his chances. An inventory of remaining stores was conducted. It found sixty to seventy liters of excess diesel fuel that could be burned off. Another chunk of surplus weight — the tattered ham bone — had already been committed to the waters off Cape Horn. *Club Med* shot north in her race against two weather systems. The first part of the strategy worked perfectly, although not for the whale wrapped briefly around *Club Med*'s daggerboard. The crew sailed smoothly around the high pressure off Uruguay, shedding layers of clothing as temperatures rose and giving the boat yet another maintenance checkup. Then it all fell apart. What the weather models had failed to predict accurately was the exact location of the depression and that it would intensify into a nasty little storm. At first Dalton, Quilter, and Badham thought they had pulled it off. *Club Med* cut through the system, sailing clear for about an hour. But weather can be cruel. The depression was unwilling to let the catamaran pass so easily. It expanded suddenly and engulfed the boat.

Dalton was now faced with exactly the conditions he had been desperate to avoid: winds blowing up to 30 knots from different directions and horrific, washing-machine seas ten to twenty feet high that hammered at *Club Med*'s beams and hulls. The boat's motion was so violent that Dalton found himself trying to sleep spread-eagled to maintain some contact with his thin foam mattress. Other sailors were thrown from their bunks, ending up on the cabin floor, wriggling in their sleeping bags like beached fish. The banging and racking of *Club Med*'s beams and hulls consumed Dalton with worry. He ordered the watches into survival mode, reducing sail and slowing the boat to a crawl in a desperate bid to ease the abuse. It was almost impossible to maintain steerage. Dalton was for once willing to give back some miles to a chasing boat. He knew *Club Med* was reaching her limits.

The catamaran was trapped in this private maelstrom for almost ten hours. The weather was so foul and the boat was jumping around so much, Badham lost contact. Dalton's instincts, as usual, proved accurate. When conditions finally eased as dark was falling, Neal McDonald went out to inspect the hulls around the main beam connection. He noticed some paint had chipped off the port hull. Paint chips like that when the hull is flexing, and McDonald could see the hull's skin rippling a bit as the boat pitched in the waves. His mouth went dry. If the bond between the carbon-fiber skin and the Nomex core had failed, the hull would lose structural integrity. That night, as he mulled over the implications, he sent his wife, Lisa, an e-mail saying he thought *Club Med* might be in serious trouble. "In my mind, this part of the boat would eventually fail and fall in two," McDonald recalled.

The next morning, closer scrutiny revealed additional areas of core failure where the main beam connected to the starboard and port hulls. Dalton was in a fitful sleep when Danby came to wake him up. "Houston, we've got a fucking problem," he announced. "You'd better come look at this." Dalton just shook his head. "I guarantee it was within a thirty-mile radius of where we delaminated *New Zealand Endeavour*," he said later. "I just had the sense that that was a badass place and it fucking delivered, too."

With only a few thousand miles to Marseilles and victory in The Race at stake, he was determined to find a makeshift repair that would see *Club Med* home. "I don't care if it's five miles or five thousand miles, we only need to finish," Dalton told the crew. He knew *Explorer* was sailing slowly in light winds for the moment and *Club Med* had a safe cushion, but he didn't want to give Peyron and Novak the slightest shred of hope and motivate them to work harder. Dalton ordered a full news blackout. No other wives were to be told about the damage, and he said nothing to *Club Med* or Multiplast lest the news leak. While Dalton stewed and cursed the place, McDonald and Danby huddled with Jan Dekker, a South African sailor who had an enthusiasm for tearing into any repairs. Dekker the Wrecker, McDonald liked to call him. Together, McDonald, Danby, and Dekker had become what Dalton affectionately called his "three-man army," the guys he relied on to fix all the pad eyes, the Plexiglas canopy, and anything else that happened to break. This would be their biggest test.

They needed some plates to stabilize the hull in the damaged area, and found them in the carbon access panels located between all the bulkheads in the two hulls. The panels, which were the size of large serving platters, separated the watertight compartments but could be removed to allow a person to crawl throughout the boat. A stack of bulkhead panels was gathered and the three-man army went to work. Holes were drilled through the hull around each weakened area. Epoxy was squirted into the holes to stabilize the core between the skins. Then two bulkhead plates were through-bolted to the inside and outside of the hull to help stiffen it. To tighten the exterior plate, Dekker had to hang upside down through a hole cut in the trampoline.

The repair was straightforward but executing it was not. As they started drilling holes, laying out the bulkhead panels, and cutting lengths of spare threaded bar to use as bolts, McDonald realized they would need a lot of nuts to squeeze the panels tight against the hull. "Right we need nuts. We've fucking got no nuts," he shouted to Danby. "Fucking get some. I don't care where they come from, just get 'em." Danby shot off to root around the boat, stealing any nuts he could find that weren't needed to keep the boat floating or racing. The ventilation fans in the engine spaces ended up hanging by a single fastener, but he returned to McDonald with a bounty of nuts. McDonald had no idea where they all had come from until some of the sailing hardware began ripping out of the deck just days from the finish.

After six hours of improvisation, multiple patches had been added to the port and starboard hulls. The repair wasn't pretty, but it might be enough to get *Club Med* home. Dalton got on the sat phone with Badham, who was miserable with worry over routing the boat into this mess. "Clouds," he told his old friend, "we can pretty much take any wind you can give us up to thirty knots, but we don't want any waves over six inches." "Right," Badham responded. "No way." Dalton, of course, was speaking tongue-in-cheek, but only just. To make it to Marseilles safely he was going to have to sail *Club Med* with tender care, holding her speed down and hoping Badham could keep her out of any extreme weather. "From there on, they were really vulnerable. They didn't like port tack and they just couldn't put any pressure on the boat at all," Badham recalled. After a few days of nervous sailing *Club Med* found the southeast trade winds. The wind came around to the beam again, and the equator lay ahead.

She needed a little luck and she got it. Dalton's radio silence had its intended effect and the *Explorer* crew had no idea that the sort of calamity they had been half wishing on the leader had come to pass. Instead of gaining hope and sailing harder, *Explorer* was battling both ennui over a race that was assumed to be over and an old nemesis, the South Atlantic High. Now, as both boats raced to the Mediterranean, *Club Med*'s lead expanded at times to more than twelve hundred miles, depending on what sort of weather system each boat encountered. The South Atlantic High was the last real weather obstacle. The Doldrums yielded as easily as they had on the outbound leg in the Atlantic. The maxi-catamarans had defused one of sailing's most notorious meteorological frustrations, and Mike Quilter was impressed. "They were just gone in the blink of an eye. In five knots of wind you can do ten knots — you get one good puff and you've gone twenty miles," he said. "You don't park unless there is absolutely no wind."

When *Club Med* crossed the Line, the crew pocketed yet another record. They had sailed south across the equator and back north again in just forty-two days, eleven hours, and fifteen minutes, beating de Kersauson and *Sport Elec* by five days. There wasn't much of a celebration; everyone was just eager to get to the finish in one piece. They weren't in the Northern Hemisphere long before Roger Badham called in with some good news. "I've got a plan to get you all the way home in seven days," he told a skeptical Dalton. He wasn't sure he believed it himself, but for days now he had been following the progress of a huge depression in the northern Atlantic. It was sweeping toward Europe, obliterating the light winds of the Azores High, and seemed to be on track to rendezvous with *Club Med*. Dalton and his crew shot north through the northeast trades. Instead of blowing at 15 to 20 knots, quite common at that time of year, they went easy on the catamaran with a perfect breeze of just 12 to 15 knots. From the trades, *Club Med* hopped onto the beautiful southwesterlies blown in by the depression and was lifted toward the entrance to the Mediterranean as if she were on an escalator. Roger Nilson could only shake his head at this final stroke of good fortune. The low-pressure system was the largest he had ever seen in the Atlantic, tailor-made for the blue cat's stretch run. "That was the last nail in the coffin. She had a ride all the way home," he said. "She sailed extremely well. And she was really in the groove." *Explorer* followed a little more than two days behind, arriving north of the equator just in time to catch the back end of the same ride. *Club Med* blazed through the Strait of Gibraltar again, paused briefly in a Mediterranean calm, and accelerated to the finish.

She arrived in Marseilles on a Saturday evening. Four hundred boats packed with spectators formed a welcoming flotilla. Radio reports had charted the big cat's approach. Then suddenly she was there, emerging from the gloom like a spaceship at 20 knots and arrowing to the line with her entire crew on deck. Helicopters put her under bright spotlights while sponsor boats crowded in. *Club Med* had raced around the world nonstop in just sixty-two days and seven hours. It was the fastest circumnavigation in history. Dalton put her into the wind and the crew dropped her sails one last time. Slowly, triumphantly, she motored past the protective stone walls of Marseilles's old port. Fifteen thousand sailing fans lined the quay and cheered her in with songs and a rain of red emergency flares. The crew, after two months at sea, were stunned by the reception.

Club Med docked at the victory pontoon and champagne was spraying within minutes. Dalton and coskipper Franck Proffit were chased down and heaved into the harbor's murky waters. Dalton climbed out quickly and led his team to a huge stage erected at the head of the harbor. Loudspeakers thundered music in a carnival atmosphere, and Bruno Peyron handed over a huge globe-shaped trophy created for The Race. Dalton seemed a little overwhelmed and deeply touched by the noise and energy of the French crowd. "It's great to be here in Marseilles, and we've annihilated the opposition," he told them. "I think it was probably our most clinical and our best win."

Explorer arrived just two and a half days later to a similar explosion of enthusiasm. Bruno Peyron had been right. A new generation of multihulls could rewrite the record books and change the basic relationship among sailors, the weather, and the Southern Ocean. Two out of six starters had completed the circumnavigation nonstop. The rest of the fleet straggled home over the next six weeks. Boats had been broken, but no one had died. The Race was over.

EPILOGUE

What we get from this adventure is just sheer joy. And joy is, after all, the end of life. We do not live to eat and make money. We eat and make money to be able to enjoy life. That is what life means and what life is for.

— George Leigh Mallory

Club Med's sprint around the world covered a total of 27,407 miles at an average speed of 18.3 knots. That was a quantum leap in performance over previous Jules Verne circumnavigations, an improvement of 20 percent. *Explorer* actually sailed faster, an average of 18.45 knots, but sailed 1,357 more miles than *Club Med* to cover the globe (a reflection of the different sailing styles of the two boats, mainly owing to the gaps in *Explorer*'s sail inventory, which forced her to sail a faster but less direct course). Dalton and his hung-over crew could not claim the Jules Verne Trophy because The Race didn't start and finish in the English Channel, as required by the Jules Verne's rules. Nor could *Club Med* claim an official World Sailing Speed Record Council circumnavigation record because she didn't start and finish in the same port. (Dalton had briefly considered diverting slightly to pass the Barcelona starting line on the final sprint to Marseilles, but it wasn't clear this would satisfy the WSSRC.)

The trophies and official recognition would have been gratifying, but *Club Med*'s crew could retire from The Race content with a de facto record and a strong argument that theirs would

easily have been the fastest boat ever if they had sailed the Jules
Verne course. An 18.3-knot average speed over the exact same
water sailed by Olivier de Kersauson and *Sport Elec* in their sev-
enty-one-day Jules Verne run would have brought *Club Med*
home even faster than on The Race's course, with its light-air
Mediterranean leg and lengthy digression through the Cook
Strait. On de Kersauson's track, *Club Med* would have girdled
the globe in just fifty-eight days. As Dalton pointed out on the
way to the finish, any Jules Verne circumnavigation that didn't
lower *Club Med*'s mark in The Race would be like "kissing your
sister."

And he was right, though he didn't dwell on the question
long. Almost immediately after finishing The Race, Dalton dove
into preparations for yet another trip around the world, this
time as skipper of a sixty-foot monohull in the Volvo Ocean
Race (the renamed Whitbread). In September he and a new crew
set out for what would be his seventh racing circumnavigation,
more than any sailor in history. It was a measure of Dalton's
toughness and focus that he could contemplate going back to sea
and the Southern Ocean so quickly. But racing boats around the
world was what he did best, even if he was a bit embarrassed
about how it looked. "That's not a record I cherish. It just shows
I am a bit too wacky . . . [and] couldn't get a real job," he admitted.

Club Med's incredible speed over the oceans delivered on
Bruno Peyron's promise of millennial performance. In the space
of two years the maxi-catamarans had raised the twenty-four-
hour record by more than one hundred miles and required
only the right weather and oceanic runway to threaten the seven-
hundred-mile barrier. Pure speed worked in synergy with the
routers, giving them unprecedented leverage over the weather.
"It's much nicer because you can do so much more," Clouds
Badham observed. "In a normal boat you just pile into the systems. In these boats you can run around them." Just as important, the boats could more or less keep pace with the favorable
systems they latched on to. *Club Med* crossed four thousand

miles of Pacific Ocean to Cape Horn riding just two weather depressions.

Speed and power of the magnitude engineered into the maxi-catamarans came with a price, though. Designers are always struggling to find the right balance between performance and durability, and in the pale Marseilles sun the morning after *Club Med* finished, the scars of her battle with the oceans were easy to see. More than a half-dozen pad eyes had been ripped out, safety stanchions had been bent over, the Plexiglas canopy looked like a jigsaw puzzle, and it was clear that multiple surgeries had been needed to keep the trampoline intact. These sorts of wounds were to be expected in a boat that had been raced for two months without interruption. But the numerous patches stabilizing the hulls at either end of the main beam were more ominous. So was a broken shroud, suffered in the final miles from Gibraltar to the finish, which could have brought the mast down if the boat had been sailing at a different angle to the wind.

These visible signs of abuse, along with the stories of pile-driving in the Southern Ocean, confirmed that Pete Goss and Adrian Thompson had at least been correct in identifying rough seas and the front beam as critical limiting factors in the quest to go ever faster. Cam Lewis arrived in Marseilles convinced that raising the beams even higher above the water was the obvious direction in which maxi-cat design would have to go (in fact, he thought the beams on his Ollier cat were too low even before The Race started).

Fossett, Morrelli, and Melvin had come to the same conclusion in time to modify *PlayStation*'s bows and front beam to almost cartoonish heights. They were never tested in the Southern Ocean; nevertheless, that design choice looked pretty spectacular six months after The Race, when *PlayStation* finally showcased her potential by sailing across the Atlantic from New York to the Lizard in just four days, seventeen hours, and twenty-eight minutes. That obliterated *Jet Services*'s stubborn eleven-year record by almost forty-four hours, a stunning improvement of almost 30 percent. Along the way, *PlayStation* also smashed *Club*

Med's freshly minted twenty-four-hour record by almost 33 miles, with a run of 687.17 miles. Fossett was back doing what he did best, happily accumulating records, and the next crop of maxi-cats out of the build sheds may well attack the oceans with *PlayStation*'s distinctive upswept, destroyer-bow look. Whatever the configuration, Multiplast's Yann Penfornis predicts the next generation's cats will be 5 percent faster.

Whether there is life in a second-generation wave-piercing catamaran is harder to tell. Pete Goss briefly spoke of his desire to build a *Team Philips* "Mark II" before fading into silence. It would take a bold sponsor to make that investment again. Even Adrian Thompson sounded an ambivalent note in the immediate aftermath of *Team Philips*'s disintegration in the North Atlantic. "The boat, which has stretched emotions, budgets, and credibility over the past two years, did not, I'm sad to say, provide the basic safe environment for survival that it should have done," he lamented.

One design question The Race did little to resolve, except in the mystical confines of various computer models, was whether a trimaran might be quicker than a maxi-cat racing around the world. Even after sailing his catamaran three quarters of the way at a record pace, Grant Dalton wasn't sure. "I don't think the cat-versus-tri argument is over; it hasn't even started," he said. "A tri would destroy these cats in the Atlantic but suffer in the Southern Ocean." Olivier de Kersauson, determined to defend his Jules Verne record against the imminent maxi-cat assault and a trimaran loyalist, prepared to help resolve the issue. As *Club Med* and *Explorer* approached Marseilles, the boat-building team at Multiplast was putting the finishing touches on a 130-foot trimaran for the French record setter, to be called *Geronimo*. Both de Kersauson and Bruno Peyron — finally free to go to sea in the renamed *Explorer* — made early plans to compete for a new Jules Verne record.

The Race fortunately failed to live up to expectations in one regard. Like the first OSTAR and the Golden Globe, it was predicted to be a killer. Andrew Bray, editor of *Yachting World,* had

put it succinctly: "Of all the round-the-world races that have
ever started, this has the greatest potential for a body count."
Bray was proved too pessimistic, which shows the value of pushing boundaries in the face of criticism. Materials technology and
the sophistication of design and simulation software, backed up
by communications, navigation, and safety wizardry, had taken
a lot of the danger out of a nonstop Southern Ocean circumnavigation. In the Golden Globe era, with its limited position-fixing
and communications capabilities, the crew of *Team Philips* could
well have ended up dead, even though they were in the heavily
traveled North Atlantic. But in the new millennium, Grant Dalton was confident enough to declare from the depths of the
South, "People talked about body counts, but these boats are
safe."

If technology had sapped some of the drama from Southern
Ocean racing by making it less life-threatening, it had added
drama in other forms. The design competition was spirited and
suspenseful. The Atlantic match race between *Club Med* and
Team Adventure was unprecedented in its closeness and in the
degree to which the crews and spectators knew where the boats
were and what was happening on them, thanks to e-mail and the
Internet. And there was beauty, grace, and power in the raw performance potential unveiled. Robin Knox-Johnston knew better
than anyone how the challenges of a nonstop circumnavigation
had changed over the years, how life aboard *Suhaili* was different from life aboard *Enza* and the maxi-cats. "It's still an adventure, but now more of a sporting challenge," he said. "We
did not know if it was possible in 1968 and most people thought
it wasn't. Nowadays we know the voyage is possible, but the
pressure is from the very close competition. The sailors these
days are the sharp end of a team, like a racing car driver; we
were the whole team." Loïck Peyron perfectly captured this shift
in emphasis from endurance to speed by scoffing at the public's
continuing fascination with long voyages. "It's not difficult to
stay at sea, to sail slow. Anybody can do that," he said. "It's
hard to stay the minimum time at sea, to go fast."

All this should not be a cause for complacency. Every sailor, like every climber on Everest, knows that despite all the advantages of technology, disaster is always lurking, that the wrong combination of bad weather and bad luck can still kill. "When someone hits a seventy- or eighty-knot storm or a freak wave, what's going to happen?" said Skip Novak. "That huge catastrophic moment is still waiting to happen, still can happen." And one flipped maxi-maxi-catamaran is all that's needed to make Andrew Bray look prescient. The Southern Ocean is too remote, too powerful, and too unpredictable to be tamed yet. Which is why some sailors always go back, and some sailors don't.

In the immediate aftermath of The Race, Randy Smyth was one of the sailors who had seen enough. Smyth is as tough as they come, a multiple winner of one of sailing's most brutal races, the Worrell 1000, a stage race sailed offshore in twenty-foot catamarans from Florida to Virginia. But his experience aboard *Team Adventure* in the vicissitudes of the South gave him pause. "You definitely feel you are living on the edge," Smyth reflected. "To do it once and get away with it, that's enough for a lifetime. If you keep doing it over and over, that's like a death wish."

Bruno Peyron, for one, wants to do it again. Plans for another edition of The Race, to be held in 2004, are under way. If he pulls it off, there will be plenty of adventurers ready to set sail. What sort of boats will they take back to the Southern Ocean? How fast will they fly?

SOURCES

SOURCES

The history of round-the-world sailboat racing lies scattered in first-person accounts, a few biographies, and innumerable articles in sailing magazines. To understand that history I trolled as many of the books as I could get my hands on and scoured dozens of back issues of *Sailing World* and *Yachting World*. These sources provided the material used to explain the background of The Race in the first half of the book.

The account of The Race itself was drawn from entirely different sources. The Race was the most wired sailing competition ever run. Each day the boats would send off e-mails, still pictures, and videos depicting life on board. All would be posted on the Web site (www.therace.org) created by race organizers, allowing sailing fans and the press to follow the competition closely. The Web site also posted position reports and radio interviews, conducted most days with most of the boats. Beyond that, skippers and crews wrote sometimes for newspapers or sports Web sites. Two of these sites, now.com and quokka.com, provided daily coverage of The Race.

The result was that an extraordinary amount of information was available even before the boats crossed the finish line. This information provided the basic narrative outline of The Race. Interviews with skippers and crews before and after the competition, at the start and finish, by telephone and e-mail, added greatly to that narrative and provided a more complete picture of the action. These interviews were critical to fleshing out the story because, although the boats sent their reports every day, many details — especially regarding tactics and any gear or boat problems — had to be left out so as not to give any advantage to opponents on the water.

One resource was particularly helpful in re-creating The Race: a software program called Virtual Spectator. Through an arrangement with The Race's organizers, VS acquired position and weather telemetry from the catamarans at regular intervals throughout the day. The software connected a user to the VS server and downloaded the data, creating a graphic representation of each boat's track over time. The software also overlaid on the graphic the position of high- and low-pressure systems. Boat position, speed and heading, wind speed and direction, distance to the finish, and distance to the leader were available at all times. VS allowed the user to go back and rerun any portion of the contest, or the whole thing. The user could also gain access to weather forecasts, showing the same evolving weather picture the routers and navigators were looking at. In short, VS provided a remarkably sophisticated graphic record of The Race — an invaluable tool in analyzing boat tactics and weather routing.

The following books were especially helpful in researching this book:

Bartelme, Tony, and Brian Hicks. *Into the Wind*. Charleston, S.C.: Evening Post Publishing, 1999.

Bruce, Erroll. *Cape Horn to Port*. New York: David McKay, 1978.

Bullimore, Tony. *Saved*. London: Little, Brown, 1997.

Chichester, Francis. *Alone Across the Atlantic*. New York: Doubleday, 1961.

———. *Atlantic Adventure*. New York: John de Graff, 1963.

———. *The Lonely Sea and the Sky*. New York: Coward-McCann, 1964.

———. *"Gipsy Moth" Circles the World*. New York: Coward-McCann, 1967.

————, ed. *Along the Clipper Way*. New York: Coward-McCann, 1966.

Clark, Arthur H. *The Clipper Ship Era*. New York: G. P. Putnam's Sons, 1910.

Colas, Alain. *Around the World Alone*. Woodbury, N.Y.: Barron's, 1978.

Cutler, Carl C. *Greyhounds of the Seas*, 3rd ed. Annapolis, Md.: Naval Institute Press, 1984.

Foster, Lloyd. *OSTAR*. Somerset, U.K.: Haynes, 1989.

Goss, Pete. *Close to the Wind*. New York: Carroll and Graf, 1998.

Hammond, Geoffrey. *Showdown at Newport*. New York: Walden Publications, 1974.

Hendrickson, Robert. *The Ocean Almanac*. New York: Doubleday, 1984.

Herreshoff, L. Francis. *Capt. Nat Herreshoff*. Dobbs Ferry, N.Y.: Sheridan House, 1953.

Holm, Donald. *The Cicumnavigators*. Englewood Cliffs, N.J.: Prentice-Hall, 1974.

Holm, Ed. *Yachting's Golden Age, 1880–1905*. New York: Alfred A. Knopf, 1999.

Jones, William H. S. *The Cape Horn Breed*. New York: Criterion Books, 1956.

Jourdane, John. *Icebergs, Port and Starboard*. Long Beach, Cal.: Cape Horn Press, 1992.

Kemp, Peter, ed. *The Oxford Companion to Ships and the Sea*. London: Oxford University Press, 1976.

Knox-Johnston, Robin. *A World of My Own*. New York: W. W. Norton, 1969.

————. *Cape Horn*. London: Hodder and Stoughton, 1994.

————. *Beyond Jules Verne*. London: Hodder and Stoughton, 1995.

Lewis, Cam, and Michael Levitt. *Around the World in Seventy-nine Days*. New York: Dell Expedition, 1996.

Lubbock, Basil. *The China Clippers*. Glasgow: James Brown and Son, 1919.

————. *The Romance of the Clipper Ships*. London: Hennel Locke, 1948.

————. *The Log of the "Cutty Sark."* Glasgow: Brown, Son, and Ferguson, 1960.

Lundy, Derek. *Godforsaken Sea*. Chapel Hill, N.C.: Algonquin Books, 1999.

Maury, Matthew. *The Physical Geography of the Sea*. Cambridge: Harvard University Press, 1963.

Moitessier, Bernard. *The First Voyage of the "Joshua."* Translated by Inge Moore. New York: William Morrow, 1973.

―――. *The Long Way*. Dobbs Ferry, N.Y.: Sheridan House, 1995.

Novak, Skip. *One Watch at a Time*. New York: W. W. Norton, 1988.

Rose, Sir Alec. *My Lively Lady*. New York: David McKay, 1968.

Slocum, Joshua. *Sailing Alone Around the World*. Purdys, N.Y.: The Adventure Library, 1995.

Southby-Tailyour, Ewen. *Blondie*. London: Leo Cooper, 1998.

Teller, Walter Magnes. *The Search for Captain Slocum*. New York: Charles Scribner's Sons, 1956.

Tetley, Nigel. *Trimaran Solo*. Lymington, U.K.: Nautical Publishing, 1970.

Tomalin, Nicholas, and Ron Hall. *The Strange Last Voyage of Donald Crowhurst*. London: Hodder and Stoughton, 1970.

Villiers, A. J. *Falmouth for Orders*. Garden City, N.Y.: Garden City Publishing, 1929.

White, Reg, and Bob Fisher. *Catamaran Racing*. New York: John de Graff, 1968.

Wilson, Derek. *The Circumnavigators*. New York: M. Evans, 1989.